Mountjoy – Th √

'Tim Carey gives a riveting account of Ireland's turbulent social and political history as seen through the distorting lens of the Joy. This is penal history told with panache.'

Dr Ian O'Donnell, Director of the Irish Penal Reform Trust

'This is a well-told, if at times, harrowing story of how offenders have been treated in Ireland over the past two centuries – in general, not a matter of pride. The light which this throws on a neglected aspect of our social history flashes a warning of the fallibility of even well-intentioned objectives centred solely on imprisonment.'

T.K. Whitaker

'A really fascinating and moving insight into life in Mountjoy throughout the past 150 years. It's all there, the good, the bad, the ugly, the humanity, the inhumanity, the humiliation, the human suffering. To understand our past this book is essential reading.'

John Lonergan, Governor of Mountjoy Prison

'As well as being a book to read it is also a good history lesson ... it's a book I'd read again, it has that edge to keep you reading on and that's important in any book. It was very well researched and nothing left out.'

Declan Donaghy, prisoner, Mountjoy Prison

Tim Carey was born in Milwaukee, USA, but has lived most of his life in Dublin. He studied History and Geography at Trinity College before going on to take a Masters in Development Studies in UCD. He is currently employed in Kilmainham Gaol Museum.

---

*To all those who have
done time or worked in
Mountjoy Prison
1850-2000*

MOUNTJOY

THE STORY OF A PRISON

Tim Carey

The
Collins
Press

Published in 2000 by
The Collins Press
West Link Park
Doughcloyne
Wilton
Cork

British Library Cataloguing in Publication data.

Typesetting by The Collins Press Ltd.

Printed in Ireland by Betaprint.

ISBN: 1-898256-89-6

COVER PHOTOGRAPHS:
Front cover – *top:* Prisoners exercising in Mountjoy in the 1920s, courtesy
National Archives;
bottom: Prisoners released from Mountjoy at the end of the War
of Independence, courtesy Kilmainham Gaol;
Back cover – *top and bottom:* Mountjoy mugshots of John Plunkett (brother of
Joseph Plunkett) after the 1916 Rising, courtesy Kilmainham
Gaol;
middle: Mugshot of 'Invincible' James Fitzharris, alias 'Skin the
Goat', on release from prison in 1899, courtesy Kilmainham Gaol.

CONTENTS

PICTURE CREDITS

The publishers and author would like to thank all those who have supplied photographs and illustrations for this book.

Courtesy Author's collection: p. 24, p. 73
Courtesy Pat Hayes: p. 126
Courtesy Kilmainham Gaol: p. 90, p. 133, p. 164, p. 167, p. 171, p. 172, p. 182, p. 183, p. 185, p. 191, p. 192, p. 196, p. 197, p. 201
Courtesy National Archives: p. 47, p. 48, p. 49, p. 57, p. 153, p. 195, p. 205, p. 206
Courtesy National Library of Ireland: p. 7, p. 10, p. 13, p. 28, , p. 36, p.38, p. 46, p. 119, p. 121, p. 175
Courtesy Hugo McVey: p. 210, p. 221, p. 229, p. 230, p. 232
Courtesy Military Archives: p. 227
Courtesy Eithne O'Byrne: p. 200
Courtesy Grainne O'Meara: p. 217, p. 231
Courtesy Jim Petherbridge, Chief Officer, Mountjoy Prison: p. 169, p. 186, p. 199
Courtesy Public Records Office: p. 129, p. 159
Courtesy *The Irish Times*: p. 82

ACKNOWLEDGEMENTS

As with any work of this nature this book has been both a solitary affair and one reliant on the support of individuals and institutions. While the contents and errors are my own I must thank a number of people and institutions for their help. Firstly Sean Aylward, now Director-General of Prisons, for his enthusiastic response to the project and his generous support and sincere encouragement. It would not be an exaggeration to say that this book would never have seen the light of day without his help. A sincere thanks is also due to the Department of Justice, Equality and Law Reform and its Policy Planning Research Unit for the generous support in the form of grant aid. In particular I would like to thank Mick Mellet and Emma Tobin. The prisoners and staff of Mountjoy Prison have been very patient with my intrusions. I would like to express my gratitude to all of them, especially Seamus Cramer for his assistance and friendship, also Jim Petherbridge, Derek Brennan, Killian Flynn and Willie Connolly. I am grateful to Governor Lonergan for his willing support of the project and for allowing me access to the prison. Thanks are also due to his secretary, Eithne Mulhearne. I would like to thank Pat Cooke and _Dúchas_ – The Heritage Service, for facilitating a period of leave that helped in the completion of this project.

In the course of the research for this book I have pestered the staff of various research institutions. Among those due my gratitude are: the Director of the National Archives, Dr Craig (especially for permitting access to the General Prisons Board files) and his staff – in particular Peter Parson, Tom Quinlan, Renah Lohen, Della Murphy and those in the reading room; the Board of Trustees of the National Library of Ireland, their helpful reading room staff, Colette O'Daly of prints and drawings and Eugene Hogan; the Public Record Office, London; the staff of the Berkeley Library, Trinity College, in particular the staff of the Official Publications desk and Donnacha MacDonnacha; Seamus Helferty of University College Dublin Archives; the staff of the Irish Labour History Museum, especially Alexis Kilbride; the staff of the Military Archives especially Captain Victor Lang and the late Commandant Peter Young for his good humour and interest.

A number of other people are due thanks for influencing or assisting this project. I would like to thank Jim Fitzpatrick, Anna Johnston, Ferdia Marnell, Phyl Mason and Niamh O'Sullivan for proofing the original scripts; Paul Turnell for kindly and diligently keeping an eye out for material in the Public Record Office; Johnny Gilmore, Andy Freeny and Barry Tierney for the loans of computers; Aileen Fallon for the legislative searches; Senator Joe Costelloe; Philip McCarthy of the Prison Officers Association; my sister-in-law, Therese, for her advice; my mother Mary and my sister Mary Kate; Maria Wooton; Hugo McVey and Grainne O'Meara and their family whose generosity with Sean Kavanagh's papers made the final chapter possible; Dr Ian O'Donnell, Director of the Irish Penal Reform Trust; Reverend McCaughey; photographer Karl Bridgeman; Tom Brady of the *Irish Independent*; Pat McBride; Pat Hayes; Connal Healy; Pat O'Byrne; Dr T.K. Whitaker; Jack Bates; Greg Heylin; James Ryan and Caroline Walsh; Deborah Smith; Gerry O'Callaghan, 'Doc' Quinn and Stephen Kirwan for sharing their experiences; the staff of Kilmainham Gaol past and present including Liz Carey, Sarah Delaney, Sinéad McCoole, Helen Murphy, Catherine O'Connor, Rory O'Dwyer, Cara Ronan and Gavan Woods. Lastly I would like to thank my wife Sinéad for her love, support, patience, editing and advice. Without her I could not have followed my longstanding dream of writing a book. For that I am immensely grateful.

PREFACE

This book evolved out of a research project on penal history that I was asked to do when I started work in Kilmainham Gaol Museum in January 1995. I soon realised that the penal history of Ireland was a story that had not yet been told. It was also a story that I felt to be of immense contemporary relevance. Kilmainham Gaol is embedded in the Irish mind as an historic political prison. While its story still resonates strongly with contemporary politics, hardly a week goes by when Mountjoy Prison does not significantly feature in the Irish media. No prison has taken up more air-time, column inches or pub talk. Like the weather, everyone has an opinion on Mountjoy. With its 150th anniversary looming on the horizon, I decided to concentrate on the story of the Joy.

During the course of my research I was constantly amazed at the wealth of material available on the subject. It is a story that I found incredibly compelling. Although the material available lent itself to an academic project, I felt this story deserved a broader audience.

The story of Mountjoy Prison is a vast one that covers 150 years and around 500,000 prisoners. Issues of penal philosophy, social reform and politics intertwine with personal details to form the fabric of its history. To describe such a complex institution each chapter focuses on one aspect of Mountjoy's history. This interrupts the chronological narrative on occasion (i.e. when the narrative 'jumps back' in time when political prisoners are first dealt with) and deals briefly with some aspects of the prison's history (for example the story of the political prisoners after the Civil War). This approach aims to give the reader a greater impression of the variety and scale of Mountjoy's history.

TIM CAREY
JANUARY 2000

Chapter One

THE BIRTH OF THE PRISON IN IRELAND

Have you ever stopped to think what a powerful weapon a key is?
Margaret Buckley, prisoner, Mountjoy Prison, War of Independence and
Civil War

Some have first-hand experience of what it is like to be imprisoned. But, for many, prison life is only 'known' through the images portrayed on the silver screen in films like *In the Name of the Father* or *The Shawshank Redemption,* or through the news media. Though we may have little or no personal experience with prisons these institutions represent something to us. When taken out of artificial cinema surroundings in which we almost invariably identify with 'the wrongly accused', 'the victim bucking the system' or 'the individual fighting against a corrupt and tyrannical prison regime', we generally have a different attitude. The prison is a symbol of law and order. Or, for those who feel the 'system' is not working, a symbol of lawlessness and disorder. It resides at the heart of some of our most deep-seated fears, including the most fundamental – the fear for our own personal safety and those of our loved ones. In Ireland no prison is closer to this core than Mountjoy Prison.

On 27 March 1850, Mountjoy Prison closed its doors for the first time. Why was it built? Today the answer to such a question seems obvious. Prisons are part of our world, part of our psyche, none more so in Ireland than 'the Joy'. But the decision

1

to build Mountjoy was not merely an administrative one, made with the stroke of a pen. The story of how it became central to our system of punishment is not straightforward. The prison we look at today with relatively unquestioning eyes has complex roots. Its form, structure and purpose were the result of a long and fitful growth. It was a growth fed by individuals, philosophies, social movements; a growth seasoned by aspirations, compromises, triumphs and defeats.

The story of Mountjoy Prison begins on the other side of the Atlantic when an American colonist raised his loaded musket and targeted one of George III's Redcoats at Concord, Massachusetts on 19 April 1775. Pulling the trigger, this unknown figure fired what Ralph Waldo Emerson in the *Concord Hymn* immortally called, 'the shot heard round the world'. It was the start of the American War of Independence and the course of political history was changed. So too was the history of punishment.

Transportation to America had been one of the main punishments handed down by Irish magistrates. From the passing of the 1718 Transportation Act until the outbreak of the American War of Independence, 13,000 Irish criminals, unwanted at home, were transported to the American colonies as 'indentured servants'[1] – so called because the paper on which the terms of their bondage were written was folded and then torn along a crooked (or indented) line, with master and servant each retaining half as a contractual guarantee. The normal criminal sentence of transportation was fourteen years and at least two-thirds of the convicts went to the labour intensive plantations of Maryland and Virginia. Irish people had been transported since Cromwellian times when they were not only banished 'to Hell or Connaught' but were also sent to the West Indies. Indeed 'banishment' as punishment went back to prehistory, but it was only after the Transportation Act that it became regular and routine practice. A substitute for the death penalty for certain crimes, it was also handed down for lesser offences to 'deter criminals and supply the colonies with labour'. An American solution to an Irish problem, it was Ireland's 'moral sewer' down which convicts were flushed to survive the harsh conditions of the colonies. Transportation was seen as a cure for 'idleness' which was thought to be the great affliction of the poor. While offering a criminal the hope of beginning life anew, it also meant the heartbreak of leaving friends and family and travelling to the other side of the world – an extremely daunting prospect for most convicts who had never before gone more than ten miles from their birthplace. The outbreak of the American War of Independence abruptly halted this stream of transportation ships across the Atlantic. After the end of hostilities the newly independent citizens of America understandably no longer wanted to receive foreign criminals (the loss of convict labour was more than made up for by the importation of slaves from Africa). The closing of this outlet to America led to what became known as the 'confinement crisis'. It was a crucial period in the history of punishment when the curious institution of the prison was transformed.

Until the confinement crisis prisons were rarely used as a form of punishment. They were used as mere holding pens, what George Bernard Shaw described as stone leashes around criminal canines.[2] Reflecting the Latin origin of the word prison – *prensio*, 'to lay hold of' – prisons were places where people were held to await either their trial or punishment. Imprisonment was not the punishment. In fact, prisons were mainly associated with the incarceration of debtors who were not criminals but were confined under a civil process. When transportation ended the prisons of Ireland were ill-equipped to deal with the confinement of large numbers of criminals for extended periods of time.

Today, prisons are managed centrally but 200 years ago law and order was largely a local issue which served the interest of, and was paid for by, the local tax-payer. The first national police force was not established until 1836 and it was not until 1850 and the opening of Mountjoy Prison that the government took a leading role in prison administration. In the eighteenth century there were over 40 prisons in Ireland under the control of the county and town Grand Juries (the local authorities and county councils of their day). The Grand Juries were responsible for their physical structures but little else. They exerted no control over internal workings: prisons were the private enterprises of their 'Keepers'. In these enterprises the prisoners were the source of income and had to pay for everything – food, drink, a bed. Extortion and exploitation underpinned the whole system. Gaolers viewed prisoners as vultures viewed their prey and it was not uncommon for a gaoler to detain a prisoner after acquittal, or expiration of his/her sentence, until he was paid for what he had supplied to that prisoner. With no attempt at internal regulation, prison conditions were atrocious. This was especially the case in the prisons of Dublin.

Newgate Prison in Green Street, which replaced the old Newgate at the end of Thomas Street, opened in 1780. Although it was then the most recently built prison in Dublin and designed by the eminent architect Thomas Cooley (also responsible for the Royal Exchange, now City Hall), Newgate epitomised the hardships prisoners endured. The descriptions of it are macabre. Sick and dying prisoners lying on stone stairs 'destitute of every assistance', 'infirm emaciated creatures' dying without anyone's knowledge, a place where morals were totally neglected as the sexes mixed more or less freely.[3] It was filthy beyond description, alcohol was openly sold to prisoners by the gaoler whose father ran a tavern across the road, money was extorted from prisoners by threatening to put them in heavy irons, the dungeons needed to be completely blocked up because 'they may in time emit their noxious vapours' and threaten disease upon prisoners and general population alike[4] and the chapel was a place of worship in name only. In 1784 it was reported in the Irish House of Commons that 'the prisoners had arrived to such a degree of audacity that it was almost impossible to come into it without being robbed'.[5] It was a 'school of iniquity' where boys as young as nine and ten, who had entered as mere novices in crime, soon 'imbibed those very pernicious principles that almost inevitably bring them to an ignominious end'.[6]

The County Gaol of Dublin at Kilmainham (about a kilometre from the present Kilmainham Gaol Museum) had been in use as a prison since at least 1715. It was 'extremely insecure, in an unwholesome bad situation with narrow contracted cells sunk considerably underground and no hospital'. The gaol was 'insufficient in point of extent, to contain the number of persons confined therein and as the windows of the prison are immediately in the street, they [the prisoners] have it in their power to confederate with their acquaintances abroad and procure instruments from them, to assist and contrive their escape through these windows; spirits and all sorts of liquors are constantly conveyed to the prisoners, who are thus kept in a continual state of intoxication'.[7] The staff only emptied the privies when the stench became overpowering. Money to pay for drink and food was begged from passers-by. One unfortunate gentleman, when handing a small coin to the felons, had his hand grabbed, a blade put to it and threatened that he would lose it if he did not hand over all his money (he duly coughed up).[8] Containing four dungeons which could hold up to two dozen felons, it was 'an ill-contrived, unproper, filthy, unwholesome prison'.[9]

The Four Courts Marshalsea, the largest prison exclusively for debtors in Ireland, was located across the River Liffey from today's Four Courts. It was condemned by Lord Annally as 'a grievance that disgraces humanity' that was 'altogether insufferable in a free country'.[10] Some rooms built for four contained twelve while some prisoners who could afford to pay the gaoler the necessary rent had five or six rooms, some being occupied by dogs, pigs and fowl, 'and others for their whores'.[11]

James St Bridewell was an 'old large prison, cold, inconvenient and out of repair' containing hard labour prisoners, 'vagabonds and lunatics'. Children were kept in the same room as lunatics, some of whom were so dangerous they needed to be chained down.[12]

The prisons of Dublin were in 'a most wretched condition'.[13] They were like bizarre hostels or inns, characterised by a strange type of disorder. 'Rapes, robberies and even murders were committed with impunity',[14] there were no uniforms, no visible regulation. Some inmates lived in opulent wealth while others lay chained and naked in dungeons, murderers mixed with petty thieves, men mixed with women, prisoners without medical attention died of disease, days were spent gambling and drinking. In many ways life inside prison was not too dissimilar to life outside – if you were wealthy you could rent the best rooms and buy the best food, if you were poor and starving you remained poor and starving. There was a continuous stream of visitors in and out of the gaols and if one peered through the door it would have been difficult to distinguish visitor from felon.

During the confinement crisis the prisons filled with 'convicts' who had nowhere to be transported (the term 'convict' was used specifically to describe a criminal sentenced to transportation or death). With transportation becoming a 'dead letter', for the first time large numbers of criminals were sentenced to the *punishment* of imprisonment. Reflecting this change in sentencing are figures relating to London's Old Bailey. In the years preceding the American War of Independence only 2.3 per cent of criminals were sentenced to imprisonment but between 1780 and 1784 this figure had risen to 34.6 per cent.[15] Without the safety valve of transportation prisons became cauldrons of fear for society at large. Escapes and riots were common. The example set by the prisoners of London's Newgate Prison in the Gordon Riots of 1780, the most serious outbreak of urban violence in eighteenth-century England, when the prisoners broke out and attacked the rich and powerful, was a salient reminder of the potentially explosive state of affairs. In Ireland the situation was not finally relieved until April 1791 when the first Irish convicts (130 men and 22 women) were sent from Queenstown

(Cobh) to the new penal colony of 'Botany Bay' aboard the *Queen*. But, during the intervening period, prisons became the subject of deep social and political concern. Light had entered the murky recesses of the Irish prison.

At the head of this interest was John Howard, the man recognised as being the founding father of the modern prison. Born in Hackney, Middlesex, in 1726, Howard was described as 'short, thin and sallow' as a boy. Inheriting a large sum of money on the death of his father, a tradesman who made good, he travelled Europe. Held as a prisoner of war in a Portuguese jail for a time, it was an experience that remained etched on his memory. Howard married twice but both his wives died. The second died just four days after giving birth to his only son (unlike the public image of the man who became synonymous with philanthropy Howard treated his son cruelly contributing to his death in a lunatic asylum at the age of 36[16]). In 1773 what had been a somewhat aimless and unfulfilling life was transformed when he was appointed Sheriff of Bedfordshire. Visiting the squalid county gaol as part of his duties, Howard was appalled by the scenes that assaulted his senses. A devout Christian had found his mission.

Prompted by 'the sorrow of the sufferer and love of my country', Howard undertook the mammoth task of investigating prison conditions

John Howard, the founding father of the modern prison.

with a view to their improvement. Later recalling the development of his obsession he wrote, 'the work grew upon me insensibly: I could not enjoy my ease and leisure in neglect of an opportunity offered me by divine providence of attempting the relief of the miserable'.[17] Driven by religious fervour Howard travelled over 50,000 miles on the unpleasant quest of poking his nose into every prison hovel he could find. Travelling on horseback (the stench of the prisons clung to his garments making his own company unbearable in a closed carriage) he abstained from meat and wine. Surviving on the sparse diet of two penny rolls with some butter, a pint of milk, five or six cups of tea (his great elixir) and a roasted apple on going to bed, he was always cheerful and serene – a condition he put down to his frugal and temperate lifestyle.[18]

From our end of the historical telescope we might imagine that Howard cut a lonely and pathetic figure, if not a ludicrous one. But in the context of the confinement crisis he became one of the most famous and respected men of his era. While he was alive Howard discouraged anyone from erecting a monument to his honour. However, after his death in 1791, a statue was erected in London's St Paul's Cathedral. The statue's inscription by Samuel Whitbread reads: 'Our national prisons and hospitals, improved upon the suggestion of his wisdom, bear testimony to the solidity of his judgement, and the estimation in which he was held in every part of the civilised world, which he traversed to reduce the sum of human misery'.

Giving terse lists of prison conditions, Howard's publications were dry as dust. Yet they were widely read and hugely influential, most notably *The State of Prisons in England and Wales* (1777). Documenting life in prisons throughout Europe they highlighted the glaring gap that existed between the well-ordered, clean and quiet prisons of countries like the Netherlands (where imprisonment had a comparatively long history as punishment) and those of Ireland and Britain which were akin to Dante's *Inferno*. When visiting Dutch gaols

Howard did not know what to admire most – 'the neatness and cleanliness appearing in the prisons, the industry and regular conduct of the prisoners, or the humanity and attention of the magistrates and regent.'[19] At the very time that the Irish and British systems of punishment were in crisis, Howard had seen his model prison system.

During Howard's first two visits to Ireland in 1775 and 1779 he exerted little influence on its political leaders. It was not until 1782 that he added his immense moral weight to the Irish reform movement when the newly-established and semi-independent Irish House of Commons in Dublin, or Grattan's Parliament as it was known, established the powerful Committee to Enquire into Prison Conditions. Irked at having little authority to effect real change within its own domain, some members of Grattan's emasculated Parliament seized on the latest *cause célèbre* – prison reform – to prove both their ability to govern and to 'cock a hoop' at the mother parliament in London. Howard was the high profile first witness called by the 1782 Committee. When he gave damning testimony on Dublin's Newgate Prison he sparked off an intense period of parliamentary investigation into exactly what the prisons of Ireland were like and how they could be improved (in recognition of his efforts Howard was awarded an honorary Doctorate of Law by Trinity College Dublin). However, this was by no means the start of the Irish reform movement. Most recently two pieces of legislation were passed in 1778 that, while being in advance of English legislation of the time, were limited in scope and largely ineffectual.

At the forefront of the Irish movement for prison reform was a small but powerful and energetic group of MPs which included Sir John Blaquire (former Chief Secretary of Ireland who built the official residence of the Chief Secretary, Deerfield House, now home to the American Ambassador), Sir John Parnell (one time Chancellor of the Exchequer and great grandfather of Charles Stewart Parnell), Luke Gardiner (MP for Dublin, property developer responsible for much of Dublin's

Luke Gardiner, one of the MPs at the fore-front of the drive towards prison reform.

classic Georgian architecture and the first Viscount Mountjoy who was to give his name to Mountjoy Prison), Lord Annally (one time Chancellor of the Exchequer) and the two Irish 'Howards', Mr Holmes (MP for the borough of Banagher) and the only significant non-political figure, Sir Jeremiah Fitzpatrick, a doctor from Kilbeggan, Westmeath. Working a double act, Holmes organised parliamentary activity and Fitzpatrick, giving detailed evidence from a medical standpoint, provided Holmes and his colleagues with ammunition. The findings of the many parliamentary investigations of the 1780s confirmed the fears of at least one MP that Ireland's prisons would be found the 'most defective in Europe'.[20] The prisons were clearly an embarrassment to the leaders of both the new parliament and the city in which it was based.

In the 1780s Dublin was a progressive, expanding and prosperous city. Slowly lurching out of the mire of its medieval past it had become the second city of the British Empire. Dublin was a newly-established European capital and its architecture bespoke its modern nature. Impressive public buildings dotted the city. The Wide Streets Commission masterminded much of the development, creating the layout of elegant avenues that converge on the present O'Connell Street and the now classic Georgian terraces, squares and wide streets. The prisons stood in stark contrast to this picture of elegance. They were the creepy-crawly underside of the well-polished stone of Georgian Dublin.

Irish prisons were damp and filthy, often with dungeons, insufficient bedding, poor food and no exercise areas. The greatest concern regarding prisons at the time was 'gaol fever'. Revelling in the squalid, filthy and overcrowded conditions, gaol fever, in reality epidemic typhus, was passed from inmate to inmate by body lice. The symptoms developed quickly and the mortality rate was high. Beginning with a slight cough, the palate, uvula and other parts of the throat reddened and swelled. Within 24 hours white ulcerous spots appeared on the tonsils and the victim experienced a general feeling of weakness and dejection. Waves of nausea and vomiting quickly followed and then, finally, death. Out of a potent blend of altruism and self-interest, leading members of society were deeply concerned about gaol fever. While wishing to relieve unnecessary suffering they were also aware that in a highly volatile economy one's situation was always precarious. Many influential people were imprisoned for debt and, as Howard had warned, 'those whose circumstances are affluent, may in time be reduced to indigence, and become debtors and prisoners'.[21] Even more importantly gaol fever was not confined to prisons. Through a prisoner's discharge or appearance in court it could, and often did, become general fever. Mr Holmes recalled many instances of magistrates and others attending court 'being swept away by the violence and malignancy of the gaol infection'.[22] Fitzpatrick called gaol fever 'a national concern of no small importance'.[23]

The reformers' zeal, coupled with the 'confinement crisis', led to a general demand for safer and healthier prisons. A rash of progressive prison legislation was passed in the 1780s to improve conditions – under the Prison Acts, Grand Juries were obliged to supply bread to prisoners, hours were prescribed during which the prisoners must have access to fires in common rooms with the Grand Juries providing £100 per annum for bedding and fuel, the sale of alcohol to prisoners was banned, healthy prisoners were separated from the sick, chaplains and physicians were appointed to visit prisons twice a week, dungeons were not used except as a punishment of last resort and, in an attempt to eliminate extortion and exploitation of prisoners, gaolers became salaried officials (£25 per annum). In May 1786 the position of Inspector General of Prisons was established in Ireland (half a century before a similar position was created in England). Sir Jeremiah Fitzpatrick was the first appointee. The Inspector General was to visit every prison once a year to ensure that prison regulations were being observed. At the end of each year he laid a report before parliament detailing the conditions of each prison. At the same time as this reinvention of the prison, other forms of punishment were in crisis.

Today punishment is hidden behind high walls but in the 1700s punishment in Ireland was normally public and usually involved the torture of the body of the convicted. Public whippings causing welts and flailing flesh were common. On 7 November 1786, four boys in Newgate Prison, 'convicted of various petty larcenies, the eldest not exceeding fifteen years of age and the youngest not more than nine or ten, were tied alternately to a cart's tail and whipped round the gaol'.[24] Ann Codd, found guilty of stripping the clothes off a child, was whipped from the chapel in St Sepulchre to the corner of Back Lane[25] (the body to be whipped was barebacked and therefore barechested). James Walsh, in 1787, was whipped from the Circular Road turnpike to Cork Bridge for attempted burglary.[26] In 1789, Thomas Bigney, Patrick Keane and Thomas Shannausy were whipped from Newgate Prison to Lazor's Hill for forcing and unlawfully entering the cellar door of Esther Dempsey.[27] James Purcell, for unlawfully administering an oath, was whipped from the Circular Road to the upper end of Harold's Cross in 1790.[28] George Dalton, 'for secreting himself in the shop of Laurence Hynes', was whipped from Kilmainham to Mount Brown.[29] These were a mere handful in the litany of scarred backs. Another 'minor' physical punishment was branding, or burning of the hand. Even punishments

Walter Cox on the pillory.

not intended to inflict pain were often accompanied by varying degrees of violence. In 1788 a man called Edgeworth was publicly pilloried (put into a standing stockade) for perjury. A punishment of shame, the display of the criminal would result in the loss of their good name. Standing in the wooden stockade, Edgeworth was the recipient of 'rotten eggs, oranges, potatoes, old shoes, brick-bats, dead cats, mud and filth of every sort'.[30]

The most extreme form of punishment was execution. Taking place mainly at the 'Hanging Tree' in St Stephen's Green, outside Newgate Prison, at Gallows Hill in Kilmainham and on Kilmainham Common, executions were manifestly public. Intended to be witnessed by the largest numbers possible, they were scheduled for Dublin's market days – Wednesdays and Saturdays – to ensure a good turn out. In this visual justice the medium was the message – this will be the result if you defy the law of King and country.

An execution was street theatre writ large. Like in all theatre everyone had a role to play. The magistrate, sheriff, clergy and taxpayers who presided over the solemn ceremony of ultimate power, represented authority. The condemned repented and confessed their crimes, some even going so far as to thank their approver (the informer who was responsible for their unfortunate situation). The crowd passively received the message portrayed when the hood was put over the head of the condemned and he, or she, was 'launched into eternity' (the familiar phrase used to describe the moment of hanging).

Executions were part of the popular culture of the time, permeating many different aspects of life – a possible relic of the period is the children's spelling game 'hangman'. The street ditty, *Luke Caffrey's Kilmainham Minuet,* tells in Dublin slang and subversive criminal cant the story of an execution from the perspective of a friend of the condemned. Caffrey had 'mill'd a fat slap' (succeeded in stealing a large amount) which he used 'to snack with the boys of de pad' (shared with fellow thieves). His friends came to 'tip him de fives 'fore his det' (bid him goodbye) and Caffrey, standing in the 'man trap' (the horse-drawn vehicle in which the condemned stood), asked them to save him from his ugly fate. They were reluctant to save such a rogue so he implored them to take hold of his body after he was hanged and cut his jugular – Caffrey quoted the common belief that such an operation would 'as de surgints of otomy tell us/... bring back puff to me bellows/And set me once more on me pins'. (A common sight around the scaffold was an undignified fight over custody of the corpse between members of the Royal College of Surgeons and the friends and family of the executed. The friends and family hoped to restore life 'by rubbing his limbs, and trying every method sagacity could suggest', without success, of course, while the surgeons, who were legally entitled to the corpse, wanted it to aid medical science. As one writer of the time put it, 'within this earthly pale, death is not the end of punishment, and although privation of life may satisfy the sentence of the law, the sentence of public feeling and opinion heaps execration on his unburied corpse and follows him from the gallows ... and attends him beneath the surgeon's knife'[31]). Then the dramatic moment when 'de clergy stept down from his side/and de gabbard from under him floated; Oh! be de hoky/It was den dat me port-royal run cold' and Caffrey was dancing the Kilmainham Minuet, the death kicks of the hanged.

The execution was a fantastically popular form of entertainment and it was not uncommon for the crushing voyeuristic masses to cause injury or death. The largest crowd in the history of Dublin public hangings was believed to have attended the execution of an informer, James O'Brien, convicted of the wilful murder of James Hoey, an 'inoffensive, infirm and defenceless man'. At his execution the crowd howled and cried with delight at the death of a fellow human being and O'Brien died, like many others, with 'no monument but the public odium – no epitaph but the public curse'.[32]

In the television age, well-managed ceremonial displays of official authority are the norm, but in the eighteenth century arrangements were not so well choreographed. While many executions went according to plan the dignitaries and symbols of offended justice were often left in uncomfortable positions as the victim was sent to the 'eternal bar'. In 1785 an execution at Kilmainham was:

> by an accident, rendered distressing to every person capable of feeling for the misfortune of their fellow creatures. In about a minute after the five unhappy criminals were turned off, the temporary gallows fell down, and on its re-erection, it was found necessary to suffer three of the unhappy wretches to remain half strangled on the ground until the other two underwent the sentences of the law, when they in turn were tied up and executed.[33]

Another hanging that broke from the script was that of one Daniel Dowling executed opposite Newgate for the murder of Charles Tyndal in 1789. On 27 July, when Dowling was sent to 'the searcher of Hearts', he 'suffered inconceivable torture previous to his death, the rope having slipped from the proper situation around his neck; for nearly a quarter of an hour, therefore, he continued to wreathe his body under great agony, a most horrid

15

... admonitory spectacle, to a great concourse of spectators'.[34]

Sometimes reprieves came agonisingly late and innocent people were certainly hanged. Indeed, for those in authority the most distressing course that events could take was for the condemned, with expiring voice, to proclaim their innocence. In one sentence, 'I did not do it', the whole concept of justice was turned on its head. It often made little difference whether the statement was true or not; the figure with the rope around its neck became victim and hero arousing the 'feelings and sympathy of every spectator'[35] and the authorities were heaped with shame and guilt. Inconveniently for the magistrates, clergy, sheriffs and taxpayers, the crowd were not always obedient spectators. Having their own sense of justice the crowd, in cases where they thought a miscarriage of justice had occurred, would fight off surgeons and military and carry the corpse to the prosecutor's door, laying it there as a testimony to his evil. The execution, a ceremony intended to enforce public order, often became a source of public disorder.

In the time of the 'Bloody Code', a body of law that prescribed death for a host of offences ranging from stealing a ham to murder, judges were often merciless in passing the grim sentence. In 1792 a sailor from London named Phillips shored up in Dublin, got drunk and stole a hat from one Patrick MacGowan. Unable to raise money for his defence in this foreign city he was found guilty. Returning the verdict the jury declared they felt death too severe a penalty for what was such a petty offence and recommended mercy. However, the judge was unmoved by their plea and, donning the black cap on his seat of power, replied that 'there was no palliation of the crime in the trivial loss of the sufferer'. Phillips hanged two weeks later.[36] In 1787 Joseph Smith and John Kelly were found guilty of feloniously entering the house of Michael Atkins of Donnybrook and stealing a number of articles including a coat valued at ten shillings. Sentencing the prisoners to death at the Quarter Sessions, Denis George remarked that 'if persons capable of entering a man's house in the dead of night, and plundering it of whatever might be in their reach, were to be treated with lenity, no honest man could be secure in his life and his property'. Kelly was in his teens and was recommended an object of mercy by the jury. However, out of motives he felt to be thoroughly humane, the judge refused such a recommendation which, he said, 'might prove cruelty in effect'. The two were 'launched off the fatal board into eternity' on 23 August.[37] One of the oldest recorded victims of the gallows was 80-year-old Peter Rigney, a previous offender, executed for stealing fat out of sheep at Ballynadrun (the sheep were alive at the time).[38] At one court session in which he sentenced eight men to death, Baron Sir Michael Smith said 'all of them had defied the laws of the country, and wickedly provoked a God, under whose protection and blessing they may have continued to enjoy personal comfort and social peace'. He claimed he felt little joy in condemning the men to early deaths and that 'his sentence was merely the echo of the imperious voice of offended justice'.[39]

In *Dublin Hanged*, Brian Henry chronicles what one contemporary account called the 'legal massacre' of the period when malefactors 'advanced like troops to their deaths'.[40] At least 242 people were executed in Dublin between 1780 and 1795[41] (at today's population level this would be the equivalent of 1,200 executions). The prospect of hell displayed in the theatre of the damned was thought by many magistrates to be the only effective way of discouraging the criminally inclined. But in the press it was reported that 'the fear of the gallows has little effect on that class of society who are daily on the high road to it'.[42] It was most disturbing for the forces of law and order that the emptying of the prisons into the graves was not working.

Dublin was a city riven by crime. It was infested with highwaymen, highwaywomen and daring footpads (highwaymen without the horses) whose blood-curdling address 'your money or your soul' was as likely to be heard in the city streets as in the rural neighbourhoods of Chapelizod, Islandbridge and along the Circular and Blackrock Roads. The Robinson gang terrorised Dolphin's Barn threatening to drive out the whole population before they were caught. The elusive footpad nicknamed 'Rí Rá' and the vicious 'Mendoza gang' were infamous. No one who had anything worth stealing was immune. Victims of crime ranged from children snatched off busy streets and stripped of their clothes to the Lord Chancellor himself who was robbed twice, once within the grounds of his own house, by 'armed banditti'. Conmen, or 'sharpers', harvested the belongings of the gullible and naïve. Dublin was awash with guns and savage beatings accompanied many robberies. Rapes were commonplace. Infants were killed by mothers who could not afford to feed another mouth. On average there were 24 violent deaths a year[43] (today it would be the equivalent of 130). Some crimes were almost picaresque in character: highwaymen bidding their victims a safe journey after their load had been lightened or the arch pick-pocket Barrington and his gang mingling at the society balls plying their lucrative trade. The poor of Dublin crammed into rookeries and, supplemented by a stream of rural migrants, were continuously on the verge of starvation – examples of what Thomas Paine had in mind when he wrote, 'A world of little cases are continually arising, which busy or affluent life knows not of, to open the first door to distress. Hunger is not among the postponable of wants, and a day, even a few hours, in such a condition, is often the crisis of a life of ruin'.[44] Add to this political violence in the form of Republican associations and journeymen illegally forming combinations (early trade unions) and a picture of a society in a severe state of flux emerges.

Lord Kilwarden, the judge who was the principal victim of Emmet's 1803 Rebellion (appropriately killed by the population of the Liberties, the 'St Giles' of Dublin, that supplied most of the corpses cut down from the gallows of the capital), in a speech which would not be out of place today, blamed the massive crime rate on 'the relaxed state of public morals' arising from the 'relaxation of domestic discipline' and the apathy, neglect and poor example set by the heads of families. He longed for the time when the clergy 'were more than nominal shepherds of the flock, inculcating the principles of Christianity by example as well as by precept'.[45] At one court session the presiding judge said the record number of defendants before him were 'sad proof of the prevalence of crimes and the insufficiency of our laws and magistracy to prevent crimes'.[46] If the savage public punishments deterred some they did not deter enough. Indeed the sheer numbers of executions were undermining their effect as the population became numbed to the sight of the hanged (one writer to the *Hibernian Journal* suggested the odd castration to provide a bit of variety[47]). In a society that lacked any sort of adequate organised police force it was a frustrating exercise for the judiciary as they often passed the ultimate sentence for petty crimes while the city was rife with murder and rapine.

There was no one moment when it was written in stone that imprisonment would be the main way that society dealt with criminals. But 1786 was a watershed year when the numbers hanged in Dublin reached their height and the most important piece of prison legislation was passed. Abandoning the usual subjects for its leading articles (such as the latest French fashion) *Walker's Hibernian Magazine* began its February edition with an unusually considered essay on 'Crime and Criminals'. Giving an overview of the punishment problem it stated that the 'wanton infliction of death can produce no advantage; the mind revolts at the cruelty of the sentence; the anguish of the criminal is supposed to exceed his guilt; and pity for his sufferings usurps the place of resentment against his crimes'. The article called for a penalty that could be adjusted to meet the exact proportion warranted by each of the numerous and ever-increasing types of offences (execution was a blunt instrument that treated a poor thief the same as a murderer). It also called for one that would make the prisoners compensate the state, to 'pay their debt' to the society that had been damaged – instead of being executed and therefore worthless, or transported and therefore useful to another society. The article put forward imprisonment, accompanied by a labour regime, as the future of punishment.[48]

Corporal and capital punishment were going out of favour. The criminal body had been regarded as a diseased part of the body politic that needed to be amputated to prevent the disease from spreading. Deprived of feelings and sensations it was viewed only as an object of retribution. But attitudes were changing in the light of medical research and evolving philosophies. The body was becoming 'the site of pain and pleasure, of choice and consent'.[49] Research into the nervous system had shown that man was a sentient being and the 'inner man' emerged as a philosophical idea. Concepts of 'benevolence' and 'sympathy', of being able to feel and understand another's pain, made torture of the body increasingly unpleasant and unpopular and in this sense prisons were the outcome of improvements in morals and the development of ideas. Imprisonment as punishment was also a reflection of the worth modern society put on 'freedom'. Valued above everything else, the denial of freedom came to be seen as the ultimate penalty. Foucault, in his classic text, *Discipline and Punish*, described imprisonment as 'an economy of suspended rights'. It was 'the penalty *par excellence* in a society in which liberty is a good that belongs to all in the same way'. Imprisonment was also convenient as it made possible a minute classification of punishment in terms of time. It offered society the 'clearest, simplest, most equitable of penalties'.[50]

The prison legislation passed in the House of Commons in the 1780s necessitated a massive prison-building programme by the Grand Juries to ensure that each county and town complied with the acts. According to Fitzpatrick the location of new prisons 'ought to be lofty, and, if possible, on a limestone gravel, in the vicinity of some running water, which may answer to keep the sewers cleansed, the floors clean, and the prison in warm weather refreshed'. While location was important so too was architecture. Before this period the prison had not evolved its own form of architecture. Now prisons were no longer buildings merely used for incarceration – castle towers, gate towers, old houses, etc. – the new prison was visibly different. It was also a place apart, removed from the towns, 'abstracted from everyday life and made very special'.[51] This was an unprecedented and since unparalleled period of prison construction. In 1788 there were 33 prison projects either planned or in progress from Donegal to Wexford and from Cork to Antrim.[52] The modern prison was born in Ireland. The sheer scale and cost of construction raised the obvious question: if we have them why not make full use of them? In response to the physical presence of the new prisons the sentence of imprisonment became increasingly common for many small crimes including stealing brass doorknockers and dogs. What had been an historical accident now created its own rationale. The prison, in a very short period of time, became an accepted and essential part of the justice system.

The reform movement that created the modern prison virtually disappeared in the 1790s under an avalanche of difficulties and distractions. Fitzpatrick, the most astute of the Irish contingent, resigned as Inspector General to take up a post in the army and Howard, the salient international figure, died in 1791. From 1791 many of the most serious criminals were transported to Australia. The outbreak of war with Republican France in 1793 concentrated attentions on national security while the ranks of the army and navy were filled with young men who would normally have filled the prisons. In Ireland the landing of French troops and the 1798 Rebellion left little room for concerns about prisons and prisoners.

The legislation passed by the Irish parliament in the 1780s was far more advanced than that of England. The Prison Acts were a remarkable attempt by central government to interfere with a local institution but real power lay with the Grand Juries who ran the prisons and controlled most of the tax base. The limitations of central government to resolve local issues like prisons were exposed as the Inspector General was rendered an impotent overseer. Having little power of enforcement the Prison Acts remained unenforced and largely unenforceable. A 1787 House of Commons Committee frustratingly reported that they were 'baffled by the difficulty and almost impossibility of fixing any responsibility anywhere' for the failure to adhere to their legislation.[53] Six years later it was reported that the Inspector General had effected few changes in the internal management of prisons.[54] However, the reform movement was also a victim of its own success. Having largely defeated gaol fever, many of the reformers lost interest. This trend led Fitzpatrick to comment in his *Thoughts on Penitentiaries*, published in 1790, that 'to permit improvement to stop now, and not touch upon the most important of its object – the reformation of the vicious and debauched and establishment of industry ... would have the appearance that the late improvements made, in great measure are from selfishness'.[55] But if the candle of reform was only briefly lit, it burned brightly.

In a very short period of time the prisons of Ireland, from being mere backwaters in the bloody pool of punishment, became central features and accounted for over half of the sentences handed down in Irish courts. Practically every county had its new or improved prison, even if many were poorly constructed with cheap materials (the most progressive and comfortable prison of the era was the one most Irish people now associate with austerity, gloom and oppression – Kilmainham Gaol). The prisons of this generation stood as monuments to the original reformers' ambition to help 'the most wretched part of the community'. They also provided the foundation for the present punishment system, at the apex of which sits Mountjoy Prison.

Chapter Two

MOUNTJOY: IRELAND'S MODEL PRISON

Those who torment us for our own good will torment us without end
for they do so with the approval of their own conscience.

C. S. Lewis

Health, security and exploitation of prisoners for private profit
were three of the main points on the agenda of the prison
reformers and by the time the movement came to a halt much
had been achieved; gaol fever, if not totally eradicated, was
much reduced; the new prisons were generally stronger; legislation was passed banning gaol fees. But prison reform did not
end there. The institution was not born whole and complete.
After a lapse of two decades prison reform re-emerged as a
major social issue with war once again providing the spur.

After the end of the Napoleonic Wars the gaols of Ireland
(and Britain) filled to unprecedented levels as victorious soldiers returned home to find few economic opportunities in a
country suffering a dramatic post-war economic slump. The
prison population in Ireland rose frighteningly from 5,792 in
1815 to 13,564 in 1818[1] (in 1787 it had been a mere 1,700[2]). This
new crisis in prisons gave a powerful impetus to the efforts of
Elizabeth Fry, an English Quaker, to pick up where Howard and
his contemporaries had left off. At the age of 33, she visited
London's Newgate Prison and witnessed scenes similar to those
that had driven Howard. Deciding that change could only come
from without, she established a Ladies Visiting Committee to

23

Mary Aikenhead, one of the founders of the Irish Sisters of Charity, who visited prisoners in Dublin.

visit Newgate and convey moral and religious instruction to the female prisoners. Sister organisations were set up in Ireland by religious organisations and well-heeled women with social consciences. These ladies visited female prisoners in Dundalk, Dublin, Armagh, Carlow, Galway, Sligo, Trim, Belfast, Carrickfergus, Derry, Omagh, Enniskillen, Roscommon, Maryborough (Portlaoise), Limerick, Wicklow, Wexford and Waterford and instructed them in morals, religion and needlework. The Ladies Visiting Committees worked in tandem with a national organisation, the Association (or Society) for the Improvement of Prisons and Prison Discipline in Ireland, established in 1819 under the patronage of the Chief Secretary. Between them they set the agenda for the resurrected cause and dominated penal thinking in the 1820s.

The second reform movement focused much of its initial attention on women prisoners who had suffered in conditions far worse than those of men. In an important departure from previous practice, matrons were appointed to govern the female parts of prisons. Until this period women prisoners had been in the charge of male staff which had led to obvious abuses. Under the legislation of the 1820s, no male members of staff, including the governor and chaplain, were allowed into the female wings except in the presence of the matron. Having immense power for women in Ireland at the time, they ruled the roost of the female wings. A matron's position was an arduous one, encompassing the role of governor, schoolmistress and trades instructor, yet unsurprisingly, in an overwhelmingly male-dominated society, she received only a fraction of a governor's salary. In the specific area of reform, the matron's job was considerably more difficult than her male counterpart's. The way to reformation for women prisoners who had 'fallen' from their great height of female virtue (a much greater fall in contemporary moral terms, from Madonna to whore, than that experienced by men) was believed to be through kindness. The matron was to cajole rather than coerce, instruct rather than regiment, convince rather than punish and, through the example of her feminine ideal, provide a model for the prisoners to emulate. It was often an impossible task.

At a time when it was becoming widely accepted that the purpose of punishment should not be revenge but the improvement of the prisoner, the issue of prisoners' rights and the obligation that society owed them came to the fore. The Association for the Improvement of Prison Discipline stated in its first report that 'society has become guilty of injustice towards the most helpless of its members' and it set about eliminating some of the prisons' many problems.[3] One of the main tenets of the second wave of reformers was that 'the principle causes of crime are to be found in the ignorance and want of education of the lower orders'.[4] Believing that the ability to read and write 'may totally alter the colour of a man's life' and be a true instrument of reformation,[5] education was amongst the most progressive changes introduced into prisons. Teaching basic reading, writing and arithmetic, prison schools were some of Ireland's first publicly-funded schools. However, attention was not merely centred on the shortcomings of life inside prison. In response to the suicides of two women who failed to find work after their release from prison, discharged prisoners' shelters were established. In these 'convalescent houses for the soul', discharged female prisoners were able to stay out of trouble until they found employment – a difficult proposition in normal circumstances but one even more fraught with failure for those with the tag 'gaol-bird' attached to them.

The primary principle of each of the reform movements was that imprisonment, given the right circumstances, could change the character of an offender from one inclined toward vice to one inclined toward virtue.[6] The debauched pre-reform prisons were hardly breeding grounds for goodness. From the heights of his moral mountain, Howard wrote, 'I make no scruple to affirm that if it were the main aim and wish of the magistrates to effect the destruction, present and future of young delinquents, they could not desire a more effectual method than to confine them in prisons'.[7] Unlike today, when we tend to look at the link between crime and punishment, the reformers were more concerned about the relationship between punishment and crime. Fitzpatrick, in his *Thoughts on Penitentiaries,* had railed against 'gaol-tuition', Lord Landsdowne labelled prisons 'universities of crime' (1820)[8] and an 1821 pamphlet claimed 'prisons in their present state afford the best opportunity of mischievous combinations. The most vicious and hardened offenders instruct and confirm in profligacy the less licentious'.[9] An 1822 Parliamentary Select Committee warned that 'it is no less the interest than the duty of every government, to take care that the individuals subjected to imprisonment, do not, by the effect of that sentence, become worse members of society, or more hardened offenders'.[10] Prisons were seen as part of a vicious circle that began with crime, was reinforced with punishment and then went back to further and worse crime. To break this cycle the reformed prison was given a mission, an almost religious purpose, the transformation of the criminal soul – in a word their 'reformation'. The official attitude towards criminals was that there was 'no individual, however depraved, that has not some good; let us cherish that good, and it will, in 99 cases out of 100, spring up in a desire for moral improvement, and for a better condition in life'.[11] In the cause of reformation the main tools used to hew at the raw material of the criminal were work and silence.

In 1810 an anonymous Dublin pamphleteer rhetorically asked 'is it not idleness that stocks our prisons?'[12] Recommending enforced work behind prison walls he continued, 'who shall pretend to calculate the effects which may be produced in the minds of culprits, by a few years constant labour with intervals of hope interposed? And will not the continual sound of machinery worked by them in the prison, deter the idle and profligate from joining their society?'[13] This concept of work, punishment and reform was not new and indeed had been the basis of the transportation system. Many of the 'excrementious masses' who had been sent to America as convicts became useful members of that society. They were held up as examples of reformation, living proof that even the lowest of the low were redeemable and, given the right circumstances, could 'become ornaments of that society of which they had been the bane'.[14] At the end of the confinement crisis an Irish Hard Labour Act was passed in 1792. Its cautious preamble read, 'Whereas it might tend to reform and render useful members of society, such persons sentenced to be transported, if such persons were compelled under proper rules and government, to work at useful trades or to labour according to their skill and ability' (the Hard Labour Act essentially established transportation without the travel but it was implemented on a very limited basis affecting a small number of cases).

In the second period of reform work gained increasing credence as a shaper of souls. Stonebreaking was one of the most common forms of labour but the classic piece of prison machinery was the treadwheel. Invented by a civil engineer from Ipswich named William Cubitt, it was based on the design of the common waterwheel (the treadwheel was several times wider). However, unlike the waterwheel, it was turned not by a flowing river or millrace – it was turned by humans. Standing on the struts of the massive wooden wheel, the prisoners held onto a horizontal bar and depressed the struts thus turning the wheel – the men becoming a mere cog of the machine. In some

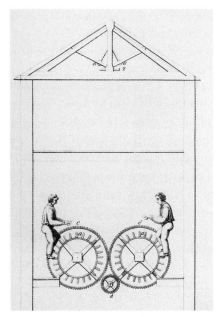

The treadwheel, invented by William Cubitt, which was developed into the classic piece of prison machinery.

prisons the power generated by the treadwheel was used to draw water from wells and grind corn but often the wheel and its turning would be the only purpose in a strenuous form of useless labour. The 'everlasting staircase' turned 12,000ft in an eight-hour day by two teams of prisoners working in tandem, ten minutes on, ten minutes off. The propensity of the treadwheel to reduce crime was firmly believed and 'the tedious uniformity of its motion added to the severe fatigue which it occasions contributed much to render it an object of the most invincible dislike'.[15] In a recommendation reminiscent of a 1950s washing machine commercial, the Association for the Improvement of Prison Discipline proclaimed 'no house of correction should be without it'.[16]

Labour in all forms was believed to be the 'most effectual corrector of evil habits',[17] particularly in Ireland where, according to one writer, 'contempt attaches itself to imposed labour'.[18] Even prisoners not sentenced to hard labour were compelled to work at various industries and crafts. Weaving was thought to be one of the best because 'the noise of the shuttle prevents conversation, and the progress of the work requires a constant eye'.[19] Work in prison also trained criminals in a trade to help them gain employment after their release. In one enlightened move inmates gained one-third of the profit they produced – it was kept aside until their release so they would not leave prison penniless and be forced to steal for their first meal. Prison work also made general economic sense as it went some way towards the financing of prisons, relieving part of the burden from the tax-payer. But prisons were not only to be houses of industry; they were also to be houses of morality. Indeed 'every prison should be a penitentiary, where abstinence and labour should be the discipline, and piety the recreation'.[20] Work had been introduced into prisons as a weapon of reform to train the criminals in the habits of labour, but keeping the prisoners busy also had the objective of keeping them quiet. In 1818 Inspector General Archer's report on Down County Gaol stated that:

> The melancholy effects of idleness are too apparent, in insolence and insubordination; could the prisoners be compelled to spend those hours in labour which they devote to recounting their past misconduct, and planning new schemes for annoying society, the happy effects would soon be acknowledged.[21]

Silence was believed by many to be the key to the reformation of prisoners. In 1776, at the start of the confinement crisis, English reformer Jonas Hanway published *Solitude in Imprisonment* in which he wrote, 'the walls of the prison will preach to the prisoner's soul and he will confess the goodness of his maker and the wisdom of the laws of his country'. The degree of silence and isolation to which a prisoner should be subjected to was the source of heated debate for decades. Some reformers like Hanway wanted to enforce complete silence and separation for 24 hours a day. Others, like Howard, felt that such a regime would eventually lead to the destruction of the individual whom they hoped to save. Fitzpatrick, a medical man less inclined towards religious thoughts and separated by the Irish Sea from the evangelical revival sweeping England, was sceptical but agreed that the less communication the better. He felt it might be more effective for old offenders, 'to whom solitude and silence will be favourable to reflection; and

29

may possibly lead to repentance'.[22] Silence was used as a double-edged sword that would both compel the prisoner to internal reflection and save him from the corrupting influence of fellow inmates.

The reformed prison became heavily laden with medical associations and religious imagery. Cut off from criminal fraternity by four cell walls, the prisoner in isolation or quarantine would, like a monk in a penitential monastic cell, be confronted with their own thoughts, see the error of their ways and ultimately be overcome by 'truth'. The Association for the Improvement of Prison Discipline summed up the reformatory powers of a room so many feet by so many feet:

> The sense of oppressive loneliness which the cell of a prison imparts becomes a moral instrument, the power of which cannot be too highly estimated. It compels the mind to render itself the subject of its own contemplation; it obliges the most obdurate and insensible to reflect seriously; it awakens repentance, and leads to sorrow and contrition.[23]

The greatest torment of prisoners in the pre-reformed prison had been the horrific physical conditions. In this new prison hell would not be the prisoners' surroundings but the prisoners' minds. During this treatment prisoners would experience, literally, a religious transformation and leave prison better people. Great importance was given to the role of the chaplain in assisting the prisoners on this internal journey of self-discovery, annihilation and rebirth. At the end of the process prisoners would be cured of their moral influenza in this new moral hospital.

Most criminals, whether city, town or rural, came from crowded quarters in cramped hovels. These were the normal conditions of the poor in which disease ravaged generations. Because crime was endemic amongst the poor it too came to be seen as a disease. Indeed the moral disease of crime was so virulent and contagious – 'no infection spreads so fast as moral depravity'[24] – that it could be transmitted through communication. With words those better versed in crime, farther down that ill road of depravity, could infect those less developed. Lice, which had carried gaol fever from prisoner to prisoner, were stopped by cell walls. The victory over fever encouraged thoughts on similar lines with regard to vice.[25] Words, the carriers of the contagion of crime, would be confined within the walls of the cell as the prisoner was effectively left in mute isolation.

In the early stages the imposition of silence proved impossible. While prison architecture had not yet developed sufficiently to enforce the rule, the staff in Irish prisons posed a further difficulty. Those managing and working in the prisons had little to recommend them as purveyors of the message of reform. Corruption, bribery, patronage and nepotism were rampant in the locally-managed prisons. Many of the staff had been prisoners before gaining employment in the prisons while others became prisoners as a result of their actions while working in prison (embarrassingly even one of the Inspector Generals, Major Palmer, found himself on the wrong side of the bars when he was imprisoned for debt[26]). In such imperfect circumstances the 'classification' of prisoners replaced silence as the working model.

Under the classification system the tried and untried, the youthful offender and old delinquent were separated from one another in wards – another hospital term – with prisoners no longer being guarded by turnkeys but by 'warders'. At night each prisoner was to have a separate cell to sleep in. By this method the disease could then be prevented from passing from the hardened criminals, those in the last inveterate stages of the disorder, to those in its first stages. Architecture was central to the classification system as the prisons were turned into 'complex atlases of vice, with each of the numerous sections cordoned off, screened and introverted'.[27] The most favoured plans were radial ones in which the wings radiated from a central area from which the governor was able to survey each section and enforce morality. In order to facilitate the classification system the 1820s saw a second phase of prison construction. Many prisons were altered and new county prisons were constructed in Down, King's County (Laois), Kildare, Meath, Queen's County (Offaly), Carlow, Westmeath, Kerry and Galway.

Classification soon came under attack from a number of quarters as a far from perfect method of control and reform. Its limitations were obvious. A criminal who had a previous unknown conviction for a more serious crime could be put into a class for minor offenders. In an increasingly complex society crime itself was becoming more complex making any sufficient classification system impossible. Overcrowding in many gaols undermined any attempt to enforce strict classification while full prisons were indicative to many that classification was simply not reforming prisoners in sufficiently large numbers. In fact many people began to blame improved prison conditions for rising crime, as ridding the prison of its physical terrors raised the question of its basic value as a deterrent to crime.

In 1830 Archibald Wilson, the Deputy Governor of the Richmond Penitentiary in Dublin, wrote a scathing attack from the inside on what he saw as the mollycoddling of Irish prisoners. Conditions that would shock and outrage us today were condemned by Wilson for being too lenient. 'Imprisonment in modern times cannot be considered punishment,'[28] he wrote. In an obvious condemnation of Elizabeth Fry, the Ladies Visiting Committees and the Association for the Improvement of Prisons he wrote that what he saw as 'soft' prison conditions were the result of the efforts of 'a number of philanthropists led away with their feelings with mistaken notions of humanity', who cared more about the well being of prisoners than they did about 'the industrious, the starving, the honest poor'.[29] Conditions were apparently so good that Wilson believed a criminal rued his life before prison. 'Why did I starve so long? Oh! that my family were here ...'[30](!?) Defending the prison system, Inspector General Palmer countered that 'accommodation in prisons has no approach to luxury, but is confined to the necessities of life', and that it was unreasonable to demand 'that when the poor are visited with hunger, cold and nakedness, the prisoner should be deprived of food, fuel and covering'.[31]

Wilson condemned the classification of prisoners and expounded the inherent properties of solitude by prefacing the publication with the maxim, 'Evil communication doth corrupt'. In the backlash against 'comfortable' prison conditions and rising crime the solitude debate re-emerged in the 1830s. Having used it as a punishment of last resort Wilson wrote, with exaggerated emphasis, that even a short period in isolation caused an astonishing change in his charges:

> I have never known it fail of humbling the most haughty, quieting the most turbulent, and breaking down the most stubborn wills and dispositions. I have often seen prisoners forced by the exertions of several strong men, struggling every inch of the way, fighting and foaming with madness, into the cell; by the next day so quiet and docile, that a child might lead them.[32]

When Wilson extolled the virtues of silence his was not a lone voice in the backwoods but part of a chorus of discontent. At the time two American prisons were engaged in a very public battle for penal supremacy on the basis of eliminating communication in prisons. In Auburn, New York, prisoners slept in individual cells at night but ate and worked in common under the Silent Association system. During the periods of association officers stood watch over the inmates waiting to punish with an instant flogging a word, even a glance. It was a regime based on tyranny and brutality. Meanwhile, its rival at the Eastern State Penitentiary in Philadelphia operated the Silent and Separate system, or merely the Separate system as it came to be known. Under this rule – a rule strongly influenced by contemplative Quaker religious practice in the city of brotherly love – it was not the staff but the architecture of the prison that kept the prisoners silent. In this 'Crucible of Good Intentions' prisoners were confined in their cells for their entire sentence. They slept, ate, worked and cried there. The only distraction was the ministration of the chaplain.

It was a perfect system of classification with each individual compartmentalised. To us the argument between the Auburn and Philadelphia systems might seem like trying to distinguish Tweedle Dum from Tweedle Dee but it was a heated debate between the two ends of the penal spectrum, those who wanted to reform and those who wanted to punish. The Philadelphia model was thought to be more humane and beneficial to reform than the Auburn method of control and in 1835 a House of Lords committee sent to investigate the competing methods put forward the separate system as the basis of future punishment. Shortly afterwards laws were passed permitting the continuous confinement of prisoners in their cells, except for periods of exercise, worship and education. In the 1840 legislation which enacted separate confinement it was clearly laid down that it did not mean solitary confinement and was 'not viewed by the Legislature as a system of harassing restraint and privation, but as a refuge to the mind not wholly corrupted, and a protection from an intercourse not more dangerous to the young offender, than painful to moral feeling'.

Up to this point Mountjoy Prison has hardly been mentioned. The concept of prison had come a long way since the 1780s – the Joy was far removed from the earlier prisons. The two reform movements had cleared the ground and laid its foundations but it is only in the 1830s that we can see Mountjoy's architect sit down, as it were, in his office to begin to shade the walls, arc the curves and fill in the empty white spaces on the drawing board of what was originally known as Ireland's Model Prison. The crucial phase was when the adoption of the separate system was linked with the winding down of transportation to Australia.

Captain Cook's discovery, for white men, of Botany Bay in 1770 seemed like proof that the Lord had once again shone bright on the British Empire. Despite going down in the lexicon of punishment as the general descriptive term for the penal colony, 'Botany Bay' itself was never used for convicts.

Captain Cook had described it in idyllic terms in his reports back to London. However, within five days of arriving there to set up a penal colony in 1787, Lieutenant Ralph Clarke wrote of the barren inhospitable landscape, 'if we are obliged to settle here there will not be a soul alive in the course of a year'. Pulling up anchor they sailed north to Port Jackson, now Sydney, and began the process of turning a continent into a prison.[33] In 1787, shortly after America won its independence from Britain, the moral sewer was re-directed south. Four years later the first Irish convicts sailed to Australia. Between 1791 and 1853, 39,000 Irish convicts were transported to Australia (9,000 of whom were women).[34] Over 200 ships, including the *Renown, Hope, Henrietta, Anne, Minerva* and *Cambden Cutter* sailed from Ireland. Political exiles like Michael Dwyer, William Smith O'Brien and John Mitchel are among the best-known transportees but only 600 of the total transported to Botany Bay fell into the political category.[35] The vast majority were ordinary criminals.

Transportation was never without its opponents. One of the most vociferous and effective of these was the Protestant Archbishop of Dublin, Richard Whately. Initially unhappy with his transfer to Dublin in 1831, Whately quickly immersed himself in Irish life. A supporter of Catholic Emancipation, he also sought reforms in the Poor Law and National Education. A philosopher, economist and churchman, Whately believed transportation to be a system more wick-ed than any convict. He campaigned in the House of Lords, published pamphlets and generally har-angued the government on the issue. For the Archbishop it was a case of anything but transportation. Criticisms of the transportation system were often levelled on the grounds of cost, that the offender was not punished by example in the country where the crime was committed and that the sufferings convicts endured on the journeys to the antipodes were unduly harsh and turned the sentence of transportation into a death sentence lottery. In addition, transportation was

Richard Whately, Protestant Archbishop of Dublin and anti-transportation campaigner.

condemned on the contradictory grounds that it was a system akin to slavery but was also an inducement to crime as people sought to be transported to start a new life down under. An essential consideration was the ties an individual had to his or her native place. A person who had nothing to lose could look upon transportation as an escape from difficult circumstances, with free passage. But it was not just the effects, or lack of, on the mother country that doomed the system. What had originally been a vast prison was now a rapidly expanding society with its own needs and requirements. Ironically, in a society built on forced labour, the one essential that was in short supply was labour. Without enough convicts to support the economy, free labour was needed but the very idea of free labour in a convict society was contradictory.

In 1837 the eventual death knell of transportation was sounded when the Molesworth Committee was appointed 'to inquire into the system of Transportation, its efficacy as a Punishment, its Influence on the Moral State of Society in the Penal Colonies, and how far it is susceptible to improvement'. Molesworth, the head of the committee, was an ambitious young radical who was vehemently opposed to transportation. The publication of his thorough and scathing report in 1838 was the beginning of the end of transportation to the antipodes. Its demise was to have wide-ranging implications for the prison system at home. With transportation in decline the question arose as to what to do with the convicts? The answer was separate confinement. The first prison built with separation in mind was Pentonville Prison in London. Known as the Model Prison it was the most important prison built in the nineteenth century.

On 22 May 1840, transportation to New South Wales was abolished. Thereafter all convicts were transported to Van Diemen's Land (now Tasmania) to work in gangs, rather than be assigned to settlers. But soon disaster loomed due to lack of work for the convicts and the fear of homosexuality amongst the gangs. In 1846 Earl Grey, Secretary of State, suspended transportation. Two years later it was revived on a new system of forced emigration. Convicts who had served part of their sentence in a penitentiary, and were thus 'reformed', would then arrive not as convicts but 'exiles' with a 'ticket of leave' which permitted them to work providing they stayed on the right side of the law.

In the 1840s Ireland fell out of step with the changes in the transportation system. To ascertain what requirements were needed in Ireland under the changed circumstances Major Cottingham, the Superintendent of Prisons, went on a fact-finding mission of the English convict system in 1846.[36] He came back with the news that Ireland needed its own penitentiary, its own Model Prison. Prior to this point the convict department had survived on the cast-offs and good will of local prison authorities. Its accommodation consisted of old prisons that the Grand Juries had abandoned and sections of county gaols. But with new demands on the part of the colonies a reluctant Irish administration was forced to take a leading role in convict management. In 1847 a law was passed enabling the Commissioners of Public Works to purchase land for a new convict prison and

Wing of Pentonville Prison in London, which became the model for Mountjoy.

£2,000 was granted by the Treasury for the purchase of a suitable site for a Pentonville-type institution for convicts. We now know this as Mountjoy Prison.

The first site chosen for the Model Prison was at the North Wall on the River Liffey near where the Point Depot is today. This site offered the distinct advantage of the speedy embarkation of convicts for their sea journey but after the handshakes were made it was condemned as unsuitable for a number of reasons; it lacked an adequate fresh water supply, the stench from the River Liffey would make it unbearable to the inmates, the site was low lying and thus prone to flooding and it was also too small. Alternatives put forward included a site in Merrion, along the Blackrock Road (the site was close to the railway line to Kingstown where the transportees could be quickly sent and loaded onto waiting ships but this area too was prone to flooding) and the conversion of Smithfield Prison (this plan was abandoned on the grounds that convicts would have to be conveyed through the centre of town allowing various contraband, 'liquor, tobacco, Lucifer matches', to be given to prisoners by the public).[37] In 1846 Colonel Joshua Jebb, the architect of Pentonville Prison and Surveyor General of Prisons in England, arrived to stamp his authority on the matter. Working in conjunction with the Commissioners of Public Works, he selected the present site on the North Circular Road. Security was uppermost in his thoughts. The site, bounded on two sides by the Royal Canal, was large enough to allow an open space at the entrance, a *cordon sanitaire*, for the defence of the building if attacked 'in case of popular excitement'. It also precluded the erection of 'low class houses' which were not only a security threat but also a health risk. The land chosen had two owners. Lord Rathdowne owned a portion but the bulk of the site was in the hands of the Mountjoy family. It was from the latter transaction, made on terms very favourable to the government, that Ireland's greatest misnamed building was given its title.[38] The cost of building the prison was estimated at £50,000.[39] Progress toward construction was slow and it was not until April 1847 that Jebb presented his plans to the Lord Lieutenant for approval. In the meantime catastrophic events in Ireland were overtaking the planned Model Prison.

The Irish Famine of the late 1840s was the great watershed of Irish history that affected every aspect of society. As a direct consequence of this last great western European famine one million people died and a further one million emigrated. Prisons were not immune to the effects of the calamity. Indeed, the spread of the potato disease and 'distress' could be gauged by the barometer of prison numbers. By 1849 there were over 100,000 imprisoned in Ireland. Conditions were atrocious. In 1849 alone over 1,300 prisoners died (the counties of Cork, Galway, Limerick and Tipperary provided over half the emaciated corpses[40]). Not surprisingly the Famine abolished 'all distinction between right and wrong' with the Inspectors General reporting that 'the annals of this country never before exhibited such a numerical array of criminal cases ... larcenies have multiplied, because ordinarily, men will steal rather than die'.[41] Exacerbating the crisis was the passing of a Vagrancy Act. It was an example of incomprehensible mistiming as magistrates were obliged to flood prisons with shoals of beggars, many of whom then used prisons as convenient and free boarding houses. The ultimate indictment of the state of the country was the fact that tens of thousands of people committed crimes to get into prison to receive food and shelter. Reporting on the situation in Ennis, County Clare, the prison governor listed several prisoners who stole rather than starved. Amongst them was one 'T.C.' who had been given twelve months for sheep stealing but was released early by order of the Lord Lieutenant when fever broke out in the gaol. T.C. immediately stole another sheep but was again released, this time on a legal technicality. Walking out of the courthouse, mustering determination with what strength he had left, he went to the nearest field, stole another sheep and drove it through the town to where the Assistant Barrister was sitting. He successfully demanded arrest and imprisonment.[42] In a futile attempt to reduce prison numbers the prison diet was reduced by twenty per cent. It was a bureaucratic decision illustrating George Bernard Shaw's dictum, 'if the prison does not underbid the slum in human misery, the slum will empty and the prison will fill'.[43]

At a time when merely living in Ireland was a death sentence for multitudes, to be sentenced to transportation was often a high award. Again in Ennis three men, 'J. O'L, J.B. and M.M.', escaped from the workhouse and went to a gentleman's field, 'made a fire in the middle of it, killed two sheep, roasted them and eat [*sic*] as much as they could. The caretaker came up to them, and they actually invited him to join them' – their object was transportation. In another case 'H.M.', a woman, had committed several crimes but had only been given short sentences. In desperation she turned to the more serious offence of arson in order to be transported and provide 'well for herself and child in a good country'.[44] Those sentenced to transportation increased dramatically both numerically, with over 3,000 sentenced to transportation in 1849 as compared to 625 in 1845 (before the onset of the potato blight) and in percentage terms with 3.74 per cent of criminals sentenced to transportation in 1845 as compared with 7.32 per cent in 1849.[45] The rising number of convicts caused grave concern and laws were passed substituting imprisonment for transportation in the case of some lighter offences, but to little avail.

The provisions for convicts in Ireland at the time were far from adequate. The interruption of transportation in 1846 coupled with the onset of the Famine caused the number of convicts languishing in county gaols to rise alarmingly. Forced to become involved in the direct day-to-day management of convicts the government established the post of Inspector of Government Prisons. With no ships to Australia local gaols that could ill afford the space were ordered to keep convicts. Sections of Kilmainham Gaol, Newgate and Richmond Bridewell were given over to government prisoners while the barracks on Spike Island in Cork harbour (built during the Napoleonic Wars and capable of holding 1,500) was given over by the Ordnance Department for the accommodation of convicts.

In 1849 transportation ships once again set sail from Ireland for Australia. However, the pressure to complete Mountjoy became even greater when the *Pestonje Bomangee* arrived at Hobart, Van Diemen's Land with 600 ticket-of-leave men on board. All convicts to the penal colony were supposed to have been 'reformed' by a course of separate confinement but it was

41

obvious they had received no such treatment. Indeed they were in such a state of immorality that they were sent straight to prison. The Governor of Van Diemen's Land was not amused with the arrogant attitude of the Irish administration towards the colony. Neither was Sir George Grey, the Home Secretary. Grey wrote to the Irish Under Secretary Reddington on the subject of the Model Prison that he 'earnestly recommends to the attention of his Excellency, the importance of proceeding as rapidly as possible, with the erection of that Prison; as, until it is completed, great difficulty must be experienced in the proper treatment of convicts previous to their removal from the country'.[46] A chastened and embarrassed Irish office then stepped up construction.

On Wednesday 26 March 1850, the Dublin *Evening Post* reported that at 3:30 the previous afternoon the Lord Lieutenant, accompanied by his Aide de Camp, Sir William Russell and Under Secretary Sir Thomas Reddington, were received at the new prison by Henry Hitchins, the Inspector General of Government Prisons, John Radcliffe from the Commissioners for Public Works, Jacob Owen, the architect and Dr Rynd, the Surgeon Superintendent. Having inspected all the arrangements the Lord Lieutenant 'expressed himself highly gratified with every department'. Mountjoy Prison was ready for prisoners.

Chapter Three

MOUNTJOY OPENS – THE MORAL SEWER CLOSES

I know not whether Laws be right,
Or whether Laws be wrong;
All that we know who lie in gaol
Is that the wall is strong;
And that each day is like a year,
A year whose days are long.

Oscar Wilde, The Ballad of Reading Gaol

On Thursday, 27 March 1850, several black horse-drawn prison vans clattered through the streets of Dublin to the new government prison on the North Circular Road. Crammed into their claustrophobic windowless compartments were 62 convict transfers from Kilmainham, Newgate and Smithfield prisons. They were Mountjoy Prison's first prisoners – the first in a list of nearly 500,000 that it has held.

Entering the prison compound, the gates slamming behind, the convicts were greeted at the front gate by the prison staff; warders, medical officer, chaplains and, at their head, Governor Netterville from Rathfarnham. The details of the first arrivals were entered into the prison register; name, crime, sentence, county in which they were convicted, date of conviction, age (if not known then estimated), height, colour of eyes and hair, complexion ('sallow', 'fresh', 'swarthy', 'pockmarked', etc.), marital status, whether they could read and write, occupation (if any), religion and when they were received into Mountjoy (today, when a person is committed to Mountjoy more or less the same information is recorded). The prisoners were then put through the intentionally degrading and depersonalising 'reception' process in which they were read the prison rules, stripped of their belongings and clothes and bathed in a carbolic solution. Their hair was closely cut, they were given a set of convict clothes and, finally, the last vestige of the convicts' identity was taken from them – their names. 'Thomas Lynch' became prisoner C.2.15 – C wing, second floor, fifteenth cell. At the end of this transformation the prisoners were marched off to their cells in this strange new world. Mountjoy life had started.

There were four wings in the prison, A, B, C, and D, each with three tiers (A1, A2, A3, B1, etc.). The wings radiated like a fan off the 'Circle', the central hub of the prison. From the Circle a member of staff could monitor the silent spaces that separated the 496 cells. Set apart from the normal cells there were twelve punishment cells of which nine were daylight cells while three were completely dark and reserved for the most refractory prisoners – mini-prisons within a prison.

The cell was the reformatory building block of the prison. On first appearances it was a simple space, thirteen feet long and seven feet wide. But the composition and dimensions of the cell were the product of decades of philosophical debate and technological development. The Irish Prison Act of 1840 that legalised the separate confinement of prisoners placed considerable demands on prison architects by stipulating that 'no Cell shall be used for the Separate Confinement of any Prisoner which is not of such a size and lighted, warmed, ventilated, and fitted up in such a manner as may be required by a due regard to health, and furnished with the means of enabling the Prisoner to communicate with an officer of the Prison'. Based on the principle of architecture against communication a prisoner was to be almost totally isolated within the autonomous unit of the cell – a womb from which he would emerge months later 'born again'. In each cell air was supplied and extracted by a series of ducts and vents in a complex ventilation system. In one of the earliest examples of central heating in Ireland, a prisoner could control the temperature in the cell by admitting more, or less, hot air through the vent connected to the prison boilers. The inside of each narrow timber door was sheeted with protective metal to prevent escape. Set into the door was a spy hole through which it was impossible to see out; outside, on the catwalks and bridges of the cavernous wings, the warders wore felt slippers over their boots to muffle the sound of their footfalls; inside, the prisoner was left with the uncomfortable feeling that at any moment a silently approaching warder would look through the spy hole. This arrangement enshrined the observation principle of Jeremy Bentham's 'Panopticon' or 'all seeing eye' developed in the eighteenth century. Below the spy hole was a larger opening called the 'hatch' through which food was passed three times a day. Above the door was a handle which, when pulled, rang a bell and flipped open a flag indicating the cell number of the prisoner to the warder on duty (today a button in each cell turns on a red light outside). High on the outside wall was a small window. To prevent escape and communication the window could not be opened. Neither could one see through. It was thought the sight of a distant tree or hillside would destroy the reformation process so the small panes were made of fluted glass which kept the prisoner blind to the outside world. The meagre light a prison window let in was best described by Oscar Wilde, a prisoner in Reading Gaol in the 1890s, when he wrote, 'outside, the day may be blue and gold, but the light that creeps down through the thickly muffled glass of the small iron-barred window beneath which one sits is grey and niggard. It is always twilight in one's cell, as it is always midnight in one's heart'.[1] During periods of work and early mornings and evenings the cells were lit by gas. Standing

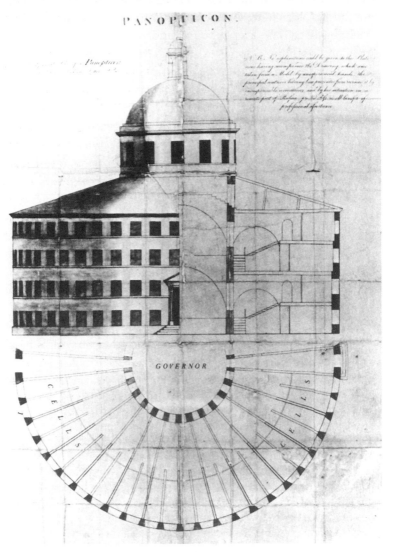

Jeremy Bentham's Panopticon, or 'all seeing eye'.

in the corner of the cell were a ceramic flushing toilet and cop-per wash-basin, water for which was supplied by a hand-driven crank pump worked by convict labour.

The principle of separation continued outside the cell. Each day seven parties of twelve prisoners made their way to the basement to work in shifts at the crank pump. Sitting in parti-tioned stalls they collectively turned the handle that ran the length of the compartments. A turn of the handle threw up one quart of water and each day it was turned 32,000 times supply-ing 8,000 gallons to the prison. Working at the crank pump was inescapably 'fraught with danger' for a lazy, unobservant or unlucky convict.[2] If one of the pump party let go of his part of the iron handle, or did not begin to turn the handle with the oth-ers, he could be struck by the revolving handle. In a report on one of the county prisons the method of injury caused by the crank pump was briefly but graphically described:

> Accidents sometimes occur in prisons where the crank by which the prisoners work the pump is continuous and undivided, and

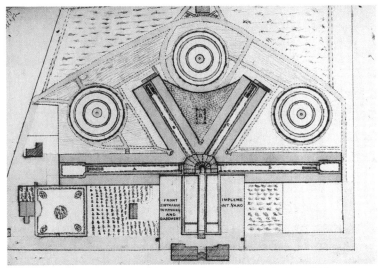

Prisoner William MacDonagh's impression of the aerial view of Mountjoy Prison.

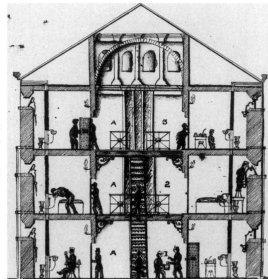

Prisoner William MacDonagh's impression of the cross-section of 'A' wing in Mountjoy Prison.

partitions separating the prisoners, have been ... put up to prevent them from seeing each other ... Under such circumstances the prisoners do not work together, and some are liable to be struck by the crank handles when the others go to work; such an accident has happened where a man was killed ... The handle of the crank pump in his stall struck him on the stomach: he was lifted over the shaft and pitched on his head on the opposite side, and never spoke afterwards.[3]

In 1852, after several injuries and the death of convict John Campbell in his stall, the crank pump in Mountjoy was replaced by a steam-powered pump.

Separation was also enforced in the 'house of God'. Instead of pews or benches lining the chapel the prisoners sat in hundreds of stalls like so many pigeons raked in rows. Partitioned on either side and at the back the prisoners closed the half doors after filing in. Once they were safely in their stalls a warder at the end of each row pulled a handle, locking all the doors until the service was over. All they could see was the chaplain and the warders perched on high stools keeping a close eye for any attempt at communication. Such dedication to keeping inmates isolated raised the question of how far this zeal for separation could go. In 1860 Baron Von Holtzendorff, a German Doctor of Law, published a report on the Irish convict system in which he queried whether prison authorities would 'one day raise a wooden partition between the graves of deceased prisoners, as if to carry the cellular system into eternity?'[4]

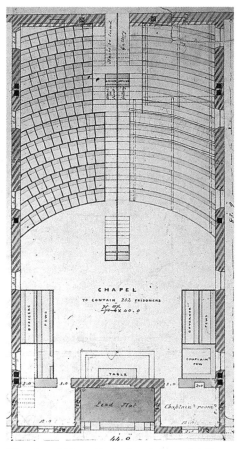

The plan of Mountjoy's chapel. Note details on left hand side of the stalls that isolated prisoners at worship.

Mountjoy was a massive piece of logistics. In addition to the cells, pump station and chapel, Mountjoy's eight acres held three caged exercise rings, fourteen baths, a number of workshops, the administrative offices of the governor, registrar, chaplain, medical officer, a library, schoolroom, visiting room, offices, stores, storekeeper's office, bread room, meat room, milk room, kitchen, scullery, kitchen coal stove, general coal store, warders' stores, officers' mess room, residential quarters for the governor, deputy governor, storekeeper, infirmary warders, as well as all unmarried duty warders. In 1853 *Wakeman's Guide to Dublin* recommended visitors to walk down the North Circular Road and see what it described as 'the new Model Prison, one of the most complete structures of its class in the British Empire'.

When the first prisoners bedded down for an uncomfortable night's sleep in Mountjoy Prison, the full stop was put at the end of the long sentence of prison reform in Ireland. Mountjoy was the last purpose-built prison in Ireland until Wheatfield Place of Detention opened in 1989. Population decline and changing economic circumstances account, in part, for the lack of prison construction. But equally important was the fact that in Mountjoy and the other prisons built at the time, the prison had been 'perfected'. It was as good as it was going to get.

In *The Fabrication of Virtue*, Robin Evans charts the evolution and development of prison architecture from the mid-eighteenth to the mid-nineteenth century – the period when the prison was hauled up from the dungeons and made into something 'special'. Prison reformers had put much of their faith in the passive walls of architecture to change the human condition. The failures of previous prisons were largely put down to the limited technical abilities of architects to produce the 'correct' environment – if only this aspect could be perfected then prison reform, and hence the reform of the prisoner, would be accomplished. The end of the prison architectural road was reached in April 1842 when the then 'Model Prsion', Pentonville Prison on the Caledonian Road, north London, opened.

Pentonville was the creation of Colonel Joshua Jebb of the Royal Engineers. Jebb had spent much of his career designing battlements and fortifications but at Pentonville he designed the 'ultimate prison'. By turning 'an issue of psychology into an issue of mechanics', Jebb made the separate system practical.[5] Generating huge interest when it opened it was one of the seminal buildings of the nineteenth century and rivalled the architectural merit of the considerably more luxurious Houses of Parliament at Westminster and the Reform Club in Pall Mall. The 'palace of felons' was toured by kings, princes, politicians and preachers. 'A most beautiful piece of prison machinery',[6] Pentonville was a massive piece of social engineering that provided the blueprint for most of the world's prisons in the nineteenth century. Within six years of its construction, over 50 prisons had been built on its principles and as late as the 1970s, 40 per cent of prisoners in Britain and Ireland were held in its offspring.

Mountjoy Prison was an almost perfect copy of Pentonville. Jacob Owen oversaw the construction of the prison and was listed as the architect of Mountjoy but his contributions consisted mainly of small finishings and details. In 1861 the Presbyterian chaplain at Spike Island convict prison, Charles B. Gibson, recalled that before Mountjoy opened, Governor Netterville 'went to London to take lessons from the governor of Pentonville on the proper working of the new machine'. Gibson sniped that Netterville felt 'himself in the position of a boy who had been made a present of a new mouse trap, full of curious little chambers, and worked by a multiplicity of springs of whose operation he was ignorant'.[7] He had to be trained to handle the new penal device that was 'too delicate for unskilful hands to touch. A few more turns of the screw, and you injure both the body and mind of the prisoner'.[8]

Pentonville was the culmination of decades of prison reform that went back to the publication of Howard's *The State of Prisons*. Described by one penal historian as a monument to the ideal of separation it was designed by Jebb as a machine to manufacture good citizens. The opening of Pentonville Prison was the crucial moment in the development of the prison when the abstract principle of separate confinement as the ideal tool to change the criminal mind was put to the test. Within a few years it was declared a failure in terms of reform. After initial optimism there was a retreat from the whole concept of a prisoner being reformed and the declared merit of Pentonville and separate confinement was not the capacity to reform but the ability to punish and terrorise. For many, the idea of reforming a prisoner, while not altogether abandoned, became an issue clouded in dark uncertainty. In 1854 even Colonel Jebb, the man who had gone to such pains to make separation possible, said the main purpose of prisons was deterrence.[9]

In January 1850 the Inspector of Irish Government Prisons, Henry Martin Hitchins, visited Pentonville to make his own impression of the separate system and how it might operate in Mountjoy. First appointed to a post in the office of the Irish Chief Secretary in 1826 Hitchins had over twenty years administrative experience. In 1847, when the Irish government was forced to take over the day-to-day management of convicts, he was promoted from his position of clerk to head the new department. His salary increasing with status, Hitchins moved from his already comfortable home at Burdett Avenue, Sandycove, on the southern shore of Dublin Bay, to the salubrious and central residence of 81 St Stephen's Green.

During his stay in London Hitchins inspected every part of Pentonville, took note of all its workings and interviewed nearly every member of staff. From impressions gained during his stay he formed the view that separate confinement was unquestionably a deterrent to crime with 'many satisfactory proofs ... adduced to me of the dread entertained by the Convict of returning to the separate cell'. On the general question of the prisoners' reform, Hitchins wrote nothing directly. But in his report he denigrated two pillars of prison reform – education and religion. With regard to education he wrote, 'there is a prevailing feeling that too much attention has been paid to secular and religious instruction and that the duties of the Schoolmaster should not go beyond the amount of information to be obtained at an ordinary Village School'. Hitchins also concluded that religion was 'a dead failure, and the Chapel seats, disfigured by grotesque carvings and gross inscriptions, attest the diligence, if not "the piety" of the Inmates',[10] (the evidence of the chapel seats could only have reinforced, in Hitchins' mind, the contents of an 1847 memorandum that recommended as little rest and sleep as possible for the inmates in the new Model Prison so they would have neither the time, nor the energy, to practice 'solitary vice' – masturbation[11]). According to Hitchins, the 'duty of labour' was the essential part of the prison regime. It would 'eradicate criminal tendency' and give the prisoners knowledge of a trade that would support them in Van Diemen's Land, or at least inure them to the concept of labour.

When Hitchins returned to Dublin he mapped out his philosophy in Mountjoy's timetable. The timetable of the prison was the crucial matrix of the daily routine. As 'the minute hand chased the hour' it reproduced the moments of each day in a metronomic regularity, the clang of bell and triangle providing the beat. Discounting the importance of education and religion, Hitchins' timetable turned Mountjoy into a virtual factory. But it was an unusual one in which the workers did not go home in the evening but stayed in their sweatshop cells.

At 5:30am the first bell of the day called the staff to assemble and the prisoners to rise. The keys to the outer gate were handed from deputy governor to principal warder who then handed them on to the gate-keeper.

6:00 – the warders and trades warders assembled on parade, the warders reporting to the principal warder and receiving instructions for the day. The number of prisoners was counted. Some prisoners cleaned the wings but most were set the task of cleaning their own cells. It was the start of the daily routine that was used a century later by Brendan Behan, playwright and Mountjoy prisoner, as the subject for a verse in *The Auld Triangle*, 'To begin the morning/A warder bawling/"Get up out of bed you/And clean out your cell".'

6:30 – the prisoners began work. Prisoners were employed in their cells as tailors, shoemakers, tinkers, mat-makers and linen and woollen weavers. The prison's output was considerable – such was the scale of production an outside building was needed for storage. Mountjoy supplied not only its own clothing and many of its other needs but also those of the rest of the Irish convict service. A substantial part of the prison's produce was sold to English companies who in turn sold them on to the colonies (much to Hitchins' annoyance the sale of prison produce in Ireland was banned to protect the free labour market). Sick prisoners, exempt from cell work, were employed in the governor's garden. The pump party made its way to the basement.

8:30 – breakfast; eight ounces of oatmeal with water added to make a quart of stirabout and three-quarters of a pint of new milk. During this period, and at all other meal times, the staff began their break only when the prisoners had their food passed through the hatch and finished their break before the prisoners.

9:45 – the warders and trades instructors assembled on parade for inspection by the governor and deputy governor. Special orders, if any, were read. Reports were received from the principal warder who then issued instructions to his officers. Prisoners worked in their cells.

Prisoners attended school in shifts between 10:00 and 12:00 (those not attending school at any given time continued working in their cells).

Roman Catholics attended mass on Tuesdays and Fridays between 12:00 and 1:00pm. Protestants attended services between 3:00 and 4:30 on Tuesdays. On Sundays, when no work was carried out, all attended Divine Worship and religious instruction.

1:00 – dinner; (except for Wednesdays and Sundays) one pound of bread and three-quarters of a pint of new milk; on Sundays and Wednesdays one pound of beef, one ounce of vegetables, half an ounce of rice, a quart of soup made from the liquid the meat was boiled in and three-quarters of a pound of bread.

2:15 – the governor and deputy governor inspected the cells and heard requests or complaints ('if any') from the prisoners. The prisoners continued to work in their cells.

5:30 – supper; half a pound of bread and half a pint of milk.

6:00 – the warders and trades warders parade.

8:00 – the cell doors were double locked for the night and the principal warder received reports from each ward. The night guard came on duty and the keys to the outer gate were given to the deputy governor.

The prisoners exercised for one hour each day, walking around in a circle a few paces apart from each other in the caged exercise rings, always under the watchful eye of a warder. They changed their linen and washed their feet once a week and, on Thursdays, weather permitting, their bedding was aired in the exercise rings.[12]

Turning the prison into a factory did not please all the prison staff. The chaplains and teachers objected to the limited time given to their interests in the timetable. Conflict was inevitable and a particularly bitter atmosphere developed between the trades department, supported by the warders, and the education department. The teachers wanted a 'Model School' in the 'Model Prison' but this aspiration was incompatible with a timetable devoted to trade and industry.[13] There simply were not enough hours in the day. Governor Netterville regarded 'the notion that a knowledge of mechanical arts will eradicate criminal tendency as a very apparent fallacy' and was sympathetic to the teachers.[14] He intervened on occasions but was overruled by those who were nominally his subordinates. The thinking of Hitchins in his office in Dublin Castle dominated Mountjoy's daily routine and he gave the trades department sanction to both disregard the governor and to bully and intimidate the teachers. As a result the education department complained of an 'inquisitorial slavery', of being 'cheated, degraded, imposed upon'[15] and of being subjected to 'repeated insults, humiliations and abusive terms'.[16] Some teachers resigned under the tirade, others were dismissed and in 1852 the school department was closed. At this point the chaplains took over the responsibility for secular education but were warned by Hitchins that whatever method they followed it should not interfere with the labour regime. The teachers and chaplains were not the only ones unhappy with the system. The medical officer, Dr Rynd, condemned the effects of prisoners being forced to work in their cells. As medical officer it was his responsibility to ensure that criminals committed to Mountjoy were physically fit to undergo their sentence. He demonstrated his disapproval of the system by rejecting up to 40 per cent of the prisoners sent to Mountjoy on grounds of 'age, delicate constitution, long previous imprisonment, or other debilitating causes'. In his reports he wrote of what were called the 'intolerable' conditions in which the prisoners suffered.[17]

The Hitchins system was an 'ordeal' for both mind and body. At the best of times life in the 'numbered tombs' was unpleasant. But the exertions of work caused a stench of body odour and the toilets were frequently blocked or misused by men ignorant of such contraptions (many of whom suffered from chronic diarrhoea caused by the unchanging prison diet). Mixing with the prisoners' own smell were the toxic fumes of the evaporating chemicals used in their work and all the while the gas lights hissed and burned, starving the cells of oxygen. Such was the concoction of stultifying odours in the cells that many staff felt unable to enter them and when a hatch was opened a 'half suffocating putrid steam' rushed out. In an eloquent protest at their conditions the prisoners broke the glass in their cell windows to get extra air (to alleviate their sufferings Netterville designed a louvred window that could be safely opened by the prisoners).[18] Despite having been vetted as the strongest and healthiest of convicts, many Mountjoy prisoners were 'harassed by attention to a trade, often unhealthy in itself in the limited accommodation of a prison cell' and plunged into depression for an indefinite period.[19] They suffered from insomnia and, after a time, 'the organs of nutrition ceased to perform their functions'.[20] In such an exhausted and dejected state the prisoners were easy prey to fever. The hospital was always full. In 1853 seven Mountjoy prisoners died and a further twelve died after being transferred from Mountjoy due to illness.[21] In the following year nine Mountjoy prisoners died.[22] In addition to the prisoners' illnesses members of staff contracted the fever with Governor Netterville reported to have been at death's door for two days.[23]

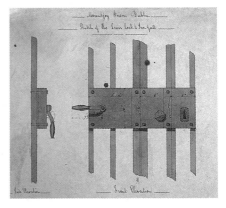

Lock on gate in Mountjoy Prison.

The convicts Rynd had rejected for admission to Mountjoy were sent to Spike Island, the 'asylum for the incurable' in the Irish convict department.[24] Sixty per cent of the convicts on Spike were 'infirm and impotent, detained in hospital, or confined in the convalescent wards'.[25] The island, at the entrance to Cork harbour, was exposed to buffeting winds and was by no means an ideal location for the weak and diseased; 'its climate is variable, and totally unsuited to the class of invalids to which the convict, and more especially the Irish convict, is particularly liable'.[26] For the most part prisoners suffered from tubercular consumption and scrofula. In 1852, 190 convicts died on Spike Island.[27]

On the other side of the bars at Mountjoy were 52 staff, most of whom were ex-police and military. Preferring men with a disciplinary background, the Lord Lieutenant's office was inundated with applications from such candidates in the run up to the opening of the prison. Michael Donnelly had enlisted in the 94th Regiment on Christmas Eve 1823 and served both in the Mediterranean and the East Indies (his father had served in the 7th Batallion of the Royal Artillery for 24 years and at the time of his application he had one brother in the 10th Batallion and another in the 28th Regiment). Stating that he was still young and had a wife and young family to support on a small pension, he asked the Lord Lieutenant to take into consideration when viewing his case that 'the life of a soldier does not supply him with the opportunity of making many friends' who could give him other employment.[28] Thomas Lonergan had joined the police after serving as a carpenter but retired after ten years because of the severity of night duty. He claimed that in the aftermath of the Young Ireland Rebellion of 1848 he had put his life in danger 'by aiding in the Prosecution of Mr Mitchel, Mr Smith O'Brien and Mr Meagher ... And being in dread to return to Clonmel, my native town in Consequence of being concerned in the prosecution ...' he asked for a position in the new government prison.[29] Among the successful applicants was First Class Warder Michael Delaney who had served nine years in the Dublin Metropolitan Police. He asked the Lord Lieutenant to bear in mind that in the last two years of his service he was acting Sergeant in the Yard at Dublin Castle, 'during which he was noticed by members of Your Excellency's Household for Courtesy and general Good Conduct'.[30] Mountjoy's Chief Warder, Cottrell Little, had been an Inspector in the Dublin Metropolitan Police for twelve years before his prison appointment. Prior to his posting in the police Little had a long military career behind him. He had enlisted in 1806 and in the course of his service was decorated for taking part in the Peninsular War, the Battle of Waterloo and the Burmese War.[31]

Hitchins considered the staff a 'respectable body of men', or at least as respectable as could be had for the salaries paid. With lower prison salaries in Ireland than in England the class of men to draw from was less than desired. A prison job was often sought by those who could gain no other employment. Hitchins claimed it would have been difficult to find better men if his staff were replaced and with this in mind he overlooked, in otherwise 'good men', the prevalence of intemperance 'amongst the class of persons selected to fill these offices'.[32] The staff conduct book for Mountjoy was littered with notes on fines and punishments of prison staff for drink-related offences. Many of these were understated as warders 'being slightly under the influence of drink' – especially if it was a second or subsequent offence. However, the case of Charles Coulon was difficult to hide. Failing to turn up for duty one morning his absence was later accounted for by an attendance in court for being drunk at Strand St. Fined 2s. 6d. by the police magistrate he was fined a further, and substantial, 20s. by Netterville when he returned to the prison. He was later dismissed for a similar offence.[33] Staff drinking problems were an embarrassment to the prison authorities who blamed much of the crime in Ireland on drink.

By today's standards the numbers going through Mountjoy each year were low. In only one year did committals exceed 1,000 – today the annual figure is closer to 5,000. In comparison with the county and town prisons of the 1850s sixteen local prisons had consistently more prisoners than Mountjoy. Although Mountjoy's prisoners came from every county in Ireland even the county gaols of Wexford and Mayo held greater numbers. The reason for this discrepancy was Mountjoy's status as a government convict prison.

Mountjoy was constructed for the confinement of criminals sentenced to transportation. These were the most 'serious' offenders and therefore accounted for only a small percentage of those convicted in the courts. Convicts sent to Mountjoy were held for a minimum period of time, ranging from eight to twelve months, during which each was confined in a separate cell. In any one year the cells of Mountjoy could only process a limited number of criminals. The county gaols, on the other hand, held prisoners sentenced for periods ranging from 24 hours to two years and their cells, although roughly the same size as Mountjoy's, could be used to accommodate one, three, four or even five prisoners at any one time (for fear of homosexual activity it was illegal to hold only two prisoners in a cell).

Mountjoy was intended as the first stop for men sentenced to transportation. After the period of separate confinement they would then be transferred to Spike Island to work in association and then be transported. But as a result of the Famine, the delay in the construction of Mountjoy and the interruption in transportation between 1846 and 1848 there was a chronic backlog in the Irish convict service. To help relieve the pressure of numbers many convicts were sent to Mountjoy for their obligatory fix of separate confinement as their last stop before being transported. Some of Mountjoy's first prisoners had been convicted as far back as 1846 and in 1852, 150 of those committed to Mountjoy had been convicted before the prison opened.

The first shipload of Mountjoy convicts left Kingstown Harbour in December 1850 aboard the *London*. The inmates chosen for the voyage were a mixture of the best and worst, those who had committed crimes in order to survive and others whose disorderly behaviour in prison warranted their transportation at the first instance. Going straight from Mountjoy to the ship, from separate confinement to the almost unrestricted communication on the *London*, caused no visible illnesses to the prisoners (it was thought such a sudden change in circumstance might adversely affect the convicts' mental and physical health). However, the ship's religious instructor, the Very Reverend Dr Geoghan, regretted the sudden transition which made his task of enforcing morality amongst the prisoners more difficult. After months of separate confinement the prisoners exploded in a bout of raucous communication telling stories of their hermit-like existence in Mountjoy and generally enjoying their freedom. Even more damaging to Hitchins' reputation was the apparent lack of capacity for work exhibited by the convicts on arrival. The sight of *London*'s motley cargo at Hobart dismayed the island's colonial Governor Denison. Struggling to maintain Van Diemen's Land as a penal colony in the face of rising local opposition (most notably in the form of the Anti-Transportation League), Denison refused to receive any more ships from Ireland.

Denison's act did little to stem opposition. Transportation to Van Diemen's Land was in its death throes. On 27 November 1852 the *St Vincent*, the last ship to set sail for Hobart left England. On 29 December 1853 Van Diemen's Land officially closed as a penal colony and, 'with a collective whistle of relief, its citizens proceeded ... to get rid of the "demonic" image of their island once and for all, by giving it the name of its Dutch discoverer: Tasmania, for the navigator Abel Tasman'.[34]

Transportation did not end with the closing of Van Diemen's Land. The last act of the 'Fatal Shore' had still to be played out. In 1850, as the history of the most infamous penal colony was drawing to an end, Western Australia announced itself 'willing to risk moral corruption for the economic advantages of transportation'.[35] However, transportation from Ireland to Western Australia had a short history. The last convict ships to leave from Ireland, the *Phoebe Dunbar* and *Robert Small*, sailed for Freemantle in the summer of 1853. Their human cargo was not well received. The Superintendent in Freemantle wrote to London that 'it was held by judicial and medical authority, that their prostrate condition, physically and morally, the result, it was conjectured, of long imprisonment, low diet, and bad training, rendered it necessary that they should be subjected to a course of preparatory discipline arbitrary in duration in some cases ... prior to their being exposed to the trials of a strange climate and novel society'. In comparison to the Irish prisoners the English ones 'maintained an exemplary course of conduct'.[36] With the Irish there 'appeared a singular inaptitude to comprehend the nature of moral agencies, or to be affected by them; neither do they seem to understand the desirableness, we will say, of self reliance, or the necessity for the exercise of habits of propriety, industry and prudence, as a means of extricating themselves from the consequences of former error ... coercion appears the only force they are capable of appreciating'.[37] On 11 September 1854 Governor Fitzgerald wrote to Sir George Grey that he hoped 'men from Irish prisons will not be sent to this

Colony with tickets-of-leave'.[38] With this note the long history of transportation from Ireland ended.

During the final demise of transportation the authorities at home had to face up to the reality which had been mounting since the Molesworth Committee – convicts could no longer be sent down the moral sewer. In 1853 one of the most dramatic changes in sentencing occurred when a new punishment, penal servitude, was established to substitute a prison sentence at home for transportation. The substitution of penal servitude for transportation meant that for the first time long-term prisoners would be held in Ireland (the longest sentence of imprisonment to a local prison was two years). This change in punishment caused 'a perfect panic on the part of the public'.[39] Now convicts, who had once been 'launched into eternity' on a large scale, would not even be launched onto a foreign shore. They would be held in Ireland and then released at home in vast numbers. Hitchins' management had been tolerated so long as the products of his system were sent abroad. But from the moment penal servitude was introduced his days at the head of the Irish Convict Service were numbered. In 1854 a letter from the Irish office stated, in a scarcely concealed criticism of Hitchins, that 'up to the present time the most approved method of dealing with convicts which has been so successfully carried into effect in England ... has been, to say the least, most imperfectly introduced in Ireland'. The hope was expressed that 'all the advantages which modern experience and science afford in the treatment of convicts' be made available in Ireland.[40]

One of the most pressing issues facing the government was the estimated 1,500 extra places needed to accommodate those who would otherwise have been transported. Various proposals were put forward to replace transportation with something similar at home. The concept of a penal island had become so ingrained that both Dalkey Island and Clare Island were put forward as solutions to the problem. In recommending Clare Island the Chief Secretary, Sir John Young, claimed its merit and penal quality was its remoteness.[41] Sites proposed for a Juvenile prison included the Curragh of Kildare and Castlereagh House in Mayo (at the time it was on the market under the Encumbered Estates Court)[42] while plans were also drawn up to increase accommodation at Mountjoy Prison to 850.[43] But before any money was spent a panel of Commissioners was appointed 'for the purpose of making a full inquiry into the present convict management in Ireland, the state of the prisons, and generally as to the steps which it may be most fit to take with a view to provide for the future management of convicts and prisoners in the altered state of the law'.[44] Two of the panel, Captains Crofton and Knight, came from England on the recommendation of Colonel Jebb. In Ireland Captain Harness of the Commissioners of Public Works and James Corry Connellan, the Inspector General of Prisons, joined them. In 1854 the four toured the convict establishments accompanied by the Irish Chief Secretary and Under Secretary, Sir John Young and Lieutenant Colonel Larcom. In May Larcom requested that the Commissioners report on Mountjoy Prison and the operation of the system of separate confinement – the key element of the convict system. During the next three weeks the Commissioners interviewed all of Mountjoy's staff, except those employed in the trades department. It was the final blow to Hitchins' reputation. Hitchins was in England at the time so what were soon to be his former staff were free to criticise his management without fear of retribution. The outcome of the investigation was a foregone conclusion as Crofton, Knight, Harness and Corry Connellan carried out what was essentially an administrative *coup d'etat*. By the time Hitchins returned the report had already been written. He attempted to defend himself but the commissioners' minds were made up. Hitchins was removed from his position and given a pension of £365 a year.

In October 1854, the Lord Lieutenant appointed three Directors to administer the Irish convict system. Two had been members of the Commission that ousted Hitchins, Captain

Crofton, who was made both Director and Chairman, and Captain Knight. The third was John Lentaigne – the only Irish member of the team. Walter Crofton, of Irish lineage, was born in Courtrai, West Flanders on 2 February 1815. Just four months later his father, a Brigade-Major in the 54th Foot Brigade, was killed in the Battle of Waterloo. Following in his father's military footsteps he enlisted in the Royal Artillery in 1833 eventually achieving the rank of Captain. In 1840 he married Anna Maria, only daughter of the Reverend Shipley of Twyford House, Hampshire, and settled down for a time in Egmont, Wiltshire, where he was appointed justice of the peace – a position that gave him some experience with prisons. Captain Raleigh Knight was 40 years old and had thirteen years military service behind him. He also had the greatest amount of prison experience of the three, having been Governor of Military Prisons in Canada and Governor of Portsmouth Convict Prison in England. The third Director, John Lentaigne, at 51 years of age, was the senior member of the group. A fellow of the Royal College of Surgeons, Lentaigne had wide-ranging administrative experience in Ireland. He was a Commissioner of Loan Funds, Chairman of the Relief Committee for Tallaght during the Famine, a Governor of the Richmond District Lunatic Asylum, Vice-Chairman of the South Dublin Union, High Sheriff of the County of Monaghan and Grand Juror of the counties of Dublin and Monaghan. On 29 November 1854 this unusually competent and experienced group took up their posts and set out to address the burning social question of the day, 'what shall we do with our convicts?'

Chapter Four

THE CONVICT QUESTION SOLVED

... a training so simple in its principles, so applicable to every human being, that its very simplicity was at first its great stumbling block.

Sir Walter Crofton, 1872

On 26 April 1855 Crofton, Lentaigne and Knight presented their first annual report to the Chief Secretary for Ireland, the Right Honourable Edward Horsman, MP. Just five months had elapsed since their appointment but in their report the Directors wrote of the many changes effected in the general management and internal workings of the prisons: the practice of sending invalid convicts to Spike Island was abandoned; many of the prison staff, including a large number of those employed in Mountjoy, were dismissed because of drunkenness[1], 'their [poor] physical conditions, their general character, capabilities and past history'[2]; stricter criteria were established for the hiring of new staff and each was put on probation for their first six months; the teaching staff, as such existed, were dismissed and replaced with suitably qualified and motivated instructors (the most significant change in staff at Mountjoy was the appointment of new schoolmaster Edward McGauran). But these were mere tinkerings with the system. Far more wide-ranging and fundamental changes were needed.

The Directors stated that their main aims were to rectify the 'deplorable aspect and apparent destitution of the Irish Convicts'[3] and to 'assimilate the treatment of the Irish convicts as far as possible with those of England'.[4] However, Crofton and the other Directors established a system of management so far from its English counterpart that it became known as the 'Crofton', or 'Irish', system. Dominating life in Mountjoy and the other convict prisons until the 1880s, the Crofton system is the single most important Irish contribution to penal history and is Ireland's only entry in the prison history section of the *Encyclopaedia Britannica*.

The Crofton system revived criminal reform when the tide of opinion was turning strongly against the idea. In 1850 a parliamentary select committee had claimed the general reformability of convicts but its findings were aimed at allaying the fears of the public when transportation was ending, rather than being founded on firm belief. Most prison management had largely given up on the idea of reform. Under the leadership of Crofton the three Directors set out to establish a comprehensive, integrated convict system that would restore the prisoner 'to society with an unimpaired constitution, and with sufficient health and energies to enable him to take a respectable place in the community'.[5] However, in a society in which transportation was still very much part of the mind set, the 'ulterior object' running through Crofton's management was the eventual emigration of the criminal.[6] In a form of 'voluntary' transportation the convicts were continuously reminded of the advantages of emigration in the hope that when released they would leave the country. It was a key part of the system of which Crofton wrote, '... we cannot too highly praise as an important element of reformation, the voluntary emigration of the well-disposed criminal when free, to lands where labour is scarce, or advocate too strongly its beneficial effects'.[7]

In the new system the Directors attempted to address the fundamentally contradictory prison questions of how a prisoner could be trained for freedom while imprisoned and how a prison system could be based at one and the same time on reform and punishment. Crofton tried to resolve these dilemmas by dividing a convict's prison time into three distinct stages, each managed in a different manner and to different ends. In many ways the staged structure of the system mirrored the transportation system it replaced but there were significant differences. The first stage of the system was nine months separation in Mountjoy Prison. The second was labour in association on Spike Island. The last stage was spent in what were called 'Intermediate' prisons at Smithfield, Philipstown, Fort Camden (in Cork harbour near Spike) and Lusk in north county Dublin. After release the convicts who stayed in Ireland were kept under police supervision to ensure good behaviour and protect the public.

The foundation of the Crofton system was separate confinement in Mountjoy Prison. The correct management of the Joy was believed to be essential 'to the success of the present intensely interesting experiment affecting the welfare of the convict population of Ireland'.[8] Mountjoy was the most complex and contradictory stage where reform and punishment intertwined. It was 'determinantly penal' and 'viewed with dread' by convicts but, 'at the same time, so many means used for his improvement tend to convince him that the end of punishment is not the satisfaction of vengeance, but the general well-being of society'.[9] Like the Roman God Janus, Mountjoy looked both backward and forward; back to the punishment of the crime committed, forward to the process of reform and the eventual release of the prisoner.

The Mountjoy stage was designed to make the convict 'docile' by crushing the criminal mind into a malleable pulp that could then be remoulded into a more acceptable form. It was aimed at convicts who had 'probably lived the life of gross animal indulgence'[10] and 'whose selfish and animal propensities have been indulged and strengthened while the intellectual and moral powers have been either wholly unexercised or subjected to false and pernicious principles'.[11] Governor Netterville, who had unhappily administered Hitchins' work timetable, was of one mind with the new Directors:

It is to the mainspring of criminal actions, it appears to me, that prison discipline should, in its first place, be directed; to the curbing of unrestrained passions, and the acquirement of those first moral principles, on which the knowledge of crafts, and habits of industry, may afterward be ingrafted.[12]

Ignoring the physical and psychological victims left in the wake of Hitchins' regime, Crofton asserted that the convicts had been 'busily and pleasantly occupied with the active employment of manufacturers'.[13] The Prisons Commissioners, and now the Directors, felt that a regime based on labour, notwithstanding whatever economic sense it made, was detrimental to the original concept behind the Model Prison, i.e., the prisoner's reformation. In the Commissioners' report the true value of separate confinement was re-stated. It was to force the prisoner:

> ... to meditate upon his own condition, to afford an opportunity to judicious instructors to reform him, by engendering to open his heart to kindly feelings, his mind to the influence of a constant sense of a future state, and to induce him to recognise, even in his confinement, the benevolence of his Creator, and at the same time whatever tends to diminish the seclusion of the prisoner tends also to diminish the reformatory influence of his instructors and the irksomeness of his punishment.[14]

Under Hitchins, Jonas Hanway's preaching walls were believed to have been ignored or drowned out by prison industry. Cell work had created a barrier between the prisoner and thoughts on his condition, eternity and the prospect of everlasting punishment. One of the ingenious parts of the Crofton system was the removal of this distraction. In separation, oakum picking – 'the most dry, most tedious, and most unchanging' of occupations – was chosen to 'occupy' the prisoners.[15] 'Stupid oakum picking', as it was sometimes called, was the pulling apart of old tarred ropes back into single strands to be used again either for new ropes or for caulking and sealing joints on ships. Likened to 'placing the mind on a treadmill ... where there is motion without progression',[16] it was a task which solitude made 'dreary and hateful'[17] and was described as 'an employment of a monotonous kind and as such is more likely to impress them as well with a sense of their position, as to add materially to their punishment'.[18] Besides being monotonous it was also quite difficult – breaking into the ropes to begin the work was often a frustrating task and the tar from the rope stuck to the fingers requiring a fifteen-minute scrub to get them into working order again. Normally a man had to pick a set quota of oakum each day or risk punishment. A convict in an English prison recalled an oakum inspection scene:

> In the centre of the hall, lighted at intervals by gas jets, stands a table containing a pair of scales and a pile of hard junk to be issued to the queue of waiting men, each of whom holds in his hands the oakum he has picked the day before. On all their faces is a mingled expression of fear and hate, for only a very few of them have completed their task. They wait with an animal expression on their faces, because it is in the lap of the Gods whether they will get the few rotten potatoes and the eight-ounce loaf of brown bread which constitutes their dinner, or not.[19]

However, in Mountjoy there were no such scenes to drive the men. Each day a warder threw one pound of oakum through the hatch but it was entirely up to the prisoners whether they worked at it or not. At the end of the day they could merely hand the untouched oakum back through the hatch, with no questions asked.

At Mountjoy, Crofton turned the accepted concept of prison labour on its head. Instead of labour being penal and used as punishment it was the very lack of labour, enforced idleness, that was made penal. An article comparing the Irish and English methods of convict management stated that 'idleness and dislike of steady work, are probably the most universal characteristics of the criminal class'.[20] Citing the example of convicts across the Irish Sea who were forced to work, grew to loathe it and then swore never to do it again, it applauded the Irish system in which 'the want of work becomes the severest punishment; so severe, indeed, that were it continued too long, the mind would give way under it'.[21] Thus, the lack of work that raised a sweat and quickened the pulse was intended to compel the prisoners to desire the distraction of work and to look on it as a reward. As such the absence of work at Mountjoy was not only punishment, it was an instrument of future training.

The idleness regime was a difficult idea for many people to come to terms with and it was not, by any means, without its critics. An obvious line of attack came from those who regarded the nine months as a chance for criminals to put their feet up and take it easy. To these criticisms Crofton replied that 'those who consider present Prison treatment operating as a "Premium to Crime", have only cursorily examined well regulated prisons'.[22] He asserted that 'enforced order, cleanliness, and regularity, however impressive of an air of comfort to a casual observer, is, be it remembered, most repugnant to the previous habits of the criminal, and most thoroughly opposed to his ideas of improvement'.[23] At Mountjoy, he wrote, 'the drunkard is made sober. The thoughtless is here made thoughtful. Conscience so long stilted is here stimulated to act. The hardened criminal, so long depending on others, is here now thrown upon himself, and finds to his costs the miserable nature of his support'.[24] The first three months were the worst as the prisoner was engulfed by a chaos of feelings – guilt, anger, fear, loneliness. It was reported that after this 'crisis in his physiological progress is passed he becomes utterly passive – without a thought or will of his own'.[25] At this stage religion came into full play.

The 1854 Commissioners stated that Mountjoy had been built, at great expense, 'to induce religious principles into the hearts of convicts'.[26] In the new strict separation of the Crofton system the inmates were frequently visited by the chaplains – one of the few breaks in the monotony of the convicts' day when they were relieved from the spinning of their own thoughts.

Under such conditions:

> The chaplain can then make the brawny navvy in the cell cry like a child; he can work on his feelings in almost any way he pleases; he can, so to speak, photograph his own thoughts, ideas and opinions on his patient's mind, and fills his mouth with his own phrases and language.[27]

Ironically, the chaplains were amongst those who raised objections to a system which was geared towards religion. William Wilson, the Presbyterian chaplain, felt prisoners who had an early education and some fondness for reading were 'decidedly improved' by the time allowed for reflection. But few prisoners had such a background and their 'unfurnished minds, dragged heavily onward during weary days and nights of monotonous, unprofitable idleness, relieved only by an occasional occupation in the cell, that failed to interest'.[28] The Catholic Chaplain Francis Cooney, wrote that while he thought separation excellent:

> ... it will, after a little, engender anything but salutary impressions ... These poor creatures are not called by God to a contemplative life, and hence their minds soon require to be relieved by other occupations. If this be denied, the almost inevitable consequence is restlessness and ennui, from which they take refuge in reminiscences no wise favourable to improvement.

Chaplain Cooney also expressed concern that the prisoners would consume their time in 'corrupting reveries that enervate the character, and in the process of time, almost extinguish religious and moral feeling'.[29] These somewhat cryptic comments are quickly deciphered when he states that the problem would escalate once the female prison opened (see below). He was referring to 'solitary vice', the often unacknowledged but everpresent part of prison life.

The period of separate confinement at Mountjoy cannot be seen in isolation from the remainder of a convict's time in prison. The Mountjoy stage provided the platform upon which the remaining stages were built, while a return to it was used as a punishment in the subsequent stages – it was hoped that the 'deterring remembrance of the separate confinement which he has endured will assist him in withstanding the temptations and seductions to misconduct when in association at Spike'.[30] Once the apparent 'animal propensities' of the convicts had been 'lulled to sleep'[31] at Mountjoy the prisoner was ready to be elevated to the second rung on the convict ladder – labour in association on Spike Island. (A small number of convicts remained in association in Mountjoy to carry out works around the prison.)

Spike Island was the Irish equivalent of England's Portland Prison. This second stage was thought to provide a relief from the solitude and close confinement of Mountjoy – prisoners were allowed to converse and work in the open air and cells were given up for large wards in the old military barracks where the prisoners slept in wooden partitions, wired in front. Employed as carpenters, masons, smiths, stonecutters and carters yoked to wagons hauling earth, stone, bricks and coal, convicts worked mainly on fortifications on Spike (some were employed under the direction of the War Office at Haulbowline – an island close to Spike – and with the Royal Engineers on the construction of the Military Hospital at Queenstown). Such working conditions were indeed penal and intended as punishment. But at Spike a 'marks' system was introduced which began to tip the scales of prison discipline in favour of reform as the prisoner was given the chance to 'work out his own redemption through his own toil'.[32]

The prison marks system was first introduced at Norfolk Island Prison, the penal pit of Van Diemen's Land, by Alexander Macononchie in 1840. Macononchie was described by Robert Hughes in *The Fatal Shore* as 'the one and only inspired penal reformer to work in Australia throughout the whole history of transportation'.[33] Born in Edinburgh in 1787, his father died when he was just nine (the early death of a father is a common denominator in the biographies of Howard,

NOTICE.

Showing the Class or Number of Marks which it will be necessary for Female Prisoners convicted under the Penal Servitude Act, 27 & 28 Vic., Cap. 47 (July, 1864), to obtain, before becoming eligible for Licence, reckoning from the date of conviction.

Class and No. of Marks to be gained for Admission to the Refuges for different Sentences.	Sentences.	Shortest periods of Imprisonment.		Earliest periods from termination of Sentence at which eligible for Licence to be passed, either in whole or part, at the Refuges.	
	Years.	Years.	Months.	Years.	Months.
Class **16 A** or **16** months in A class,	5	3	4	1	8
„ **24 A** „ **24** „	6	4	0	2	0
„ **32 A** „ **32** „	7	4	8	2	4
„ **40 A** „ **40** „	8	5	4	2	8
„ **56 A** „ **56** „	10	6	8	3	4
„ **72 A** „ **72** „	12	8	0	4	0
„ **96 A** „ **96** „	15	10	0	5	0

Prison notice showing table of marks to be earned by female convicts.

Crofton and Maconochie) and he was brought up by his uncle, later Lord Meadowbank. Following an eventful career in the Royal Navy – for two years Maconochie, like Howard, was held as a prisoner of war – he was the first person appointed to the post of Professor of Geography at University College London. Acquainting himself with members of the English Society for the Improvement of Prison Discipline he was asked to go to Australia to survey the convict system and investigate the possibility of reforming it. In his report he did not damn transportation as a punishment as such but he did outrightly condemn the transportation system as it existed. His report was an important piece of evidence used by the Molesworth Committee of 1837-8. Dismayed at a punishment that did not take into account the conduct of a prisoner, Macononchie believed that a convict's sentence should be indefinite and dependent on reformation. Influenced by an idea of Dublin's Archbishop Whately – that convicts should associate 'work with freedom and independence with that labour'[34] – Macononchie introduced a marks system when he was appointed Governor of Norfolk in May 1840.

The marks system was based on the principle that 'the fate of every man should be placed universally in his own hands'. As a convict earned marks through his own labour he not only ameliorated his conditions but also shortened the time he spent in prison. In its most basic form a prison sentence was not counted in time but in work – one analogy used to describe the idea was that every step on a treadwheel became one step out of prison. After a stint of just two years on Norfolk Island Macononchie was dismissed from his post by less enlightened individuals and faded into relative obscurity. However, his marks system was adopted by Crofton and the Irish Directors, albeit in a watered down version called 'progressive classification'.

A convict's time at Spike was divided into several stages through which he could progress. A prisoner who passed through each stage could significantly reduce his time on Spike. A prisoner sentenced to four years penal servitude could finish at Spike nine months before the expiration of his sentence, while someone sentenced to twelve years could leave three years before the end (in 1857 a similar system was introduced at Mountjoy in which the convict could reduce his time spent in separation from nine months to eight months). On average a convict spent four-fifths of his prison time on Spike but a convict who did not earn enough marks to rise through the various classes stayed there for the remainder of his term.

When most convicts entered Spike they were placed in the third class for between two and six months (the lowest class was the probation class reserved for those guilty of misconduct at Mountjoy). The time spent in this class, and each of the subsequent ones, was largely down to the individual. Every month he earned a number of marks based on conforming to the prison discipline, conduct in school and industry at work. Ledgers were kept documenting the convict's progression and each man was reminded and informed of his progress through a badge system. A convict wore two badges. On his right arm was a registration badge which gave his sentence and registration number and length of sentence (i.e. PS/15000/4 – Penal Servitude, number 15000, four years). On his left arm was a conduct badge which displayed the class he was currently in, the total number of marks needed to progress to the next stage and the number of marks already gained. The conduct badge provided a constant reminder to both staff and convict of his progress.

Rising from one class to another resulted in a change of clothing (the third class wore a plain frieze uniform, the second class had blue cuffs and collar, the first class had red cuffs and collar while the advanced class wore a brick-coloured uniform) and a change in the type of conduct badge worn (in the third class it was yellow with black figures, in the second, light blue with black figures, in the first red with black figures and in the advanced class it was white with bronze figures). The change in outward appearance was intended to act as an incentive to progression but a more powerful stimulus was the easing of conditions, less onerous work and greater freedom entailed in rising to a higher class. If a convict finally reached the advanced class (it was originally called the 'exemplary class' but it was felt that such a label was unsuitable for convicts) he spent a minimum of twelve months there. After this period he became eligible for the third stage of the system but was only transferred to it after Crofton himself had received a favourable report on the convict.

The third and final stage of the system was made up of what were confusingly called the 'Intermediate' prisons – Fort Camden for mechanical labour, Smithfield for artisan labour and Lusk for agricultural labour. It was at this point that the Crofton system deviated considerably from established prison practice. It was the most 'peculiar' feature of the Irish system where the emphasis was emphatically on reform. Unusually, this reform was not only aimed at the convict, it also targeted the prejudices the general public held about convicts.

The most famous of the Intermediate prisons was at Lusk, twelve miles north of Dublin. Lusk became world famous and a well-worn path was beaten to it by international penologists and students of social science. Not since the opening of Pentonville had attentions been so focused on one prison. Originally intended as the site for a juvenile convict prison it was given over for use as an Intermediate prison when legislation was passed to establish juvenile reformatory schools in Ireland. After an area of common ground had been cleared of squatters the first convicts arrived at Lusk on 2 April 1857 and started to erect two large iron sleeping huts and farm outhouses and clear an area for a parade ground. It was the beginning of the first experiment in what we would now call an 'open prison'.

A typical day at an Intermediate prison was broken down into $9^1/4$ hours work, $2^1/2$ hours recreation and meals, $3^3/4$ hours instruction and prayer and $3/4$ hour cleaning. Although the days were $16^1/4$ hours long the regime at the Intermediate prisons was considerably more relaxed than during the previous stages.[35] The driving idea behind the Intermediate prisons was 'individualisation'. Here, it was stated, the convicts were treated as 'Christians' with a reputation to lose, rather than inherently untrustworthy criminals.[36] In these prison institutions there were neither handcuffs nor carbines. Permitted to grow their hair long, the prisoners peeled off the convict garb and donned their own clothes. Each week they earned a gratuity of half a crown, six pence of which they were allowed to spend as they liked – on tobacco or extra food. Each Sunday when the convicts went to the local church they put a halfpence in the poor box while the rest was kept aside until their release[37] – a fund that the authorities hoped would be used by the released convicts to purchase one way tickets to a foreign country or distant colony.

At the Intermediate prisons the final lessons the establishment wanted learned were drilled into convicts – principally that they should lead a good, honest life and that they should emigrate. No opportunities were lost to ram these points home. Examples of lessons in dictation at the Intermediate prisons included: Intemperance, Suicidal Spirit of – 'Those men who destroy a healthful constitution by intemperance and an irregular life, do as manifestly kill themselves as those who hang, or poison, or drown themselves'; Labour – 'Do not live in hope with your arms folded. Fortune smiles on those who roll up their sleeves and put their shoulders to the wheel that propels them on to wealth and happiness. Cut this out and carry it about your vest pocket you who idle in bar-rooms or at the corners of streets'; Adversity – 'Adversity over one, is the greatest glory, and willingly undergone, the greatest virtue.' Instructive evening lectures were important elements in the convicts' final education. Interspersed with talks on the physical geography of the world were moralistic tracts on 'Conscientiousness Regarding Debt', 'Temperance', 'Revenge, Miseries of', 'Howard the Philanthropist: his Life and Times', 'Misfortunes, Self-Created', 'Humble Birth no Obstacle to True Greatness' and 'Swearing: its Evil Consequences'. In light of the ultimate aim of the system – the emigration of the discharged prisoner – practical lessons were given to help, and indeed encourage, the convict to leave the country; 'The Advantages of Emigration to the Unfortunate', 'The Qualifications of a Successful Emigrant', 'When and Where we should Emigrate', 'New Caledonia as a Field for Emigration', 'Emigration, Canada', 'Emigration, the

Road to Prosperity and Independence'.[38]

The Intermediate prison at Lusk was said to resemble a small cottage factory or model workshop where the supervising staff were more foremen than warders. In this relaxed atmosphere the prisoner was forced into a position of moral responsibility for himself, in a sense becoming his own gaoler. Having to show true habits of honesty, the prisoner needed to be guided by 'an inward sense of duty, in the mind' rather than by external restraint.[39] Under such training it was envisaged that the released convict would 'go forth a good MAN, not a good PRISONER'.[40]

As the convicts' time progressed and they earned sufficient marks the regime that dictated their day was even further relaxed. In order to place their characters under greater strain the convicts were exposed 'to the love of pilfering and the thirst for drink'[41] when sent unaccompanied on messages outside the prison. The unusual sight of convicts passing through the streets on messages 'involving honesty, punctuality, and, attention' became commonplace.[42] Eventually the stage was reached when prisoners worked outside the prison during the day and only returned at night. Of these it was remarked that 'there was nothing to distinguish them from the ordinary labourer, except, undoubtedly, in most instances, a more thoughtful aspect, and a countenance that might be described as more awakened'.[43] At Mountjoy four justices from Wakefield, visiting the Irish experiment, were caught by surprise when a sight was presented:

> ... strange to eyes accustomed to the ordinary mode of dealing with prisoners. A small number of men, perhaps 20, were employed in working a portion of ground outside the prison, but within the boundary wall. They wore no distinct dress, but we were informed they were convicts, who had been sent from the Intermediate Prison at Smithfield to execute the work. It being just dinnertime, they shouldered their spades, the door was opened, and off they set, to walk a mile or more through the streets of

Dublin, to their own prison at Smithfield, without physical restraint or guard of any kind, except the one who was superintending them, himself only armed with a spade.[44]

The Intermediate prisons acted as a powerful incentive to a convict in the earlier stages. When American prison reformer E. C. Wines visited Spike he spoke to many of the prisoners and found that Lusk was 'ever in their thought and on their tongue' and 'that coveted goal, and respect and esteem beyond it, keeps up heart in them and produces alacrity and cheerfulness at their work'.[45] But for some prisoners the free reins of the Intermediate prisons were too much to bear and they asked to be returned to Spike where 'physical restraint, which was continually before their eyes' kept them in check rather than 'be obliged to make the more painful effort, which the taking of the responsibility of their own actions would entail'.[46]

The public employment of prisoners and the relaxed discipline of the Intermediate stage was not only aimed at testing the prisoners. Crofton was aware that no matter what was done in prisons only some prisoners would emigrate while a large number would remain in Ireland 'with equal intention of well-doing'.[47] However, under normal conditions the very nature of imprisonment mitigated against the convicted criminal being accepted again into normal life. Strong doubts remained in the mind of the public as to the actual reformation of the prisoners irrespective of what the prison authorities claimed. As the Wakefield Justices remarked:

> Everybody knows that they must have committed a serious crime to be sent there. Of what was done within those mysterious walls the public knew little, but they saw that the prisoners were kept in by strong gates and grated windows, and if at any time seen abroad, were seen in chains.[48]

The Intermediate prisons were run on the principle that 'the more the public see of the prisoners ... the better'.[49] They were intended to inform the public, and employers in particular, that the convict was cured and could be 'restored to his country an altered and reformed being, and entitled to take his place again in society'.[50] Crofton, who sympathised 'with the public which refused to employ criminals who were ill-trained and untested, and with the well-disposed criminals who suffered in consequence',[51] used the Intermediate prisons as 'moral sieves' where the lifestyle of a free person would be simulated, in a controlled manner, and as shop windows where the public could see evidence of the prisoners' reform. Hence the term 'intermediate'.

At the end of his period at the Intermediate prison a prisoner was released on licence. If he chose to emigrate he was granted an unconditional discharge, but if he stayed in Ireland he was governed by strict rules until the remaining portion of his sentence had expired. Under the rules for a man discharged on licence the convict reported to the local constabulary on arrival in a district. The constabulary then monitored his life and reported to headquarters any misconduct or evidence that 'he is leading an idle, irregular life'. Each time the convict moved he had to sign off at one police station and then sign on in the new district. Any breach of these rules resulted in the licence being revoked and the convict returning to prison to finish out his sentence.

***

In September 1858 a female convict prison, distinct and separate in its management from the male prison, was added to the Mountjoy complex. The original discussions about the proposed Model Prison contained many references to it being a prison for both sexes. Such was the crisis in the late 1840s, the prison was reserved to deal with the more pressing and numerous problem of male convicts. However, in 1851 letters passed between Dublin Castle and Downing St outlining the inadequate facilities for females and the consternation they caused on arrival in Australia. Held in county gaols, Cork Female Convict Depot, Grangegorman, and later Newgate Prison (Newgate had lurched its way through the prison system since 1780) separation could not be carried out, thus the moral training of women was deemed 'out of the question'.[52] In June 1851 it was decided to build a female prison on the separate plan at Mountjoy. Two years later plans drawn up by architect James H. Owens were presented to the Lord Lieutenant for approval. Five years later 450 cells were ready for the reception of female convicts.

Mountjoy's first women prisoners were transferred from Cork on 20 September 1858. They were under the supervision of Delia J. Lidwell who had been in charge of the Cork Depot but transferred with the prisoners to become the first superintendent of the female prison at Mountjoy. Over the next eight days 248 women made the train journey under guard from Cork – one woman escaped.[53] The women from Grangegorman and Newgate soon joined them in Mountjoy. The first prisoner committed to Mountjoy Female Prison was Margaret Boland, aged nineteen, single and with no trade, sentenced to life in Cork city for murder. Others in the first batch included Johanna Guernon, sixteen years old, a servant, convicted at Nenagh for 'assisting and aiding in a rape' and Mary Kelly, 60 years old, a widow with three previous convictions, whose life sentence for killing sheep had been commuted to twelve years penal servitude.

Under the Crofton system female convicts passed through stages of progressive classification similar to those of the men. The marks system, again dictating the position of the prisoner on the convict ladder, was described by Lidwell as 'the most powerful incentive to good that in my experience has yet been tried'.[54] She remarked that 'though it is quite possible the majority of them could not explain it if required, I may say there is not one who does not fully comprehend the cause and disadvantage of losing a mark, and who will not be ready to remonstrate if deprived of it'.[55] In 1863, Mary Carpenter, the most famous female prison reformer since Elizabeth Fry, wrote of her

Aerial photograph of Mountjoy Prison, 1949.

observations made during a visit to the women's prison:

> ... from the first the prisoner is made clearly to understand that her gradual rise into a higher class and greater comforts, as well as being received into the refuges [see below], and her eventual restoration to society in a favourable position will depend solely on herself, not on her simply abstaining from the breach of prison rules, but on her absolute effort to overcome her vicious inclinations, and to co-operate with those placed over her in the work of reformation.[56]

Like the men the women began their sentence with a period in separation. Walking through the separation wings was described by one visitor as a 'dismal occupation':

> The long white corridors and walls unrelieved by a patch of colour; narrow iron staircases running here and there to upper stories and galleries; long rows of cells, with closely locked doors, and a little window in the middle through which the matron can peep, or the prisoners make any necessary known. Pacing up and

down a corridor containing a number of these cells, is a matron dressed in black, whose countenance and manner show you she is fair, resolute, patient and prepared for emergencies.[57]

Isolation was thought to act more severely on women so they were kept in separation for just four months. At the end of this stage they were 'allowed the luxury of having the cell doors open, and thus seeing all that passes in the occasional passage of a matron, or some other official; yet this slight break in the dread monotony of solitary confinement is valued, and looked upon as a reward'. In the third class the doors were only open half the day, one side of a wing in the morning, another side in the afternoon, 'so that the prisoner cannot see her opposite neighbour'.[58]

Of the change in lifestyle experienced by the female convict on entering the prison Mary Carpenter wrote:

> Her food has been as self-indulgent as her circumstances would permit; as stimulating as possible, and very irregular. She is now obliged to be content with food which in her present morbid condition is distasteful or even disagreeable to her, and taken at regular intervals. She is perfectly careless about cleanliness and order, perhaps has seldom employed cold water on her person, and shrinks from it.[59]

Unlike the men who benefited from a change in geography and environment when passing from the separation stage to associated labour at Spike, the female convicts remained in Mountjoy. The women were principally employed at shirt making for large manufacturing houses. In each year the profit from the female convicts defrayed about twenty per cent of the annual cost of running the prison. In the advanced class prisoners worked in association in the laundry – which serviced both the male and female prison – or generally around the prison.

Entombed in Mountjoy for most of their sentence, one of the only contacts the women had with the outside world came during visits made by nuns from the Sisters of Mercy to the Catholics and respectable Protestant women to prisoners of their faith. Initially, the convicts were visited individually in their cells but this practice was soon stopped by Lidwell who felt the women looked upon it:

> ... rather as an opportunity of talking than of learning, and after a little time there is a tendency on the part of the prisoner to seek to become too familiar with her instructress. In time they began to regard the attendance of their kind teachers in the light of the visits of condolence than admonitions to prevent them from a recurrence to their evil ways.[60]

After the individual visits were abandoned the Sisters instructed them together in a class. Despite the collection of 'wild, desperate women, with great physical strength and easily roused passions', the Sisters would not permit a prison official to attend these sessions.[61] In addition to being taught morals the women were instructed in the rudiments of education.

The management of the women mirrored to a great degree the path laid out for male convicts. But there was one element of life in the women's prison entirely absent from the male prison – children. Many convict women brought young children with them to prison – the first batch of 248 prisoners from Cork was accompanied by 24 children. In 1867 Fanny Taylor, a visitor to the prison, described the nursery as 'the most affecting site in Mountjoy':

> There are collected together the poor little creatures whose mothers are in jail. Some were sleeping in cots, others toddling about the floor, others a little older learning their letters. They were clean and nicely cared for, and looked happy enough; many of them very pretty, and all with the innocent baby faces which appeal to every heart. Poor little beings, what a strange fate is theirs; there for a brief space sheltered from the storm, but soon to go out and make experience of life in its roughest, bitterest aspect. How soon from many of them the innocence of childhood will be snatched!

Perhaps raging in the cells above, or in the 'punishment cells', tearing about like wild beasts, were the mothers of some of them ... I know not how any one could look at these rosy, smiling faces, without shedding tears. It is at least a merciful arrangement which permits them being cared for during these few years, and taught holy lessons which may linger as fragments in the memories of some.[62]

Each Sunday the mothers – unless under punishment – were allowed to spend the afternoon with their children. The children were permitted to remain in the prison until they were four years old (later changed to two years) when they were sent either to relatives or to the workhouse. Children were not only brought into Mountjoy in the arms of their mothers. The first child to be born in Mountjoy, Mary Flaherty, was born on 2 May 1858. She died eight months later. 1859 and 1860 were two of the darkest years in the history of the prison when twelve of the 27 children born into the prison died (the reason for this is unclear but the annual reports told of the totally unsuitable hospital accommodation which must have contributed to the high death rate). Prisons are gloomy places at the best of times but during these years the name of the prison must have seemed most cruel to its inmates.

After passing through the various stages at Mountjoy the women were not entitled to release on licence. Instead, they were sent to either the Sisters of Mercy Refuge at Goldenbridge or the Protestant Refuge at Hcytesbury Street. According to one writer, 'the industrious and well behaved ... earn something better than a mere premature dismissal. To turn them loose upon the world, with probably no prospect before them but vice and starvation, would be but an ill reward ... The reward, therefore, offered to the convict for completing her tale of marks is not absolute freedom ...' As with the Intermediate prisons for men, transfer to the Refuge was intended strictly as a reward for good conduct – 'the hope of getting there, the hope for the future, is the star that rises on the dark night of despair and recklessness and leads them on to exertion'.[63] The government gave the Sisters five shillings a week for each prisoner. It was a sum insufficient to cover even the day to day costs of the establishment. When the Refuge opened the Sisters were forced to procure a loan to build a large laundry and convert outhouses, lofts and sheds into dormitories.

The refuge at Goldenbridge, or St Vincent's as it was sometimes known, was a descendant of the refuges of the 1820s established for the reception of discharged female criminals. It was also inspired by similar institutions on the continent such as the one attached to the St Lazare Prison in Paris. The Superior at Goldenbridge was Mother Mary Magdalen, or Miss Kirwan as she was normally called. Kirwan established the refuge just days after being asked by Crofton (it was opened by Archbishop Cullen in March 1856) and in the subsequent years they collaborated closely on the new experiment (there was a female juvenile reformatory school run by the Sisters at Goldenbridge but this was managed separately). Kirwan was described by E. C. Wines as 'brimful of genius, heart, energy, enthusiasms, good sense and devotion to duty. She combines gentleness with firmness and piety with worldly wisdom in a remarkable degree'.[64] While one should retain a degree of scepticism for praise heaped upon people in such positions, Miss Kirwan seems to have been a remarkable woman with a strong sense of humanity. In an unusual break from the overbearingly pious prison administrators of the time Kirwan claimed to hate mock self-restraint and at the end of a day of work she would allow the women to 'dance jigs, sing songs and amuse themselves just as they please'.[65]

Goldenbridge attempted to address the same issues as the Intermediate prisons – the emigration of the convicts or their re-integration into society. Like the male convicts in the final stage, the females earned gratuities which could pay their passage abroad – often Miss Kirwan herself would buy a ticket for a deserving woman or one who needed to be saved from the clutches of unscrupulous friends and family. For those women who chose to stay in Ireland the prospect of finding employment was even more difficult than for men. Baron Von Holtzendorff wrote that 'the obstacles to be overcome are twice as great with them as with regard to males, because the sphere of action for female employment is much more limited, the wages considerably less, and the temptations to an immoral course of life more powerful'.[66] Another writer described the difficulties facing a discharged female convict:

> If a poor woman endures her sentence patiently, and keep the prison rules, she goes out at the end of her imprisonment with very little prospect for the future, save that of dishonesty. What is to become of her? She has no character. Who will employ a discharged prisoner? ... For men there are a dozen modes of hard, rough outdoor employment to which they can turn; but take away from a woman domestic service, charring, and laundry work, and there is nothing left to her but wretched needlework, at which even respectable women can hardly earn their bread. It must seem almost like a mockery to speak to a poor prisoner of the mercy of God, when the mercy of her fellow-creatures is so strongly withheld.[67]

To address the particular problems faced by women, Miss Kirwan refused 'to receive them at all unless she could hold them until she felt a good degree of assurance that they were strong enough, so to speak, to go alone, and would not be likely to relapse again into crime'.[68] At the same time the influence of Miss Kirwan, it was hoped, would rub off on the women and make them once again acceptable to society. While at the refuge the women were taught domestic housework so that they could readily fill any servant position. With the reputation established by Kirwan and the public knowledge that it was not necessary to control the women with 'the formidable appliances of a prison'[69] during the last stage of their sentence, it was hoped that respectable families would employ the convicts. For those who emigrated, the Sisters of Mercy's worldwide network of religious orders was utilised to assist the women in finding work.

Chapter Five

MOUNTJOY PRISON LIFE

Little do Irishmen know the wretchedness of imprisonment.
John K. Casey, Fenian prisoner, Mountjoy Prison

To look at the history of Mountjoy during its first decades without setting it in its broader context would give an incomplete picture. Mountjoy was one component of the unique Irish convict system. But the management of the separate system at Mountjoy showed many similarities with the other prisons of Ireland. To facilitate the separate system old cells were modified and new cells were constructed in all Irish prisons while the county prison for Antrim – better known in later years as Crumlin Road Prison – was the only county prison entirely built on the Pentonville plan. This pattern mirrored similar developments in Britain, Western Europe and the United States. Though these separate systems were different in outward appearance, the skeletons of prisons run on the separate system were the same.

The mid-nineteenth century was the era of prison history when the prison authorities ruled with an iron fist and inmates were subjected to a level of daily control perhaps second only to that exerted over members of the armed forces. Isolated from the rest of society, an island with an ever-changing population, Mountjoy life was an artificial one manufactured by the prison acts and structured by the prison rules. The most significant piece of legislation passed by the original reformers – the 1786

Prison Act – had specified just thirteen prison regulations. By 1867 the rule books for both Mountjoy male and female prisons ran to over 120 pages. The regime in Mountjoy was as far removed as possible from that of the eighteenth-century pre-reform prison. The debauchery, corruption, filth and chaos of the eighteenth-century prisons were distant memories as Mountjoy's life gravitated between the cardinal points of health, punishment, education and religion.

Concern for prisoners' health was the most basic part of Howard's prison legacy and it became a cornerstone of Victorian prison administration. However, conditions in Mountjoy were by no means ideal. The Mountjoy files reveal infestations of insects in the kitchen, rats in the cells and staff toilets. In December 1866 cholera broke out in the male prison affecting nine prisoners, four of whom died – 'in all the cases there was the usual vomiting, purging, cold blue extremities, huskey voice, sunken eye, thirst, cold tongue, and breath etc'[1] – and the temperature in the cells was eight degrees Celsius on November nights.[2] From reading these and other files it is apparent that the building and the system that ran it were far from perfect. But the very fact that the defects attracted so much attention testifies to the seriousness with which the authorities viewed the physical health of the prisoners and the conditions in which they were kept. In the 1870s a young George Bernard Shaw was invited by a warder to visit Mountjoy. He later recalled:

> I accepted the invitation with my head full of dungeons and chains, straw pallets and stage gaolers: in short, of the last acts of *Il Travatore* and Gounod's *Faust*, and of the Tower of London in *Richard III*. I expected the warders to look like murderers, and murderers like heroes. At least I suppose I did, because what struck me most was the place was as bright and clean as white-wash and scrubbing and polishing could make it ...[3]

Cleanliness was the most obvious aspect of prison management.

Typical prison cell in the late nineteenth century.

Conveniently it was also one of the most easily achieved. The cells were regularly scrubbed with the versatile bar of soap which the prisoners also used to clean themselves and their eating utensils. Daily convict crews, made up of prisoners who had finished their separation period, washed down the landings and halls of Mountjoy. Frequent whitewashing disinfected the prison. Indeed such was the extent of whitewashing in Victorian prisons that the sight of many inmates was damaged by the glare of the gaslight among the gleaming walls – to alleviate the problem the wash was later toned down with blue and brown pigment.[4] Another improvement was the removal of cell toilets from Mountjoy in the late 1860s. Poor sewage had frequently caused the cells to fill with the offensive odour of human waste and all were relieved when pots were put into cells for urine and earth closets were installed in the hall for 'stooling' (the soil, mixed with excrement, was removed to Lusk and used as human manure on the convict farm).[5]

Of all the daily aspects of prison life none was more closely examined and considered than food. In the belief that the 'God of the criminal is their belly'[6] the prison diet attempted to strike a balance between what was necessary for the survival of an inmate and what would act as an inducement to crime. As penal historian Philip Priestley wrote, 'food in the Victorian prison was weighed on scales as delicate as those of Justice herself'.[7] In Mountjoy a prisoner's weekly allowance consisted of 15 pounds 6 ounces of solid food and 12½ pints of liquid. The quantity of bread, soup, milk and meat pushed through the hatches of Mountjoy was the result of 'long and careful experiments, made by scientific men and disciplinarians, with the object of discovering the exact minimum which would suffer the criminal to pass through prison free from disease'.[8] While the quality and quantity of food was labelled wholesome, nutritious and adequate by the authorities prisoners often had a different view. Sufficient to sustain life, prisoners never enjoyed the sensation of being full. Michael Davitt, writing of his time in an English convict prison, called the prison diet 'a scale of scientific starvation'.[9] During the Land League campaign Charles Stewart Parnell, imprisoned in Kilmainham Gaol, witnessed the 'half starving' of prisoners.[10] One ex-prisoner from Mountjoy, 'E.H.', when giving evidence to a Penal Servitude Commission in 1879, was less than complimentary. The food, he said, 'was dreadfully bad sometimes, and sometimes good'[11], the meat at times 'putrid', the 'bread was half baked only in order to make weight, and it could not be eaten, if one did eat it, one could not digest it', while 'it was the most extraordinary thing, but I never once found the taste of tea from the fluid that they had there which they called tea, it was a horrible compound'.[12] The low diet debilitated their system making the prisoners brains' feeble and susceptible to the influence of the prison. It also made them more susceptible to disease. More directly its monotonous repetition caused chronic diarrhoea. This dehumanising 'ordeal by skilly' was the most prevalent illness in the prison. Most were treated in their cells with an altered diet supplemented by an oil and laudanum draught but each year dozens needed to be admitted to the prison hospital.

In the women's prison the prisoners' health was particularly difficult to maintain because of what the medical officer described as their 'character', previous pursuit in life (many diseased prostitutes) and the fact that the women, unlike the men, passed their entire sentence in Mountjoy.[13] As female Superintendent Lidwell wrote:

> While the male prisoners have the hope of variety and enlargement, owing to the number of prisons ... there is scarcely any such encouragement for female prisoners. This is the only Female Convict Prison in Ireland. It comprises the old, the lame, the blind, the half deranged and violent convicts from every part of Ireland. For all the only hope of a change for the better is in the refuges, but these accommodate a comparative few.[14]

The length of time that the females were confined in Mountjoy Prison placed great demands on both the prisoners and the female hospital (the original hospital was totally inadequate to cater for the number of broken-down prisoners). For some physical decline meant an early release from prison if the medical officer determined that 'the disease has been caused and is aggravated by confinement' and that the prisoner's life was 'in actual danger ... [and] would probably be prolonged if liberated'. Often these prisoners were released only to be buried a short time later by their family. In many cases the physical effects of confinement insidiously undermined their health, prematurely ageing them. The prison registers sometimes reveal telling information. In 1863, when Mary Nugent (alias Crowley) was committed to Mountjoy for seven years she was described in the prison register as 25 years old with dark brown hair and a fresh complexion. Released seven years later, she was recommitted to Mountjoy in a matter of months. However, on this occasion she was described as '38', with grey hair and a sallow complexion.

Overall responsibility for the health of the prison rested with the medical officer. His duties included the inspection of prisoners on arrival to assess their suitability to the Mountjoy regime, a weekly tour of the prison to ascertain any possible threat to the health of the inmates and frequent visits to the kitchen to inspect the food and its preparation. From the prisoners' perspective his most important duty was the daily examination of the 'complaining sick'. For most prisoners the sick parade was not the beginning of the end of prison life. However, it did provide a break from the monotony of the cell and offered the potential of transforming their prison life. The medical officer could detail prisoners to work in the governor's garden, increase their diet or grant more time at exercise. Highest on the list of prisoners' desires was a ticket to the Infirmary where prison life seemed a distant echo in a relaxed atmosphere. Here the luxuries of fish, beef and fruit, beer, wine, port and brandy were supplied to convalescent prisoners to improve their constitutions and restore their vital energies.[15] The regard in which the medical officer and the Infirmary life he governed were held was articulated in a poem confiscated from prisoner William Hendersen, one of Dr McDonnell's patients, in 1862:

> With books you'd endow me
> And Pen, Ink and Paper
> Thus Steer me from sadness
> I might well caper
> And if I would ask it
> No doubt you would grant me
> Beef, Soup and potatoes in manifest plenty.
>
> ... in keeping with Instincts
> I sharply judge by
> You've never been found wantin'
> In just sympathy

In conduct befitting
A true gentleman
As nutur'd e'er was
In this generous land.[16]

At Mountjoy the prisoners, deprived of more than their freedom, were not subjected by design to overt physical discomfort. This sanitised prison gave the illusion of a 'neutral' world. But sitting uneasily at the heart of the Victorian prison was the acute problem of mental health. Intended to transform criminals into spiritual beings, imprisonment mentally unhinged many people. Remarkably, suicides were rare. Most who took their own life did so by hanging, one warder reporting on his unpleasant task, 'I hat [*sic*] the sheet Cut and took him down'. The cause of these deaths was not put down to the effects of the prison system but to prisoners 'labouring under a fit of temporary mental derangement'.[17] However, successful suicides were merely the tip of a small iceberg of mental illness in Mountjoy. There were many failed suicide attempts – these were generally judged to be 'feigned' in order to gain better treatment or a transfer from Mountjoy – and a small but disturbingly steady stream of traffic made its way from the prison to the lunatic asylums.

After a sentence of penal servitude was passed on a prisoner standing in the dock, a quick departure was made to the convict prison. At Mountjoy the first slam of the cell door rarely failed to make an impression. Even the bravest of men, willing to face imprisonment and death for their principles, found that most disturbing. Peadar O'Donnell, a republican prisoner held during the Civil War, later wrote of his feelings when his Mountjoy cell door closed for the first time: 'I was as full of panic as a child, who, searching nervously in the distant corner of a barn at night time, is trapped by a gust of wind which slams the door and puts out the candle; it was as bad as that'.[18] During the separation period of nine months, prisoners were allowed just one twenty-minute visit. In addition to this brief and vital contact each convict could write a letter on arrival and thereafter every three months. But neither visits nor letters were free flows of communication. A warder superintended all visits while the governor and relevant chaplain read all incoming and outgoing mail, the contents of which were strictly controlled:

> All letters of an improper or idle tendency, either to or from Convicts or containing slang or other objectionable expressions, will be stopped. The permission to write and receive Letters is given to the Convicts for the purpose of enabling them to keep up a connection with their respectable friends, and not that they may hear the news of the day.[19]

Almost completely cut off from the outside world, prisoners commonly described the experience as being buried alive, the sounds from outside prison as fistfuls of earth thudding on their closed coffins. Under such conditions the day-to-day existence in prison was a battle against time. An inmate in one of the local prisons in the 1880s wrote:

> Prisoners are strange things. They make much of the companion-ship of a mouse or spider, and learn from them the lessons of patience, and hope, and courage. They will make a shrub or flower, a bird or rat a subject of engrossing interest. Joy to the unoccupied mind is anything of life that will speak to it by its own methods of existence, of the great problem of life and death, and of the Great Author, who is revealed in all things. How deprivations may be endured, how miseries might be mitigated, what indomitable patient perseverance the most fragile are capable of, were some of the lessons read to me by the unflinching energy of a blind fly.[20]

During nine months isolation – over twenty million seconds – the prisoner faced a daily choice between killing time or being killed by it. Sean Milroy, a prisoner in Mountjoy in 1915, warned those who enter the 'Palace of Bolts and Bars', 'don't forget to take your imagination with you when you go or you are in for the devil of a time'.[21] On the effects of cellular confinement Milroy wrote:

Solitude behind a doubly-locked door, with only a few feet of space to walk backward and forward in, has a powerful tendence to make one a philosopher. Happy the mortal thus situated who has a clear conscience, but woe to him whose conscience is of the kind that tortures, lashes and upbraids with guilty reckonings. For it does seem to me that never does man and his conscience come into closer intimacy, more delicate friendship – never does it seem to whisper in his ear or array itself before his mental vision more than when he is thus shut off from humanity, and stripped of all expedients for time-killing so prolific in social intercourse, save those which his own mind can devise.[22]

Many prisoners in Mountjoy lost their battle against time. In 1884 a member of the Cross Commission of Inquiry into Prison Conditions in Ireland thought insanity in Mountjoy 'one of the most serious points' which had been brought to their attention. He stated that 'it ought to have attracted the notice of the authorities to a greater extent than it appears to have done'.[23] However, not all those who worked in Mountjoy turned a blind eye to the mental distress of the inmates. Standing out for their humanity were the Roman Catholic Chaplain Cody from Kilkenny, and the medical officer, Dr MacDonnell, a fellow of the Royal College of Surgeons. Chinks in the prison armour, they frequently complained of what they saw as the unnecessary and inhumane treatment of convicts. In 1870 Cody wrote:

The separate discipline in Mountjoy, may, I admit, improve some minds, may help towards attaining purity of heart and solidity of character, but I believe it has, in many cases, the effect of gradually causing depression of spirits, nervousness, and causing, what is most to be deplored, loss of controlling power by which a man governs his imagination, course of thought, and inferior appetite ... to subject prisoners to the separate discipline for eight months is calculated to injuriously affect them mentally as well as physically.[24]

Some prisoners' mental and physical condition began to give way 'after four months, and most after six'[25] – as one prisoner-poet wrote, 'Strange that the soul and brain lose power so very quick/That palsy stiffins still the work of every sense'.[26] Concerned with the situation, Cody wrote to his prison superiors, 'I am confident that the Government do not desire the demoralisation of any of Her Majesty's subjects'.[27] Many became 'irritable, peevish, sullen, morose, and gloomy, liable to burst into passion on the most trifling provocation, fancying every one to be an enemy, and quite unable to control their bursts of frenzy'.

Some prisoners became mentally unsound and had visions of people visiting them in their cells at night.[28] One 'suffered mania with delusions, was very noisy and often troublesome, and constantly praying ... he would pray until he would froth out of the mouth'.[29] A female convict was admitted to the hospital in March 1871 'in a fearful state of perturbation, and in a very severe shivering fit'. The next day she was declared well but soon became 'strange' and violent and 'thought herself to be an Archangel whom we should not touch with our polluted hands, and that all her acts were done under divine inspiration'.[30] Another female 'E.H.' suffered from paranoia – a condition peculiarly associated with the separate system – and thought herself 'an object of persecution by her fellow prisoners, and the objects of plots against her life'.[31] In 1870 another female prisoner described as 'a violent self-willed individual and easily excited' with a history of injuring herself, was reported by the medical officer to be 'now lying quite naked in the cell, in order to preserve her from the cold, I consider it necessary to have her clothed and tied down on a bed, and she must be restrained with handcuffs to prevent her injuring herself'.[32] The Presbyterian chaplain at Spike wrote:

> Some men came from Mountjoy to Spike Island Prison ... with what the Scotch call 'Bees in their bonnets'; and I have reason to believe that two or three of them caught the bees in the cells of Mountjoy. One of these men hears strange whisperings, all the lamps in the prison are bobbing at him, and touching the end of his nose. But what is of more consequence, he thinks I am pulling the strings, or arranging the machinery ... another man, who

imagined he had discovered the freemason's [secret] sign, and that a warder in Mountjoy, who was a freemason, was endeavoring to poison him, committed suicide, at Spike, though closely watched and handcuffed.[33]

Like the problems of physical health, mental disease was particularly acute in the female prison. Destined to spend their entire sentence in Mountjoy – staring at the same walls, doing the same work, eating the same food – they were often helpless prey to mental illness. Women, considered to be more sociable than men, were also thought to be especially susceptible to mental illness. Frequent committals to the hospital for mania and hysteria forced the authorities to provide extra stimulus to the dulled senses. The diet was varied and extra employment (tailoring, washing, plaiting and splicing coir for mat-making) was introduced to enable some change to be made from the constant sewing and knitting, which had been their principal employments[34] – in 1868 the women of Mountjoy made a staggering 42,864 shirts.[35] Despite these modifications a survey of mental illness in Mountjoy Prison between 1879 and 1884 recorded that 2.59 per cent of women became insane after their committal to Mountjoy (the figure for men was 1.52 per cent).[36]

If many prisoners became insane as a result of their confinement, large numbers of those who filed into Mountjoy were either mentally ill ('odd', 'eccentric') or mentally handicapped ('weak-minded', 'half-thick') on committal. Contemplating the plight of these prisoners is difficult and unpleasant. Thrown into an alien, constraining world, oblivious to the rules they broke, not capable of comprehending the impersonal power that governed their day, this group accounted for the majority who filled the punishment cells and penal class. In an internal memorandum Chaplain Cody wrote, 'separation in the case of weak-minded prisoners only tends to exaggerate their disease ... I know of few places more calculated than Mountjoy Prison where its gloomy appearance, peculiar construction and surrounded as it is by high walls, cannot fail to exercise a depressing influence on the minds of such a class'.[37] According to the Catholic chaplain, 'the small number of refractory prisoners cannot of course be thought of without pain ... they keep the establishment in a constant state of unpleasantness. It appears that their reasoning faculties are impaired, and some are commonly spoken of as mad'.[38] A typical example of those prisoners considered neither sane nor insane was Rosanna Hynes. During her five years of confinement she was continuously under punishment. Along with a catalogue of other prison offences, she 'injured' prison property to the tune of £24. The list of damage read: panes of glass – 144, rugs – 27, blankets – 78, aprons – 1, bed covers – 3, bed ticks – 16, quart tins – 6, sheets – 8, pillow covers – 4, boss – 16, towels – 7, neckerchiefs – 2, tin plates – 1, canvas suits – 5, capes – 1, spoons – 1, petticoats – 2, jackets – 1.[39] Individuals like Hynes put prison officials trying to enforce order in a difficult position. Delia Lidwell explained the predicament in one report:

> Doubtless the persistent misconduct of some of the convicts renders it difficult to reconcile their conduct with their perfect sanity; but to allow misconduct to pass unpunished, except in cases when it is perfectly clear that the mental state of the convict is such as renders her a certain extent irresponsible, would result in serious and continued disorder in the prisons.[40]

The mentally ill stood at the coal-face of prison punishments at Mountjoy but about twenty per cent of prisoners in separation and 40 per cent in association were punished. The explicit aim of the prison system was to make the convict docile and obedient. Often the prisoners stubbornly refused to be cowed into submission. The most common breach of prison rules was for communication. Though a mouse made a big noise in the separate prison all attempts by warders, on the back of decades of prison reform, came to nothing in the face of the prisoners' determination to communicate. They tapped out a Morse code on walls and on the partitions in chapel, talked like ventriloquists, whispered through the cell vents and shouted out windows. Second to communication was the trafficking of 'lady nicotine'. Despite the official attitude that 'the narcotic was so perilous as dynamite'[41] – not for health reasons but because it indulged the prisoners – and the war waged against it (each day two prisoners were picked at random from each landing and strip searched in the hunt for illegal substances[42] while every two months the whole prison was searched) the smuggling of tobacco was one of the most common breaches of prison regulations.[43] Risking dismissal warders 'treated' with prisoners (trafficked in tobacco and other goods) and when prisoners were committed they smuggled in the banned substance by swallowing it or concealing it up their rectums.[44]

The range of prison offences was vast. All of the following were recorded at Mountjoy – lifting floorboards in cell and concealing wool, wasting water in cell, allowing trousers to take fire in cell, threatening to kill a warder, being up at a cell window, assaulting a fellow prisoner, threatening to report an officer, speaking improperly to officers, attempting to cut the bars of the cell with nitric acid, giving dinner to another prisoner, giving ludicrous answers in class, unnecessary talk and laughing in association, having a small piece of brass in possession, whistling violently, not working satisfactorily, wrestling, having a piece of oakum secreted in cell, malingering, disorderly and noisy when going to cell, having a small bit of paper and pencil not issued, giving a slip of paper to another prisoner while at school, making use of an irritating expression, larking with a fellow prisoner, having in possession an old newspaper, altering trousers without leave, demanding to go to the penal ward, singing in cell, writing down the words of a song on a slate, ringing bell violently, disobedience, insubordination, throwing a cloak over the exercise wall, immoral language, attempting to assault an officer, using vile and abusive language to an officer, using unusual language.

Punishments given to prisoners varied with the seriousness of the offence. The least serious warranted a loss of marks or bread and water diet for up to 28 days (although this was rarely resorted to, the usual being three). Then came the dark, unheated punishment cell in the basement into which the prisoner was flung naked, with only a small rug for warmth. On one occasion the medical officer found 'a prisoner in one of them looking very miserable. He was stooping forward with his hands thrust between his legs, his extremities were cold, his features shrunken, he shivered, and his teeth chattered. He had the appearance of a man labouring under serious illness; indeed, the leaden hue of his face and sunken eyes looked like that of a patient struck with Asiatic cholera. I inquired what ailed him; he said he was cold, very cold; that no bed or bedding, except for a single rug, had been allowed him during the night, that he had lain on the floor, with no other bed clothes than a rug to cover him, and that he was cold to his very bones'.[45] For the most serious offences (assaulting an officer, persistently feigning suicide, homosexual sex, breaking windows) male prisoners could be subjected to the unpleasant ritual of corporal punishment inflicted with either the birch rod or cat-of-nine-tails. Intended to act as both punishment and example, corporal punishments were held in a yard or corridor within earshot of the other prisoners:

> The sentence is read out by the Governor to the prisoner – and in the case of the cat he is ordered to strip to the waist – a leather collar is fastened round the neck to protect the nape of the neck and large blood vessels, a broad belt also of leather, is fastened around the loins – and the culprit is fastened to the triangle – each ankle and knee being separately strapped to the two anterior legs of the triangle or to the cross bars. The wrists are secured by straps attached to a cord which runs through a wheel at the apex of the triangle, the hands being drawn upwards over the man's back.
>
> All being ready, the Governor gives the order to the officer selected – to do his duty [In Mountjoy a warder was paid 10s for this task]. The Chief Warder counting the lashes in a loud voice

and writing down each lash as it is given.

In addition to the Governor – Medical Officer and officer or officers actually inflicting the punishment – the Chief Warder and some six discipline officers are present frequently – the Deputy Governor and deputy Medical Officer, where there are such officers, also.

In the case of the birch rod, the procedure is much the same, but the prisoner keeps his shirt on, the buttocks only being exposed. A board is fixed on the triangle over which the prisoner bends and the hands are drawn forwards instead of upwards, the feet are kept close together, instead of straddled – a pad is sometimes put between the upper part of the thighs in the crotch to protect the scrotum, if this is pendulous.

After the punishment is over, the prisoner is released as speedily as possible – a piece of soft linen or lint spread with vaseline or olive oil is applied and the prisoner removed to his cell.[46]

On the other side of the penal coin was the prison staff. Although exercising great power over the convicts the staff were almost as much prisoners of Mountjoy as the prisoners themselves. Working long hours, the Irish prison staff were particularly badly paid. Taken from the same labour market as police constables, warders were only paid 17s a week compared to 28s a week for a constable. They too were harnessed by a strict regime of punishments mainly based on a scale of fines for the lesser offences, suspension or dismissal for the more serious ones. Each prison officer had a misconduct sheet detailing each infringement of the prison rules – talking with another officer while on duty, being one minute late, allowing prisoners to have in their possession prohibited articles, leaving a water tap running, allowing prisoners to wear their caps improperly, falling asleep on duty, etc. In 1867 a marriage bar on female staff was introduced and thereafter they had to leave their job if they wanted to marry. The conditions in the female prison resulted in a very high turnover of staff. Those who stayed were, in a way, married to the prison. Having to find emotional support within its confines, some engaged in surreptitious lesbian liaisons with prisoners. In 1866 some of the female staff were dismissed for 'becoming too familiar with prisoners'.[47] In August 1872 Superintendent Lidwell came across a cell door ajar. When she went in she found a matron sitting down with prisoner Catherine Cooney kneeling at her feet with her arms resting on the matron's lap. In his report Director of Convict Prisons, Captain Barlow, wrote, 'it is perfectly clear to me that very undue familiarity exists between some of the Matrons and the Convicts'. He warned that any further irregularities would lead to dismissal.[48]

Working in a prison was by no means an easy occupation. In one report it was written that 'the duties of Prison officials are at all times harassing, often dangerous, it is not going too far to remark that they, probably of all Civil Servants, have no relief, excepting during absence on leave, from continuous anxiety'.[49] The work was dominated by periods of boredom (one Inspector of Prisons described the job of a warder as 'hideously monotonous work'[50]) but ever present in the daily routine was the fear of being attacked by one of the prisoners. Violent outbursts were not uncommon. A prisoner resisted being searched by kicking and screaming and 'at the same time he swore that he would have the life of every bloody warder he could catch, and kicked Warder Finnamore in a most Savage manner in the "Privates", the warder fell and was obliged to leave the cell from weakness'.[51] Another warder was stabbed several times with a scissors by a prisoner who swore that 'by his holy J- C- that he would take his life'.[52] Violence was not restricted to the male prison. Attacks by female prisoners were also frequent. In 1874 there was 'a mutinous atmosphere' in the women's prison. After a particularly serious incident in which one staff member was viciously attacked (she was unable to work for some months) the women were warned that any further attacks would result in their hair being cut short until discharge and they would not be entitled to go to the refuge.[53]

When looking back in time through the 'penal spy-hole' one must be careful not to become voyeuristic. Concentrating on the oppressive and painful elements of prison life would give a false view of the reformed prison. The official files and reports tended to concentrate on the more unpleasant or unusual parts of prison life. However, there were other aspects that tried to improve the prisoner. They often worked away quietly in the background. Uniquely Victorian prison administration, founded on the separate system, satisfied both sides of the penal divide. Being 'determinantely penal' it appeased those who wanted to punish. Yet it was also 'perseveringly kind' and had its laudable elements.[54] The nineteenth-century prison was built on 'moral' foundations. One of the most important of these was education.

Within 48 hours of their committal to Mountjoy convicts were examined to assess their educational attainments. Not surprisingly the majority were found to be either wholly or partially illiterate. In the belief that ignorance was a cause of crime, one of the main aims of the prison system was to give the prisoners a basic education to enhance their employment prospects after release. For six hours each week the convicts were taught according to the primary school curriculum (the schools were regularly visited by an Inspector of National Schools). Some prisoners rebelled against this forced education, telling the schoolmaster that 'they would never have it said that they got any learning in a gaol-school, or from the English government' and contemptuously wondering 'how other prisoners could be so mean as to take the Government learning; that although he was a prisoner, he was not quite so mean as all that and that he had some little pride left'.[55] But most, previously deprived of education, saw it as an opportunity. Indicative of their respect for the schoolroom was their good behaviour in class – a punishment for breach of rules in class was rare. By the time they finished their 'gaol-tuition' over 90 per cent were able to read and write – they proudly penned 'this is my own writing' at the bottom of their first letter.[56] Some even advanced to writing complex essays on 'Moral, Science or Intellectual' topics. In 1862 Thomas Hanlon submitted *An Essay on Slang or*

Counterfeit Language in which he wrote:

> During my sojourn in this institution, I had from time to time to
> remark that among the majority of the inmates with whom I have
> been associated, there prevailed a fault, which degrades the char-
> acter of him with whom it is predominant, as much as it hurts and
> irritates the feelings of those who meet its reproach ... for language
> is too exalted a term for such gibberage ... slang is not only the
> signe of the vulgar, but of the blaguard and gail bird, and who
> would respect the blaguard, muchless he who lost his character by
> being an inmate of a Convict prison.[57]

A visitor to one of the women's classes described the sight of
elderly women, 'grey and shriveled, with the hardened countenance of ignorance and depraved age, busy over the very rudiments of education – a second childhood being brought to book
in a manner as melancholy as it is fantastic'.[58] Another visitor
wrote that 'it was curious to see women of every age, even to
the grey-haired, standing in classes with spelling-books, like so
many children, many of them able to read but little, but eager
and interested in the employment, which broke the monotony
of their days and gave them some new ideas'.[59]

The prison school served a variety of ends beyond the
inmates' strict educational development. The prisoners were
made conversant with the marks system and were urged to be
'humble, submissive, and industrious' in order to 'shorten their
confinement by their own exertions'.[60] The teaching of geography fulfilled an important element of the convict system, the
eventual emigration of the criminal. It was also the most popular
subject in Mountjoy – perhaps giving the prisoners food for
thought and allowing them to at least mentally escape the physical confines of the prison. Though when first presented with a
map many looked on it 'as some mystical representation of the
earth, and believed it impossible for ignorant men like them to
ever comprehend',[61] they soon learned the outlines of the world,
Europe and Ireland and 'something of the customs, manners and
productions of the different countries'.[62] Edward McGauran, the

first schoolmaster under the Crofton system, felt that 'erroneous notions regarding wages, rise and fall of provisions, competitions in trades, railroads and machinery, have been made a public source of poverty and crime'. In addition to the Bible in each cell McGauran asked that prisoners be supplied with a copy of Archbishop Whately's *Easy Lessons on Money Matters* to learn the folly of such social evils as strikes and trade unions.[63] McGauran pointed his finger at the ideas circulating amongst the poor of Ireland that their plight was the result not of their own actions, but of the social structure that stacked the odds against them. To dispel these 'myths', special emphasis was given in Mountjoy's education to 'the nature of relations between the employer and employed, the constituents of value, and the great advantage of machinery to every one, particularly the working people, the lasting benefits of education, and the means by which wealth is honestly acquired, accumulated, and transmitted from father to son'.[64] Intermittently the prisoners were examined on such subjects by staff and visiting dignitaries.

Education was closely related to religion, the second element of prison life designed to improve the convicts who were thought to be 'lamentably ignorant, not only of the simple elements of education, but also their duties to God, to society, and to themselves'.[65] School time was used to 'engender self-respect so as to induce shame',[66] to make prisoners 'steady, sober, and industrious members of society'[67] and to uproot 'perverted notions of "right" and "wrong"'.[68] A crucial role of the prison teacher was to promote as far as possible the moral improvement and instruction of the prisoners. The schoolmaster ploughed the field of 'ignorance' for the chaplains by teaching prisoners the meanings of such words as 'virtue, vice, righteousness, iniquity'.[69] Literacy also opened their minds to the books chosen for them by the chaplains (*The Life of Israel, Tales of Christian Testimonials, Loretto of the Choice, Loss of the Sacraments, Life of St Patrick, Legends of the Commandments, Knights of St John, Robinson Crusoe, Popular Church History, Gerard the Lion Killer,*

The Anxious Inquirer, Memorials of Captain Hedley Vicars, 97th Regiment, The Sunday at Home).[70] This religious pioneering role became a source of conflict in the 1860s when Edward McGauran renounced his Catholic faith in front of his class and announced his conversion to Presbyterianism. After McGauran's revelation, Chaplain Cody thought the school 'pregnant with evil for the Roman Catholic convict'. Rumours circulated that Catholic prisoners were being 'tampered' with by the Presbyterian schoolmaster. In 1862 convict John O'Driscoll wrote to Chaplain Cody that the schoolmaster had told the class that 'the Church of Rome has without doubt allowed gross faults to creep into her system'. According to O'Driscoll's letter McGauran was 'certainly thwarting the minds of his Catholic pupils imbibing his latitudinium principles into their minds trying to make them suck the poison of his freewheeling religious opinion – This will never answer the poor Catholics of Mountjoy'.[71] Sensitive to the charge of proselytysing in a predominantly Protestant-dominated institution (after McGauran's conversion Delia Lidwell was the only senior Roman Catholic in Mountjoy) the Directors ordered the transfer of McGauran to Spike Island.

When committed to Mountjoy all convicts were classified according to their religion and were forced to attend the service of their faith. The majority were Catholic (accounting for about 80 per cent), then Protestants and the smallest congregation, representing between two and three per cent were Presbyterians (mainly from Ulster). For many years these three main religions were the only options given to a prisoner. Failure to conform to one of them was deemed insubordination and was punished. According to one article 'the meaning of that is this – that if a man is a Quaker, or belong to any of the great dissenting communities, or be a Jew, or Mahommedan, or, as may unfortunately happen, an Atheist, he must select one of three religions, every one of which he disbelieves, and conform to a creed which to him is a mockery ... Such a prisoner must if he wishes to escape punishment, with his jail clothes, assume a jail religion'.[72] In 1865 when the well-known Fenian 'Pagan' O'Leary was committed he refused to register a religion and was put into a punishment cell for a month and examined for insanity.[73] Nearly all prisoners professed themselves to be members of one faith, but their knowledge of religion was often sketchy, sometimes non-existent. In one year the Catholic Chaplain reported that one-quarter of his charges were ignorant of 'the principles of religion'. In a nominally Christian country many of those who entered Mountjoy had lived outside the loop of the formal churches. In 1855 Reverend Black, the Protestant Chaplain, wrote, 'I found all deplorably ignorant of the simplest doctrines, promises and precepts of revealed religion; they were Christian only in name, living without God, without Christ, and without hope – wanderers in a world of iniquity, uncaring and uncared for'.[74]

The chaplains employed every tool in their repertoire 'to explain to each individual the mischief of the vile motives by which their conduct had been hitherto actuated, and to set forth the objects and hopes by which as immortal beings, they ought to be influenced'.[75] In the cell and chapel they harangued, admonished and instructed prisoners 'to reflect on such subjects as divine revelation presents. By these means the most hardened criminal has been taught to know himself as an accountable creature, guilty before God'.[76] Like missionaries in a distant heathen land the chaplains set about familiarising the prisoners with the basic tenets of their religions. The totally ignorant were specially instructed to prepare them for Confirmation. Regularly bishops and archbishops, including former anti-transportation campaigner Archbishop Whately, ventured into Mountjoy to confirm the convicts. Every Friday Catholic prisoners attended confession, many leaving with their eyes full of 'penitential tears'.[77] In 1875 a three-day mission was conducted in the women's prison by the Vincentian Fathers, 'at its close almost all approached the Sacraments of Penance and Holy Communion with the intention of gaining the jubilee'.[78] In May 1871 Chaplain Cody married convicts James Hennessy (alias Dwyer) and Margaret Dwyer[79] (most prisoners had common-law marriages and many of the children brought into Mountjoy by their mothers were illegitimate in the eyes of the Church).

There were many examples illustrating the failure of religion. In 1861 Delia Lidwell requested that the practice of giving female prisoners Bibles and prayer books on release be stopped because they were immediately pawned or sold.[80] Prisoners in separation were allowed only religious books and thus viewed them, and religion, as part of their punishment.[81] In 1858 a note of a most 'disgustingly obscene nature' written by convict John Craughwell was found in the Chapel's holy water font. Its contents included:

> Do not let Moloney be sticking his prick in your arse ... John Craughwell ... is a divil for fucking himself ... he is killed from it ... Pat ... you have the arse fucked out of yourself there is a lump on your back from that. Can't you do as Tom Corragan told you. Shut your fist and put your prick into it rub it in and oute very hard believe me your nature will come. Spit your hand and make it wet, this will do well as if you had a woman's cunt.[82]

In 1879 ex-prisoner 'E.H.' told the Prison Commissioners of the failure of religion:

> We learn evil more easily than virtue, and the elevating sentiments of the chaplain are quickly effaced by the blighting and insinuating whispers of the prison fiend. I saw on one occasion a young prisoner approach the altar to participate in a great sacrament of the Catholic Church. That very day I observed an old prison inmate making love to him.[83]

In his Mountjoy cell on 15 April 1867 John Keegan Casey wrote lines summing up the visions the chaplains were attempting to create on the fly leaf of *Visits to the Blessed Sacrament* – from the Italian of Saint Liguori, 'O LOVE divine! O sweet o'erpowering love!/With which my Jesus comes to visit me/A sinner steeped in crime and misery,/To lead me to the blessed home above'.[84] But they were not ignorant of the difficulty of the task that their prison congregation set them. Although believing that 'religion alone can reach the root of the evil which lies in the heart'[85] they often had to satisfy themselves with what limited successes they could achieve. Chaplain Black, recognising the realities of the situation, consoled himself with the thought that 'there is joy in the presence of the angels of God over one sinner that repenteth'.[86]

For all the rhetoric of the prison reformers religion, fundamental to every prison plan since the 1780s, had been given an unrealistic mission. Standing in the way of the mass religious transformation of Ireland's criminal souls were a number of insurmountable questions. How could the prison produce perfect Christians when so many outside prison were not? How could the prison system produce God-fearing souls out of some of the most depraved and vicious people in society? How could enforced religion produce true repentance? How could the light of God be seen through the cloud of prison life?

Chapter Six

END OF REFORM

Penal history is littered with unfulfilled promises, abandoned hopes, and discarded institutions ...

Sean McConville, penal historian, 1995

From the 1780s until the second half of the nineteenth century punishment had seemed a very simple idea. Thoughts of deterrence and reform, backed up by philosophical arguments, had propelled prison management along a uniform and clearly defined path. Prison theory had promised much. Indeed such was the faith of some reformers that they believed the natural consequence of feeding criminals through prisons would be the elimination of crime, and ultimately, the elimination of prisons. When transportation to Australia ended, the prison became the undisputed centre of punishment. At the same time prison architecture had been perfected and prison management reached its height. However, just as the prison 'came of age' it was judged a 'failure' against the measuring sticks of deterrence and reform.

Prison history reached a turning point in the second half of the nineteenth century when prison theory foundered upon the rocks of the human condition. Those involved with prisons would never again be so united in their ideas nor so convinced they would work. The prison reform movement disintegrated while a retreat was made from the great claims made on behalf of bars, cells and high walls. The Crofton system was the last national prison system around which there was any sort of consensus. By the 1890s the last vestiges of his system had disappeared. It was not the only victim of this sea change. By the end of the century the separate system, the very basis of the modern prison, was being abandoned and issues of management were being decided with reference to merely functional and bureaucratic considerations. The reasons for these striking changes are complex but lurking in the shadows behind each was the defiant figure of the criminal who stubbornly refused to be changed by the prison.

When the Crofton system was established it was heralded as one of the great contributions to prison management and caused huge interest. In 1857 the Third International Prison Congress, held in Frankfurt, called for the general adoption of Intermediate prisons.[1] In Switzerland prisons were established on the Irish template. The Elmira Reformatory in New York, which was to act as a model for other American states, was structured on Crofton's mark system. Over 200 articles were written on the Irish convict system, the majority of which were overwhelmingly favourable; *The Economist* declared 'the method adopted by Captain Walter Crofton in the Irish Convict Prisons to be the true solution of the most difficult social problem of the day';[2] French penal reformer Count Cavour wrote that it was 'the only efficacious means of discountenancing vice and checking crime';[3] Mary Carpenter proclaimed 'a grand experiment has been tried, the success has been indisputable and triumphant'; American prison reformer E.C. Wines wrote that under the Irish system 'the prison is no longer a grave for the living but is transformed instead into a moral sanatorium, in which human beings, dead to virtue, may begin a new life';[4] even Ireland's nationalist minded *Freeman's Journal*, in a bout of penal patriotism, claimed the Crofton system was 'one of the grandest triumphs our countrymen have achieved'.[5]

Statistics relating to the Irish system appeared to confirm that Crofton had succeeded where others had failed. Of the 1,250 male convicts released on licence between March 1856 and

March 1860, only 77 had their licences revoked.[6] By 1861 less than five per cent of the women who had passed through the refuges had been recommitted to a convict prison.[7] Between 1853 and 1862 committals to Mountjoy fell by more than half. In 1870 the average daily number of convicts in Irish prisons had fallen to one-third of the 1854 level. Mountjoy Prison, filled to capacity during its first years, actually began to empty. Such was the fall in numbers that in 1873 two empty wings of the male prison were boarded up to save on coal and gas[8] and one-quarter of the staff were let go in 1874.[9] It was indeed a remarkable turnaround. But, while he was a deeply committed and inspired administrator and his system of convict management was methodical and considered, Crofton had not found the talismanic key to criminal reform. In 1862 Crofton retired from the Irish Convict Service because of poor health (on retirement he was knighted for his efforts at convict reform). It was an opportune time to leave. His reputation was at its height but it was resting on very unsteady foundations.

In 1863 Reverend Gibson, the Presbyterian Chaplain at Spike Island, wrote a booklet entitled *Irish Convict Reform, The Intermediate Prisons, A Mistake*. Gibson was Crofton's most caustic critic in Ireland. While preparing the booklet, he wrote to Crofton's English equivalent and rival, Sir Joshua Jebb, for support. In writing Gibson was honing in on the professional chasm that existed between Jebb and Crofton over Crofton's system. Jebb was one of the few in the penal world who doubted the merits of Crofton's system. As Crofton noted in one article, 'there is a new feud between Britain and Ireland – a grand protest against anything like a union between the two countries'.[10] It was a debate that would not last long. Gibson's booklet was one of the last writings dedicated to the Crofton system. In it Gibson called the system a 'failure' and declared that Crofton may have held the reins of the convict department when numbers were falling 'but the chariot was rushing down a fearful incline at the heels of those pale horses, FAMINE, DEATH and DEPOPULATION'.[11] While one may have reservations about Gibson's motives (he was in part spurred by Crofton's positive attitude towards Roman Catholics) and his mathematics (both Crofton and Gibson juggled with statistics) his publication was not too wide of the mark. No thorough modern-day assessment of the Crofton system has taken place. The question, did it really achieve what no other prison system has been able to do, has not yet been definitively answered. Certainly the Crofton system cannot be dismissed out of hand – he made great improvements that are still evident in prison systems. However, if one gave credence to claims that it caused the spectacular change in the Irish situation (as Richard Hinde does in two articles in the *Irish Jurist* from 1977) one would, in turn, have to deny that the Famine had originally led to the dramatic increase. This was simply not the case. The decline in convict numbers in Ireland was largely a reflection of improved social and economic conditions and massive emigration in the decades after the Famine.

A large percentage of the first convicts to pass through Crofton's system had dazzled the prison world with evidence of reform. Miss Kirwan kept a file of letters from women who had passed through her refuge after completing their Mountjoy stages. In the letters the women told of how they had been saved from a life of ignominy, vice and shame.[12] However, they were largely the victims of extraordinary social and economic circumstances. Between one-third and one-half of the convicts who passed through every stage of Crofton's system emigrated when released – the ones who emigrated were dubiously pronounced 'reformed'. Of those who stayed in Ireland many led crime-free lives not because of prison mechanics but because the society they were released into was one in which they did not necessarily have to steal in order to live.

When the Famine convicts were being released a new type of convict emerged who was little affected by the Crofton system. As early as 1852 straws were seen blowing in the wind when it was noted that the convicts were 'the real pests of society habituated to vice and crime'.[13] In 1856 convicts passing through Mountjoy were different than before, they were 'less tractable and more restless' than convicts of previous years.[14] On another occasion it was noted that the 'greater proportion of those convicted appear to be of a more abandoned class'[15] and were 'more inclined to violence, and less reclaimable'.[16] Overall convict numbers had plummeted but when the system was confronted with the new criminals, statistics relating to convict reform became less and less favourable to Crofton. In 1862 when 209 convicts were discharged, there were 97 recommitted.[17] In 1867, total convictions were half what they were ten years before but recommittals had nearly trebled.[18] In 1868 only 25 of the 185 men committed to Mountjoy had never before been convicted of a crime (68 had been convicted six times or more).[19]

These 'new' convicts were markedly different from the Famine convicts. No longer were the vast majority from rural areas – they were the 'idle and dissolute roughs' habituated to lives of crime and based in the large cities and towns.[20] A survey of the Mountjoy Prison registers shows the transformation – in 1851 only five per cent of convicts sent to Mountjoy were from Dublin but by the late 1870s they accounted for nearly half of Mountjoy's committals. In 1879 Captain Barlow, Vice-Chairman of the General Prisons Board (see below) standing in front of a Commission on Penal Servitude said, 'they are what they call in Dublin (I think it is a new institution that has come from America to a certain extent) corner boys'.[21] In 1874 Delia Lidwell reported from the female prison that 'there is a proportion of violent women here whose violent tempers it seems impossible, either through kindness or severity, to bring under control; they are generally those who have lived their lives in cities and towns, in every kind of dissipation and drunkenness'.[22] In 1882 the Right Honourable the Recorder of Dublin

F.R. Falkiner outlined the courtroom phenomenon of the hardened urban criminal in an article entitled *Our Habitual Criminals.* In it he claimed they were infected with the 'moral malaria of our lower streets' and became more and more contaminated with every flux and re-flux between prison and street.[23] In the prisons they were noted to be markedly different from their rural counterparts. Indeed such was the distinction between the two sets of prisoners that plans were put forward to keep Dublin and Belfast convicts separate from the rural convicts in Mountjoy.[24] One Mountjoy prisoner claimed that a rural criminal looked upon an urban thief with 'horror, he would not touch him'.[25] These 'dregs of the town' were seemingly impervious to reform and cut the ground from under Crofton's system.

It would be wrong to unduly criticise Crofton and his system. Now largely unsung in the country whose convicts made him famous, Crofton deserves recognition for his successes: Crofton ran his prison system with an enlightened attitude and undoubtedly contributed to the reform of some. He treated prisoners as individuals rather than an undifferentiated mass and he invented the open prison. At worst his system merely failed when confronted with the type of criminal that had frustrated other prison systems. However, this failure was one of the defining moments of prison history. For a brief period of time in the late 1850s and early 1860s, the Irish convict system had seemed to offer practical evidence of convict reform at a time when other prison systems were disappointing. The prison reformers had been dazzled by the decline of prison numbers in the early years of the Crofton system. When it ceased to produce remarkable statistics of reform their vision was shattered. The reformers had been searching for the perfect solution to the problem of crime. Anything less than this was not good enough. Thus when the Irish system did not prove to be the complete solution, it was abandoned by the reformers. When the Irish convict system ceased to be a rallying point for the prison fraternity the cohesion of the reform movement was lost. Indicative of this fundamental change was the fact that in London in 1872 the International Prison Congress, the first since 1857, could not agree upon a way forward for the prison.[26]

As the situation in Ireland 'normalised' in the decades after the Famine, penal administration took on a fatalistic demeanour. The birth and development of the prison had been framed by eloquent phrases. When the prison failed to live up to expectations, a deep scepticism permeated the administration of prisons. Pessimism is rarely articulate and the story of the prison's 'failure' is documented not by carefully chosen words but by their absence. The most poignant indicator of the failure of prison reform was that, as the years passed, Mountjoy's annual reports became shorter and shorter. What had once been the forum for the Governor, chaplains and medical officer to wax lyrical about the reform of the criminal mind was eventually reduced to terse statements of facts and reams of the 'Gradgrindian' statistical tables. The Directors' opening addresses, which once ran to pages, were now down to a few paragraphs. Weighed down with routine and inertia, they frequently began with comments like, 'the working of the Irish Convict system for the past year has been so entirely similar to that of the previous year that but few remarks are called for by me'.[27] The Directors were by no means alone. Practically everyone involved in prisons became disillusioned. In 1878 the record for brevity was set by Presbyterian Chaplain Robert Hanna when his report on Mountjoy amounted to just thirteen words. Against the background of the prison's disappointments, the once clear-cut issue of punishment found itself in a terrible muddle. On a practical level nothing illustrates this more than the contradictory relationship that had developed between the county gaol and the convict prison.

The sentence of 'penal servitude' in a convict prison was designed for the worst criminals convicted of the most serious crimes. The sentence of 'imprisonment' to a local gaol was for the least serious offenders. But, paradoxically, the regimes in the local prisons were much harsher than in the convict prison. Reformation was thought to be the work of time and the maximum sentence to imprisonment, as opposed to penal servitude, was just two years. Such a short stay in prison was not deemed enough time to reform so the regime in the local prisons was emphatically on the side of deterrence. The catch cry of the local prison in the second half of the century was 'hard labour, hard board and hard fare'. The diet was less than in the convict prisons (no meat was allowed), prisoners stayed in separation for their full term (up to two years), there was no remission of sentence and prisoners spent their first month on a hard wooden 'plank bed'. The cruelly pointless shot-drill exercise epitomised the regime of the local prisons.

The shot drill exercise consisted of prisoners lining up in a prison yard 4-6 paces apart behind a four-inch high block holding a triangular pile of cannon shot. To one side of each prisoner was an empty block. On the words 'prepare for shot drill' every prisoner stood to attention. On the word 'lift' every prisoner stooped 'without bending the knee' and raised the shot in front of him in line with the elbows, standing to attention. On the command 'one' every prisoner stepped a full pace to the right/left with their right/left foot. The warder counted off the number of paces until the prisoners were behind their second block. 'After a pause of slow time' each prisoner stooped down as before, without bending the knee, and placed the shot 'on the block without any noise, by opening the fingers and allowing the shot to slip through close to the block' and then rose smartly to attention. After another pause of slow time the prisoners returned to the original position 'in the same number of paces; without a shot'. The exercise was continued until the whole pile had been carried. The procedure was then 'simply reversed'.[28]

Charles Stewart Parnell, when giving evidence to a Prison Commission, quoted one judge who told a man when sentencing him to two years imprisonment, 'that very few persons went through this term without suffering permanently in mind

Hard-labour yard in Kilmainham Gaol.

or in body, and very often in both'.[29] Even after legislation was passed lengthening the sentence of penal servitude to seven years for a second felony Captain Barlow stated that prisoners convicted a second time should be sent to a local prison which, he believed, would be more of a deterrent.[30] Some criminals, when being sentenced, asked to be given penal servitude rather than a shorter term of imprisonment. This led to the obvious conclusion in the press that penal servitude could not be a very severe punishment. Responding to such charges Mountjoy's Protestant chaplain commented, 'little do such writers know what penal servitude is in its stern reality, and less do they know of the sentiments and opinions of prisoners themselves on the subject'. Yet having defended the harshness of penal servitude the chaplain summed up the difficulties of those who put their faith in the prison when he asked, as if to himself, 'why are there so many returned convicts when penal servitude is so severe and dreaded by criminals?'[31]

The first prison reformers had painted with wide philosophical brushes on the broad canvas of punishment. The ultimate realisation of their vision was the regime at prisons like Mountjoy. While the colours used by the eighteenth-century philanthropists and the administrators of Mountjoy were of the same hue, the overall pictures of theory and reality were undoubtedly different. The prison's test was whether it would succeed in its primary aims of reforming prisoners and deterring people from committing crime. When the prison disappointed it was not, of course, abandoned as an institution. In the absence of an alternative the prison remained the salient feature of punishment but there was a fundamental change in thinking.

The incapacity of the prison to solve the problem of crime meant that the criminal and the prisoner would be permanent fixtures of society. For the protection of persons and property it was necessary to discover who they were and to document their identities. As the century progressed an increasingly sophisticated noose of officialdom tightened around the neck of the criminal population. In 1869 the Habitual Criminals Act was passed. Under this legislation an alphabetical list was compiled of the names, physical descriptions and criminal histories of persistent re-offenders. Every year 1,700 copies of the register were distributed to police stations, prisons and post offices. Between 1870 and 1890, over 10,000 names appeared. In the 1860s photography was introduced into Mountjoy.[32] Later detailed anthropometric physical measurements of prisoners were taken to add to the bank of information on the criminal population. These measurements included the length and breadth of head, face, ears, either foot, fingers of either hand, cubit of either hand, the prisoner's height when standing and when sitting and the size and relative position of every scar and distinctive mark upon any part of the body.[33] It was a cumbersome, time-consuming and error-prone method (even a couple of millimetres out in a measurement could make any search futile). In 1903, after the head of Irish prisons and a clerk from the Dublin Castle offices went on a familiarisation trip to Scotland Yard, the far more convenient and efficient method of fingerprinting was introduced into Ireland. The warders at Mountjoy were the first to be trained in the new system.[34]

The documentation of prisoners went some way towards finding out exactly who they were. Directly following on from

120

this was the new subject of criminology that asked the question 'why do criminals commit crime?' Criminologists, led by Italian Cesare Lombroso, put the criminal rather than the form of punishment as the central area of concern. The early criminologists did not exclude agencies such as free will but they did hold that criminals were not normal human beings who could be held responsible for their actions. They believed crime was largely a function of dynamic laws relating to one's physical attributes. These, it was believed, bore 'as correct a relation to the rules of cause and effect, as that fire will explode gunpowder, all conditions being equal'.[35] Under their theories the characteristics of a murderer were thought to be a deficiency in the frontal curve of their head combined with a projecting occiput and receding forehead. Thieves had enlarged orbital capacities and bulging foreheads. Sexual offenders had bright eyes, rough voices, overdeveloped jaws, swollen eyelids and lips and were 'occasionally humpbacked'.[36] These ideas were not new but dated back to eighteenth-century thought. One publication directly relevant to Ireland published before Lombroso's was Frederick Bridges' *Phreno-Physiometrical Characteristics of James Spollin*. Spollin was tried but found

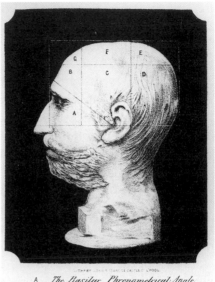

A   *The Basilar Phrenometrical Angle*
B   *The Anterior Basilar Section*
C   *The Middle Basilar Section*
D   *The Posterior Basilar Section*
E   *The Posterior Coronal Section*
F   *The Middle Coronal Section*
G   *The Anterior Coronal Section*

Phreno-physiometrical image of James Spollin.

innocent of the murder of George S. Little at Dublin's Broadstone railway terminus in November 1856. After the trial Spollin and his eldest son went to Liverpool from where they hoped to travel to America. To raise funds Spollin gave Bridges, a phrenologist, exclusive rights to take 'a cast of his head and Photographic Portrait'. For his part of the deal Bridges paid their fare to America. Bridges found that although Spollin had been found innocent of the murder his head measurements had shown that in fact he did carry it out.

The popular development of criminology was a direct result of the prison's failure. Once established it further undermined the very idea behind prisons. If they could not reform or deter because of scientific laws then what was their purpose and how should they be run? The Gladstone Prison Committee of 1894-5, under the supervision of Home Secretary Asquith, marked a turning point in the history of the prison. Prompted by the poor moral condition of prisoners who left the convict and local prisons of England and the high number of recommittals it found that the prison had done little to either deter or reform hardened criminals. Even more damning was the committee's opinion that terms of imprisonment and penal servitude had brutalised others. The committee felt that 'the system should be made more elastic, more capable of being adapted to the special cases of individual prisoners; that prison discipline should be more effectually designed to maintain, stimulate or awaken the higher susceptibilities of prisoners, to develop their moral instincts, to train them in orderly and industrious habits and wherever possible to turn them out of prison better men and women physically and morally than when they came in'.[37] The Gladstone Committee undermined some of the most fundamental tenets of the nineteenth-century prison. The soldiers of prison reform – silence, strict control, deprivation – that had been marched up the hill were being called back. From this point on imprisonment became increasingly lenient. The prison began to be divorced from its historical roots. The first changes were small but significantly they undermined what had been the accepted basis of prison reform. In the cell windows clear glass gradually substituted opaque glass. The prison dress was made 'smarter and neater' and prisoners who could afford it were entitled to wear their own clothing. The period of separation for convicts was reduced to between one and three months. Remission was allowed for prisoners in local gaols. The time male prisoners in local prisons were subjected to the hideous torture of the plank bed was reduced from one month to fourteen days while it was abolished altogether for children, women, male prisoners over 60 and those deemed to be of 'good character'. Well-conducted prisoners were allowed to associate at labour, visits and letters were increased and the diet was improved. Convicts were allowed to retain photographs of their 'respectable' relations and friends in their cells and copies of an illustrated weekly publication containing news of the main events were given to well-conducted long-term prisoners months before their release to help their reintegration into society. Non-productive labour such as oakum picking, shot drill and the treadwheel were abolished (the last treadwheel was taken out of use in Sligo Prison in 1895).

As belief in the prison's ability to control crime was being eroded and the ideas that structured its daily routine were being taken away, issues of prison management became devoid of ideology and philosophy. In the most significant change in overall prison management all prisons were nationalised in 1878. Just a couple of decades before such a drastic and dramatic step would not have been contemplated without strong philosophical and ideological reasons to back it up. However, the change in ownership was not made with reference to any grand thoughts; it was made on the grounds of uniformity of punishment and, more importantly, dismal economics.

Since the eighteenth century local prisons, catering for the vast majority of prisoners, had continued to be run by the local authorities. Although the Inspectors General of Prisons became increasingly powerful as the nineteenth century progressed, the Grand Juries retained a large degree of autonomous control over their prisons. As a result the plethora of local gaols did not form a national system of punishment – the strictness of the regimes varied from one county gaol to another. In an age when the world of travel was being revolutionised by the train it was thought that criminals hatched plans to commit crimes in jurisdictions with lenient prison systems. By making punishment uniform it was envisaged that 'vagrant criminals' would be made 'more amenable to discipline than heretofore'. By centralising prison management it was also hoped that optimum use could be made of resources, which would lead to an overall reduction in the tax bill.

On 1 April 1878 a General Prisons Board (GPB), headed by a Chairman answerable to the Chief Secretary of Ireland, was established to manage Ireland's convict and local prisons (similar legislation set up a similar body in England). The prison system that the board inherited in 1878 was outdated and anachronistic. There were 38 prisons and 98 bridewells in Ireland. Built for a larger population that lived in a more turbulent time, there was massive excess capacity in the Irish prison network. In 1879 a survey comparing the English and Irish prison stock revealed glaring differences. In Ireland there was one prison for every 71 prisoners while in England there was one prison for every 294 prisoners. Ireland had twice the number of prisons for its population in comparison with England, while the rate of imprisonment in Ireland was significantly lower than in England (there was one prisoner to every 2,037 people in Ireland, in England it was one to every 1,125). Immediately on coming into office the GPB set out to close prisons. In their first year they closed 51 bridewells and twelve local prisons which had had a daily average prison population of just a dozen prisoners.[38] In subsequent years there were times when it seemed their only rationale was the closing of prisons and the reduction of costs. As the number of committals continued to fall and sentences became shorter, more prisons became obsolete. By 1914, when the annual prison population in Ireland had fallen to just over 10,000 (a mere ten per cent of the Famine levels) there were just Mountjoy, the Maryborough convict prison, fourteen local prisons, one borstal (opened in Clonmel in 1906), one Inebriate Reformatory for 'habitual drunkards' and five bridewells in operation.

In an era when the prison was stripped of much of the potential to reduce crime and convict numbers were falling, the changes which heralded the end of the famous Crofton system were made with little fanfare. In 1880 the Irish convict rules were adapted to mirror the English rules (English prison officers came to Ireland to instruct the warders in Mountjoy in a new marks system).[39] In 1883 Spike was closed because it was impossible to keep discipline on the island (there had been two near mutinies). In 1886 Lusk was closed because it was too expensive to run. In 1891 Goldenbridge closed as a refuge. The once famous Irish convict system had ceased to exist. On 23 June 1897 Crofton died with little notice at the age of 82 in Oxford.

Under the GPB the status of Mountjoy, once Ireland's 'Model Prison', built with a very specific purpose in mind, was shuffled like a penal deck of cards. In 1878 the surplus accommodation in Mountjoy was given over to long-term male and female local prisoners transferred from the various county gaols. In 1883, when Spike was abandoned, Mountjoy's female convicts and long-term local prisoners were sent to Grangegorman. Both prisons at Mountjoy were then merged into one male convict prison. But in 1888, with numbers declining, the convicts were concentrated in the original male prison as the original female prison at Mountjoy became the local gaol for Dublin's male prisoners (Richmond Prison closed in 1888 and Kilmainham Prison then accommodated untried prisoners until it too closed in 1910). In 1897 Grangegorman female prison closed (it became part of Richmond lunatic asylum) and the female prisoners were transferred back to Mountjoy. Finally, in

Construction of Maryborough Convict Prison, by convicts. This new construction signalled the demise of Mountjoy as a convict prison – and its new status as a local prison.

1902, all convicts were transferred to Maryborough (now Portlaoise). Mountjoy was then made the prison for Dublin's male and female local prisoners. This series of changes was nothing but numbers management – there was not an ounce of philosophy in sight.

Changing the status of Mountjoy from convict to local prison made it an official place of execution (those sentenced to death were technically 'convicts' but death sentences were carried out in local prisons in the area where the crime was committed). Although in continuous decline execution remained a conspicuous part of the criminal justice system since the eighteenth century. As the decades passed most of the laws that had prescribed the death penalty were repealed. By the end of the 1840s the ultimate punishment was only carried out on those convicted of murder. As a result, the numbers executed became a mere fraction of what they were in the last years of the eighteenth century – between 1859 and 1863, 21 people were sentenced to death in the whole of Ireland, with just eleven of these actually executed.[40] Periodic campaigns to abolish capital punishment had come and gone but in 1868 the heat was taken out of the capital punishment debate for nearly a century when public executions were at last banned. The last public execution in Ireland was on 19 April 1866 when John Logue was hanged outside Downpatrick Gaol. Much has been made of the significance of this change but V.A.C. Gattrell in *The Hanging Tree* argues that while the passing of the 1868 Capital Punishment Act may have advanced civilisation, it did little to further the cause of humanity. Private hangings had eliminated voyeuristic mobs congregating on the streets but the removal of the crowd from the death scene did not necessarily mean the death was less painful, horrific or, of course, final. By removing the crowd the privatisation of executions also removed the only support for the condemned. After 1868 they died surrounded only by strangers.

After the Capital Punishment Act, genuine efforts were made to make the execution a more precise, and therefore shorter and less painful, exercise. To reduce the chances of 'messy' hangings caused by the incorrect length of rope used, hangman James Berry set out a 'Table of Drops'. The table was designed to ensure that the length of rope used would result in the quick death of the victim, rather than slow strangulation, without the drop being so long as to mutilate the condemned. Dubbed the 'Hangman's Ready Reckoner' by one opponent of capital punishment, it detailed the length of rope that should be used to hang a person of any given weight. Based on the equation 840 divided by a person's weight in pounds (i.e. a prisoner weighing 140 pounds required a drop of six feet) adjustments could be made with reference to the prisoner's build, age, size of neck muscles, etc. As the local prison for Dublin city, Mountjoy's first execution took place on 7 March 1901, when John Toole was launched into eternity for the murder of Lizzie Brennan (alias Toole). The drop should have been four foot six inches but because Toole was stout and well built a drop of six foot nine inches was used.[41]

Besides becoming a place of execution, turning Mountjoy into the local prison for Dublin changed its entire character. As a convict prison the numbers received by both Mountjoy male and female prisons never exceeded 1,500 but as the prison for Dublin it often received over 10,000 a year. Their arrival in prison was a spectacle 'to a person unacquainted with prison affairs, the appearance of the occupants of a prison van on reception into prison must always come in the nature of a surprise, consisting largely as they do of human derelicts, drink sodden and mentally or physically deficient'.[42] As the local prison for Dublin, Mountjoy now received far more than any other prison in Ireland. In 1910 the committals to the male prison represented 30 per cent of total male committals in Ireland, while the female prison received 52 per cent of females committed to Irish prisons. The nature of the work inmates were employed at changed with the departure of the convicts. While the long-term penal servitude prisoners could be properly trained and entrusted with major works (such as the construction of the 60 warders' cottages outside the prison) the work for the local prisoners was more menial – mailbag-making (for the General Post Office), brush-making, mat-making, sackmaking, shoemaking, weaving, carpentry, joinery, labouring, painting, whitewashing, stone-breaking, wood-chopping (to supply firewood to government offices), washing (for the Dublin Metropolitan Police, some military barracks, the Royal Hibernian School and other prisons), baking, nursing sick prisoners and repairs.

As a convict prison Mountjoy had received prisoners for a minimum of eight months. As a local prison the majority prisoners were in for less than three months. The short sentences

'Table of Drops' used to calculate the length of rope used to hang people according to their weight.

Executions — Table of Drops. (April 1892)

The Length of the drop may usually be calculated by dividing 840 foot-pounds by the weight of the culprit and his clothing in pounds, which will give the length of the drop in feet, but no drop should exceed 8 feet. Thus a person weighing 140 pounds in his clothing will require a drop of 840 divided by 140 = 6 feet. The following Table is calculated on this basis up to the weight of 210 pounds:-

Table of Drops.

Weight of the prisoner in his clothes.	Length of the Drop.		Weight of the prisoner in his clothes.	Length of the Drop.	
lbs	feet	inches	lbs	feet	inches
105 and under	8	–	142	5	11
106	7	11	144	5	10
107	7	10	146	5	9
108	7	9	148	5	8
109	7	8	150	5	7
110	7	7	152	5	6
112	7	6	155	5	5
113	7	5	157	5	4
114	7	4	160	5	3
115	7	3	162	5	2
117	7	2	165	5	1
118	7	1	168	5	0
120	7	0	170	4	11
121	6	11	173	4	10
123	6	10	177	4	9
124	6	9	180	4	8
126	6	8	183	4	7
127	6	7	186	4	6
129	6	6	189	4	5
130	6	5	193	4	4
132	6	4	197	4	3
134	6	3	201	4	2
136	6	2	205	4	1
138	6	1	210	4	0
140	6	0			

When from any special reason, such as a diseased condition of the neck of the culprit, the Governor and Medical Officer think that there should be a departure from this table, they may inform the Executioner, and advise him as to the length of the drop which should be given in that particular case.

judges insisted on handing out were a cause of concern for the prison authorities. A prison writer commented that 'short sentences, taken as a whole, are the curse of our prison system, the despair of its administrators, and one of the most powerful, if not most powerful, aids to crime'.[43] In one report the chairman of the GPB wrote that, 'now that the punitive side of prison treatment is being subordinated so much to the reformatory side, and that prisoners are made so comfortable in prison, these short sentences have little or no deterrent effect'. In another report it was written that, 'to send prisoners to gaol for 24 hours, or perhaps three days, who have been 200 or 300 times in prison before, amounts simply to a delusion. All these prisoners must be washed and cleansed, and probably sent to hospital, from the effects of drink, to be there cared for and attended to, and rendered physically fit for re-indulgence in crime after a short rest in gaol'.[44] Charles Cook, when visiting the male local prison at Mountjoy remarked 'we saw the men about to be discharged whose time was up – a ragged regiment truly! Answering to their names, they were once more allowed their liberty, and were not slow in taking their departure from what has been called "Her Majesty's Hotel"'.

In January 1922 Mountjoy Prison was handed over by the outgoing British administration to the Provisional Government. Prison numbers had declined considerably. While in part due to the buoyant war-time economy, the enlistment of many males of the 'criminal age' and the concentration on imprisoning political offenders, the decline in numbers was first and foremost the result of legislative changes that affected imprisonment. Among these was the 1907 Probation of Offenders Act (replacing the Probation of First Offenders Act, 1887), the Fine or Imprisonment Act 1899 (which provided for the reduction of sentence on part payment of a fine), the 1907 Prisons Act (which authorised partial remission of sentences for good conduct and industry) and the 1914 Criminal Justice Administration Act which allowed extra time for the payment of fines. These pieces of legislation all combined to significantly reduce prison numbers. By the time the provisional government took over there were just eleven prisons in southern Ireland (the Northern Irish prisons were managed by a new northern executive). Each had massive excess accommodation. While the total prison places in Ireland was 2,361, there were less than 600 prisoners. Mountjoy's accommodation was 900 cells but it held just 237 prisoners.

Chapter Seven

NEGLECTED BIOGRAPHIES

... if our lot had been not so small in this world we might not occupy a place in a prison but be members of Society. And it is a bitter reproach to me that the Lord made me like a man and that I have not acted so.

Thomas D'Arcy, Mountjoy prisoner, 1863

Prison diaries and jail journals written by Ireland's political prisoners are well represented in Irish historical bibliographies. However, the first jail journal written in Ireland by an 'ordinary prisoner' was not published until 1945. Entitled *I Did Penal Servitude*, its author was the appropriately anonymous convict 'D.83222'. Shame, poor education and an apparent lack of interest on the part of the public has left almost a complete absence of material written by ordinary prisoners. At the same time the descendants of those who suffered imprisonment for the cause of Irish independence cherish relics from this glorious past. When it comes to ordinary prisoners it is a far different case. Their total absence from our history is the result of a conscious process. They are not merely forgotten. The story of a criminal relative is hidden – the proverbial skeleton kept locked in a cupboard.

When attempting to uncover the stories of the ordinary prisoners the volumes of prison registers are tantalising sources of information. Turning the pages of a Mountjoy Prison register is, at first, an exciting exercise. Each individual, crime and description appears as a mini biography. However, with time they begin to disappoint. Though they include every prisoner, the brief facts noted year after year by the prison registrar actually tell very little. Of more value are the 166 boxes of Convict Reference Files held in the National Archives. There are thousands of files in the boxes. The majority have not been opened since they were filed away – their pages permanently folded by time into quarters.

The convict files generally follow an established formula. In each is a letter addressed to the Lord Lieutenant called a 'petition' or 'memorial' – the terms were interchangeable. Explaining the position from the prisoner's point of view, it asks for either the release of the prisoner or a shortening of sentence. The pleas were often accompanied by supporting signatures of priests, landowners, shopkeepers, Justices of the Peace and other influential people to lend weight. In almost all cases the memorials or petitions were penned by a legal figure paid for by the prisoner, their family or friends. They were entitled to write just one memorial a year, although in many cases prisoners would have only been able to afford one every few years, if at all. In these memorials and petitions it was common practice first to admit the justness of the sentence but then go on to explain its unjustness. The language used was formal, polite, ingratiating, self-deprecating and often in the third person. One typical petition ended:

> Your Petitioner thereby humbly Prays Your Excellency will be graciously pleased to extend your Clemency to Petitioner by remitting him to his family thereby enabling your Petitioner to spend his future life in Loyalty to his Queen and with honesty to his Neighbours, and though his mind will be ever embittered by the remembrance of his crime, yet his heart will always abound with gratitude to your Excellency.[1]

Once the memorial or petition was received in Dublin Castle the judge who tried the case would be contacted for his opinion. Contained in most files are the judges' letters giving their views on whether the prisoners should be released – sometimes the

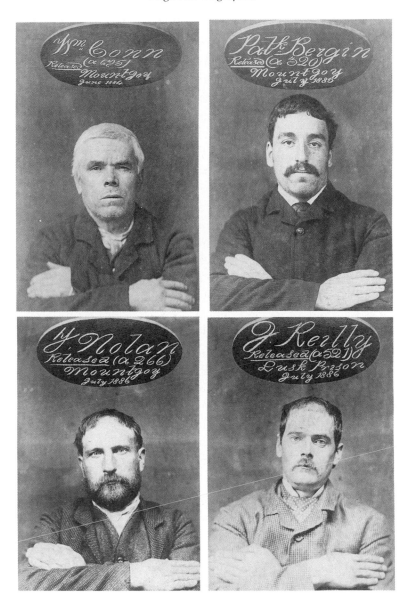

Mugshots taken between 1884-1886. The information above their heads details their name, convict number, the prison they were released from and the date of release.

complete trial transcript was attached to back up their opinion. In a small minority of cases they recommended mercy and the prisoner's wish was granted. In 1857 Michael Doherty was sentenced to life for burglary in Limerick. He had been given such a severe sentence because in 1850 he had been sentenced to ten years transportation for sheep stealing and had been released early when clemency was shown. Doherty claimed that he had turned to crime on the second occasion because of a relapse of an 'inward malady' which meant he could not practice his trade of shoemaker. Since he could not work he wanted 'to obtain for himself in Prison simple bodily sustenance rather than enter the Workhouse'. He was released on licence in June 1870 at the order of the Lord Lieutenant.[2] In the same year John Dixon was discharged after serving just over a year of a five-year sentence for stealing rhubarb valued at one shilling and six pence. He had originally been sentenced to twelve months imprisonment. However, out of an 'overwhelming feeling of shame' and a belief that he could not show his face in Belfast again, he asked for – and was given – five years penal servitude instead. In his memorial he wrote that he keenly felt the 'degradation to which his indiscretion has reduced him and having an almost certain prospect of being placed in a position of repairing his lost reputation in a foreign country', he humbly implored the Lord Lieutenant to release him. The judge who tried his case recommended release. Dixon left prison on 19 September 1870.[3] In 1855 Thomas Allen, aged seventeen, was convicted of stealing a pair of boots and a pair of shoes in Dingle. He was sentenced to four years penal servitude. In August 1856, the prisoner's uncle, Michael Ahern, wrote a memorial stating that his nephew had been in the Tralee Union Workhouse for a number of years and that 'he has neither Father, or Mother, living, nor sister, he has only the one Brother, who is in America'. His brother had sent seven sovereigns to pay passage across the Atlantic. On 11 September 1856 Governor Netterville received a letter stating that the prisoner should be discharged.[4] These were the exceptions. In the bulk of cases, the judges wrote, 'this man is not a proper subject of mercy' or 'there are no mitigating circumstances' – these comments were underlined in red by the government clerk. It was rare for the judges' recommendations to be ignored but it was not until the condemning lines, 'Let the Law Take its Course' or 'The Law Must Take its Course' were written on the cover of the petition that the judgement was final. The Governor then informed the prisoner of the verdict.

Throughout the prison registers and the Convict Reference Files there is a seemingly endless list of petty and pathetic crimes, broken only by the rare exception. They confirmed Edward Gibbon's assertion, in *The Decline and Fall of the Roman Empire*, that 'most of the crimes which disturb the internal peace of society are produced by the restraints which the necessary but unequal laws of property have imposed on the appetites of mankind, by confining to a few the possession of those objects that are coveted by many'.[5] It is hardly surprising that poverty is a common denominator in the lives of many of those who slept in the prison's cells. Mountjoy was almost tediously filled with the 'have nots'. However, though poverty was the main cause of crime, the finger was also pointed at alcohol.

In its 28th annual report the General Prisons Board wrote of what it saw as the strong link between poverty, drink and, in consequence, crime:

> Many among the illiterate classes turn to drink as the only means of passing their unoccupied time. They have no idea of any pursuit or even amusement in which to spend their surplus energy, and seek the association of the public house. There are others, perhaps the majority, who have no desire to work, and whose drunken habits are the result of their idleness, and for these the training to habits of industry is essential. Sloth and intemperance often react upon each other; drink is the cause of idleness, and idleness the cause of drink.[6]

In 1878 Mountjoy's Protestant Chaplain Robert Flemyng wrote

that the 'undoubted cause of most crime is to be traced to the drinking habits of the people ... While public houses are still so numerous, crime will flourish, criminals will increase, families will be disgraced and ruined, and the sober, honest, and industrious taxed to support prisoners ...'[7] In another report he claimed that while crime could be put down to a number of factors – moral weakness, poor education, etc. – an important cause was the 'terrible temptation of that nursery of crime and misery, the gigantic source of lamentation and mourning and woe – the public house'.[8] Petitions and memorials to the Lord Lieutenant seemed to bear out these views. In 1873 William Jackson was given seven years penal servitude for stealing 'two chemises' from a washing line. Writing to the Lord Lieutenant he begged 'to state emphatically that he was under the influence of drink at the time and incapable of understanding the guilt of his actions'.[9] In 1866 Eliza Burns, a Limerick dressmaker, 'addicted to intemperal habits', was convicted of stealing a communion cloth from St Michael's Church in Limerick. By way of explaining the crime she wrote that, 'owing to family affliction she unfortunately took to drink and while under the influence of which she took the altar linens from the Chapel at Limerick, the enormity of which she now deplores'.[10] Patrick O'Malley was convicted of writing a threatening letter to a landlord warning him that he would be killed if he raised his rents. O'Malley wrote to the Lord Lieutenant, 'That Memorialist foolishly, but as he thought at the time, harmlessly wrote those letters while under the influence of drink, having no object in doing so, as he was altogether unconnected with land or any other calling, being at the time of this unfortunate occurrence an humble village Schoolmaster'.[11] Drink was given as a reason or excuse for committing serious crime but when Mountjoy was made into a local prison, thousands were committed for 'drunkenness'. In 1900 half of Mountjoy's prisoners were deemed to be 'drunkards'.[12] In June 1899, in an attempt to address the particular issue of drink, a State Inebriate

Reformatory was established in Ennis. It was specifically intended for the reception of criminals who were not insane but, 'by reason of habitual intemperate drinking of intoxicating liquor, at times dangerous to himself or herself or to others, or incapable of managing himself or herself, or his or her affairs'.[13]

To reduce the causes of crime to mere poverty and drink would oversimplify what remains the extraordinarily complicated question, why do people commit crime? If it were only poverty, why were all the poor not criminals? Why were rich people imprisoned? Can one give common cause to all of Mountjoy's prisoners? Can one find a link between Mary Agnes, who served twelve months for fraud in 1912 and killed her sixteen-month-old baby in the prison hospital, 'by striking its head against an iron bedstead and on the floor'; John Broderick from Mayo convicted at 60 years of age of the rape of a child of eleven years; Thomas Greelish given three years for 'conspiracy to cheat at cards'; Ambrose Davis given five years for attempting to commit buggery; Catherine Driscoll who was released from Mountjoy in 1865 after serving seven years for stealing seventeen ducks and seven hens; Robert Colbourne who, though present on the 'heights of Alma, and at the Battles of Inkerman and Ballaclava', was convicted of desertion in front of the enemy during the Crimean War; Jane MacMahon given five years in a Belfast court for running a child prostitution racket; and five boys convicted of the manslaughter of an Assistant Teacher at the Trim Industrial School in 1912? It is not possible to perfectly classify and compartmentalise the prisoners of Mountjoy but there are certain trends that do stand out from the mass of crimes and statistics. One of these was the imprisonment of women.

Each year the women sentenced to penal servitude and confined in Mountjoy represented about one-third of the total convicts committed to the Mountjoy complex. Rates of recidivism (the re-offending of a convicted criminal) were particularly high amongst women. For them it was hard to break free from patterns and habits of criminality once established. When imprisoned they often became outcasts from respectability and embarked on lives of petty crime. In 1877, of the 60 women sentenced to penal servitude, half had had their licences revoked or had previously served terms of penal servitude while many others would have served terms in a local prison. Some of the women were imprisoned so often they were doing what penal historian Sean McConville described as 'life by instalments'. Among them was Hannah Flanagan who was given four years penal servitude in Mountjoy in 1858 for vagrancy. She had over 130 previous convictions. In 1861, 48-year-old Mary Burke was convicted of felony of three shillings and six pence and given four years penal servitude. She was a widow, had no occupation and had been in prison on 163 previous occasions. Eliza McGinnis, a knitter from Limavady, married with eight children, was convicted of larceny on a succession of occasions spanning nearly two decades. In 1862 she was sentenced to one month, in 1865 three months, 1866 three months, 1867 two months, 1869 seven days and twelve months. In 1871 she received her first sentence of penal servitude, for seven years, in Mountjoy. In 1875 she was released on licence but this was revoked. In 1878 she served three months in a local prison and in 1881 she was given another five years penal servitude.[14]

While the term 'labourer' was put down for a large percentage of Mountjoy's male prisoners, a wide variety of occupations were represented in the male registers: sawyer, porter, sweep, servant, farmer, weaver, hostler, shopman, miner, painter, slater, basket-maker, stonecutter, shoemaker, flax dresser, butcher, baker, netmaker, lime-burner, herder, soldier, cooper, mat-maker, peasant, tinsmith, groom, farrier, tinker, tobacconist, horse jockey, hoosier, schoolmaster, pedlar, barber, brogue-maker, gasfitter, slater, dairy boy, apothecary, shepherd, bookbinder, messenger, postboy, collier, bootman, confectioner, cobbler, nailor, draper, umbrella maker, woolcomber, brushmaker, cattle jobber, cabinet maker or simply thief and pick-pocket. For women the range of occupations was much more limited. At that time the women of Ireland had few economic alternatives to becoming a wife, maid, thief or prostitute. There are few statistics that more graphically portray the difficulties experienced by women in nineteenth-century Ireland than prison numbers.

The sheer scale of female imprisonment in Ireland in the post-Famine period is unparalleled – in other European countries women generally accounted for between ten and twenty per cent of prisoners while in America, where economic opportunities for women were incomparably greater, they represented as little as four per cent of the prison population.[15] In Ireland in 1854, of the 60,000 prisoners in local jails, over 26,000 were women.[16] Breaking down the statistics into provinces, Connaught and Ulster had the fewest women prisoners in comparison to men, while women accounted for the majority of the committals to prisons in Leinster (one of the main reasons was the large numbers of prostitutes associated with the garrisons of Dublin and Kildare). As the nineteenth century came to an end the total number as well as proportion of criminals sentenced to penal servitude declined dramatically (this was the result of both a decline in crime and an increasingly lenient attitude towards offenders). This was particularly the case with women. In January 1866 there were 479 women serving sentences of penal servitude in Mountjoy[17] but in 1897 there were just 37.[18] However, indicative of the continued plight of Irish women were the numbers of women confined in the local prisons. While women received fewer and fewer long-term sentences, the numbers committed to local prisons serving short-term sentences remained relatively high. When Mountjoy was made into the female committal prison for Dublin it took in thousands of women every year for mostly petty crimes. In 1912-13 the female prison received 4,780 committals which represented just over half of the total number of women committed to Irish prisons (the male prison received just 6,121 prisoners out of a total of 19,834 males committed to prison in Ireland).[19] Meanwhile the pattern of female recidivism continued. In 1906 nearly half of the women committed to Mountjoy had previously been convicted more than twenty times, while less than one-fifth of the male prisoners had this number of previous convictions.[20] The phenomenon of the returned female prisoner led Margaret Buckley, a republican prisoner held during the Civil War, to write of 'Eileen', a Mountjoy prisoner:

> This woman was an expert laundress. I was shown some of her work and it compared favourably with any I have seen turned out by first-class commercial laundries. Yet, here she was, her skill wasted, body and soul degraded; spending a few days every month outside drugging her senses, giving full reign to indulgence, and then facing back to Mountjoy to expiate in work the crime of being alive. She had no dread of coming back; she was actually encouraged to return, and it was the only home she knew.[21]

During Mountjoy's first decade, hundreds of boys and girls passed through its doors. William Dwyer was convicted of burglary and robbery in Galway in 1853. He was twelve years old and just three feet eleven and a quarter inches tall. Charles Rice, whose occupation was put down as 'thief', was given six years for larceny in Antrim. Owen O'Sullivan from Kanturk, County Cork, was fifteen years old when given fourteen years for felony of a plate. Fifteen-year-old Honora Lynch was given six years for killing sheep. Mary Lyons aged fourteen served three years for felony of purse and money. The decade after the Famine was indeed a particularly bleak one for the children of Ireland. In 1853 over 12,000 children were imprisoned in Ireland. The main cause of crime amongst these 'Juvenile Delinquents' was put down to 'neglected childhood'. The Famine had robbed them of one or, in many cases, both parents. Of the 12,000 child criminals in 1853, nearly one-sixth were 'absolute orphans' and over 3,000 had lost one parent. Many others had simply been abandoned.[22] A large proportion of this army of child criminals lived among the 'low lodging houses' of Dublin.[23] These 'City Arabs' accounted for 20,000 convictions in Dublin between 1849 and 1853.[24]

While the courts did not, in many cases, make any distinction between child and adult, children sentenced to penal servitude and imprisoned in Mountjoy were not treated like adult prisoners. Convicts under fourteen years of age endured the separation stage for one month, the fourteen to sixteen year olds for two months and the sixteen to eighteen year olds three months.[25] Isolated as far as possible from the adult convicts, they were employed as tailors, shoemakers, garden labourers and carpenters in Mountjoy (they were also kept in Philipstown Prison). Despite the better conditions of the juvenile class it was also the most vicious and unruly – many seemed intent on breaking the rules and regarded themselves as 'outcasts, without hope, and beyond amendment'.[26]

In 1858 the Reformatory Schools (Ireland) Act established reformatory schools for under-sixteens. On 21 December 1858 High Park Reformatory for girls in Drumcondra was the first one opened in Ireland. A reformatory school sentence was the equivalent of 'child' penal servitude (going hand in hand with these institutions were the Industrial Schools established for the training of 'young waifs and strays' that had not yet, but, it was thought, undoubtedly would find themselves at odds with the law[27]). Walter Crofton, son of the convict chairman, in his first report as Inspector of Reformatory Schools, stated that a 'keystone' of the arch of the reformatory system was 'Parental Responsibility'.[28] The idea was that although the state took control of the children their parents were not absolved of responsibility. Parents who could afford it were obliged to contribute to their child's upkeep in the reformatory. Inspector Crofton declared this to be the 'means of improving the habits of some of the parents who can no longer with impunity squander money in intemperance, while the State is performing a duty that they have very seriously neglected'.[29] A parent's failure to pay could, and often did, lead to imprisonment.

After the establishment of reformatory schools, children virtually disappeared from the registers of the convict prisons. However, they were still sent in large numbers to local prisons to serve terms of imprisonment. Indeed, for many years, a term in a reformatory school was often preceded by one or two weeks in prison – it was hoped that this would give the children a taste of what their future would be if they did not mend their ways. After the GPB made Mountjoy into a local prison it once again received children on a large scale. In 1889 over 200 children under sixteen (fifteen of whom were under twelve) passed through Mountjoy en route to the reformatories. The crimes for which these children were committed included maliciously breaking gas lamps, stealing two pairs of boots, stealing a mouth organ (value nine pence), begging in a public thoroughfare, larceny of a purse and illegal possession of a blanket. In 1902 the situation improved somewhat when the Youthful Offenders Act came into effect. Under this legislation the courts could remand children to family members willing to receive them. It was also no longer legal to send a child to prison as part of a reformatory school sentence, while children under the age of twelve could not be sent to a reformatory school for a first offence. In 1906 a borstal was established in Clonmel for sixteen to 21-year-old males. This was inspired by the borstal experiment in England, which was based on the Elmira reformatory in America. Elmira, in turn, had been inspired by the Crofton system. In 1908 the Children's Act (which still governs our treatment of children today) banned sentences of imprisonment for offenders under fourteen years with limitations on imprisonment for fourteen and fifteen year olds.

Closely allied to the issues of women and children was that of family support. In an era when family ties were often necessary merely to survive, the imprisonment of a key family member could spell ruin and disaster for others. In 1856 Thomas

Kinch, who had been a member of the constabulary for four years, was given four years for receiving stolen goods which were the property of Major Caldwell, the Limerick County Inspector of the Constabulary. In his petition he wrote that his 'Young Creature of a Wife' was 'very nigh her Confinement' as a result of his imprisonment.

His wife also wrote to the Lord Lieutenant explaining her position: 'having been brought up by respectable parents who now reject her as an outcast, and disgrace to her friends, Memorialist humbly hopes, that His Excellency will take her deplorable case into his kind consideration and grant the speedy release of her husband, and not let memorialist in vigour of her youth become a prey to all the evil which must eventually await a female unprotected and unprovided for'.[30] John Devine, of 35 Blackpits, Dublin City, was the father of eighteen-year-old Patrick Devine sentenced to four years for forging and uttering a Postal Order valued two pounds and ten shillings. He wrote to the Lord Lieutenant, 'That Memorialist is a poor labouring man in a very delicate state of health occasioned by his son's foolish act which has preyed on his constitution and having a wife and eight children who are almost depending on Memorialist's exertions for their support are now in a very destitute state'.[31] Widow McCarran's son was convicted of manslaughter. She wrote that she had endeavoured, 'by honest means to support a helpless family left me by my husband who is now dead eight years'. Her son, Hugh, had been employed by a local farmer and was her only support. She appealed that, 'Petitioner worn with age and infirmity ventures to approach Your Excellency, soliciting your humanity in releasing to me my son, who promises to live for the future a moral and quiet life, to be a loyal and faithful servant'.[32] In 1859 Thomas Halfpenny was sentenced to six years for robbery of arms. His father John, asking for his son to be released, wrote from Nobber, County Meath, that, 'he must shortly expect to be ejected out of his little holding and end his days in the Work House' if his son was not released.[33] In 1872 Bridget Walsh of

Marrowbone Lane wrote praying for the release of her eighteen-year-old husband Albert, sentenced to five years penal servitude for assault 'while in a state of intoxication'. She explained that she too was just eighteen and had a child of three months with 'no person to look to for support'.[34] In 1882 James Lawlor (alias Murphy) was convicted in Belfast for possession of a stolen cartwheel and sentenced to seven years. A trained carpenter, he was transferred from Mountjoy to Kilmainham Prison to carry out some carpentry work (he built the altar in the Catholic Chapel before which Joseph Plunkett and Grace Gifford were married hours before Plunkett's execution in May 1916). From Kilmainham, Lawlor wrote to the Lord Lieutenant that his mother had died in Belfast, leaving the rest of the family orphaned, the eldest of whom was seventeen. He feared that if he were not released to care for them they would soon be driven to crime and end up in prison.[35]

The most basic function of the prison was the successful removal of criminals, at least for a time, from circulation. In prison they no longer represented a threat to society. However, there remained the issue of what would happen when they were released. When transportation from Ireland ended in 1853 it was superseded, in part, by the encouraged emigration of convicts from Crofton's system. After the demise of Crofton the idea of banishing criminals to a distant country became, if anything, more institutionalised. In the terminology of the bureaucrats it was known as 'emigrating' or 'migrating' a prisoner. Finance for this procedure was supplied by a combination of the prisoner's gratuity, a grant from the Discharged Prisoners' Aid Society and a supplement from the Charity Funds. Thousands of prisoners, both convict and local, left Ireland in this manner.

In 1892 25-year-old John Barnes served two months hard labour in Mountjoy for stealing nine pairs of boots. In his application for assistance to emigrate he told the GPB that he had been nearly seven years in the army during which time he had fought in Egypt and Burma. In 1888 he was discharged in

Bombay. 'Now Honourable Sir,' he wrote to the Chairman of the GPB, 'since the year 1888 I have been constantly coming into Prison. I have no one belonging to me in Dublin and I can't get any work to do and I do be going about the city of Dublin starveing ... If you grant me this money your humble Servant will pray for you and the Members of the board all the days of his life.' Barnes was successful in his application – it was later confirmed to the GPB that on 16 April he had sailed from Liverpool for Halifax, en route for Quebec.[36]

In 1895 Convict John Dempsey wrote to the Board that he had 'got no friend in this country to do anything for me or get me employment'. In response to a query from the GPB as to whether the prisoner was married or not (the Board would not 'emigrate' a married man) Governor Sheehan replied that he was convinced the man was single, as 'it was for converting to his own use some articles the property of a girl he had promised to marry that he was convicted'. He also wrote that he believed Dempsey 'is earnestly desirous of earning an honest living in future, but thinks it impossible to do so in Dublin'. Indeed, such was his determination he was prepared to leave in November and risk the Canadian winter rather than return to his old associates in Dublin. Dempsey had earned a gratuity of four pounds eight shillings and six pence and the Prisoners' Aid Society granted two pounds, while nearly three pounds was provided out of the Charity funds. On 7 November 1895 he sailed from Liverpool on the *SS Lake Huron*, bound for Quebec.[37]

Many prisoners were given assistance to emigrate to the vast British colony of Canada, which provided quick access to the USA. In most cases it is not known how emigrated prisoners fared in their new land. However, light was shed on the life of one of Mountjoy's ex-prisoners in 1909 when the Governor of Mountjoy received a letter from the Mattaewan State Hospital for Insane Criminals in Albany, New York. Confined in the hospital was one Dennis Sullivan. In the letter the hospital's Secretary, T. E. McGarr, asked the Irish authorities to pay for the return of Sullivan to Ireland 'in view of Sullivan's history and the circumstances under which he came to the United States'. McGarr explained the history of his patient. Sullivan was born in Cork on 7 April 1857. When he was just five years old he was put into a workhouse where he remained until he ran away at the age of thirteen. After finding work for a time, he was given fourteen days in prison and five years at the Sefton Reformatory in 1871 for stealing a chicken. As punishment for trying to abscond from the reformatory he was sent to Cork jail for a year. After his discharge he went to work but was back in prison on three occasions for larceny. Then, in 1877, he was given five years penal servitude for four counts of larceny. In 1882, shortly after his release, he was sentenced to another five years. After discharge he found himself in Mountjoy for petty larceny. When Sullivan's sentence expired he was given financial assistance by the Irish prison authorities to emigrate to Canada.

The day after he arrived in Halifax Sullivan entered the United States. Going to New York, via Boston, he found employment at Ward's Island Hospital where he stole $400 from the hospital safe. He was sentenced to three years in prison but after his mental condition was examined, he was committed to the New York State Hospital for Insane Criminals. Secretary McGarr, obviously unhappy at having to deal with what he saw as an Irish problem intentionally transferred across the Atlantic by the General Prisons Board, wrote, 'You will observe from the foregoing that Sullivan is a very undesirable addition to our population and the Commission earnestly hopes that you may arrange at an early date for his deportation'.[38] Mountjoy's Governor referred McGarr to the diplomatic service. The outcome of the case is not recorded but it is highly unlikely that any action was taken. The prisoner was not forced to emigrate, he was merely 'assisted'. Initially he went to Canada and only later, of his own free will and without the knowledge of the Irish authorities, entered the United States.

***

Between 1850 and 1924 Mountjoy received in the region of 250,000 committals. Even if the total number of individual prisoners was less than this (many were in Mountjoy on more than one occasion) it remains a staggering statistic. If each committal is very conservatively estimated to have spent one month in Mountjoy the total amount of time done in the Joy between 1850 and 1922 was more than 20,000 years. The history of those who passed through Mountjoy is a story of truly epic proportions. To an extent, selecting certain cases for special attention is an arbitrary exercise. The following are just some of the more notable and better documented members of that vast cast who passed through the doors of Mountjoy.

CATHERINE HENNESSY

In 1851, Catherine Hennessy pleaded guilty to the charge of assisting in the killing of a child in Buttevant, County Cork. She was 24 years old, married with two children and appeared 'to have been of the labouring class'. The murder was described as 'a most cruel one, a female infant between two and three months old having been buried alive'. The killing took place when the baby's mother, Elizabeth Curly (alias Fitzgerald), was bringing the illegitimate child to its father, Amos Brook, a private in the 47th Regiment. Hennessy accompanied Curly on the journey. On the way plans radically changed. The baby was brought to a deserted house and covered with earth. She suffocated. Curly was transported to Australia for life while Catherine Hennessy, also given a life sentence, stayed in prison in Ireland. Beginning her sentence in Cork prison she was transferred to Mountjoy in 1858 – she was the 454th female prisoner committed to Mountjoy.

For a prisoner given a life sentence there was little prospect of an early release. At the time they were required to have served a minimum of ten to twelve years of a life sentence before their case could be reviewed (this was later changed to twenty years). In addition to this technicality Hennessy faced a further difficulty. It was said that in the area of Buttevant there was considerable feeling against Hennessy – an early release would not be popular. After nearly fifteen years in prison a possible breakthrough occurred when the local parish priest asked for Hennessy to be released back to her friends and family. He also asked the local population to forgive and forget. The prisoner's mother, spurred to hope by the priest's action, wrote to her in December 1866:

> ... I thought you would be home with me long ago. My dear daughter I now enclose a certificate from a clergyman stating that both your brother and I are most willing to receive you. There is nothing would give us greater pleasure than you should be once more at home with us. I never cease praying to God that in the goodness of his mercy he would again give you to me. May the Almighty God reward Mrs Lidwell for her kindness to you. She will always have my blessing. Humbly trusting in God I await the time when I can see you.
>
> I remain dear daughter
> Your affectionate mother
> Mary Daly

The raised hopes of mother and daughter were dashed when the Attorney General decided that returning Hennessy to the scene of the crime 'would be very objectionable'. After this bitter disappointment Superintendent Lidwell, in a highly unusual departure from normal practice, wrote a petition in her spidery handwriting on behalf of Hennessy. In it she stated that while the 'petitioner now fully understands the enormity of the crime which she committed and admits the justice of the sentence awarded', most of the blame for the crime rested not with Hennessy but with her 'more wily and crafty accomplice'. At the bottom of the petition Hennessy put an 'X' for her signature. The plea was not successful.

In July 1871, the Mountjoy medical officer reported that Hennessy was declining in health and that her debility was caused by long confinement. Poor health at least offered the prospect of release. However, sick prisoners were not released until the prison authorities were satisfied they would be looked after adequately by family outside prison. Attempts to contact the family in Buttevant drew a blank. They had left Cork and could not be traced. Perhaps, after the failed intervention by the priest, they were run out of the area or maybe they just gave up hope and could not bring themselves to tell the prisoner. Whatever the cause, their disappearance had serious implications. Since she had no one willing to look after her, Hennessy could not be released. In 1873 Lidwell wrote a final futile petition on behalf of the prisoner with whom she had spent time since 1851. Four years later Hennessy was admitted to the women's prison hospital. She died on 3 March 1877. The cause of death was given as 'old age and debility'. She was 50 years old, had spent more than half her life behind bars and was buried in the grounds of Mountjoy Prison.[39]

MAAMTRASNA

Of the thousands of petitions and memorials addressed to the Lord Lieutenant very few received his personal attention. They were dealt with in a routine manner within well-established parameters. It was only the more difficult and controversial ones that crossed the desk of the Crown's representative in Ireland. One that he dealt with personally was that associated with the 'Maamtrasna prisoners'. The Maamtrasna Convict Reference File is the largest in the National Archives. The case also has the dubious distinction of being one of the most infamous miscarriages of justice in nineteenth-century Ireland.

Maamtrasna is the complex story of the savage murders of five members of the Joyce family in Maamtrasna, County Galway (now in Mayo) on 17 August 1882. *Maamtrasna: The Murders and the Mystery* by Jarlath Waldron details the circumstances of the killings. Perhaps more than any other serious crime, the Maamtrasna case skirted the grey line that divided political and criminal acts in Ireland. The establishment believed the murders were the result of a debt owed to one of the secret 'Ribbon Societies'. This, however, was only partly true. Entangled in this tale were disputes over land and sheep, as well as the general animosities of an often bitter rural society. Ultimately the court case hinged on the testimonies of two of the suspects who turned Queen's evidence. The manipulation of these witnesses makes chilling reading. Only one of them had taken part in the attack but they gave identical stories that were based on what the prosecutors wanted proved more than on what happened. The first three men tried were sentenced to death, one of whom, Myles Joyce, was completely innocent. They were hanged in Galway Prison. On the advice of their parish priest, Michael McHugh, the remaining five defendants, in order to avoid the death penalty, pleaded guilty. Each was sentenced to death but their sentences were commuted to terms of penal servitude for life.

The plight of the prisoners became the subject of great controversy. Their case was championed by the Irish Parliamentary Party MP, Tim Harrington. In 1884 the two men who had turned Queen's evidence gave information to the Archbishop of Tuam that appeared to exonerate at least some of the prisoners. When these new revelations were made, Harrington published *The Maamtrasna Massacre: Impeachment of the Trials*. In it he called for a complete review of the case. The Lord Lieutenant, Lord Spencer, opposed all calls for release. His view was at least partly coloured by the events of two years previous. On 6 May 1882, the day he arrived in Ireland to take up residence in the Phoenix Park, he watched from the window of his Viceregal Lodge the Invincibles assassinate his Chief Secretary and Under Secretary. The sight made a deep impression on him. Spencer believed the Irish to be completely lawless. Confirming his impressions were over 60 unsolved murders in the country. Someone had to pay the price to stem the tide of anarchy. In response to the calls by Harrington and others for the case of the prisoners to be reviewed Spencer wrote that it was 'a pity one-tenth part of the time and energy expended in endeavouring to discredit the action of the officials was not employed in assisting them to discover the authors and perpetrators of this frightful crime'. All pleas for clemency were rejected. What became of those in prison? When Michael Casey began his life sentence he was 63 years old. Freely admitting that he was present at the murders he denied having taken any active part in them. He also claimed that the men in prison with him were all innocent. In poor health – in 1893 he described himself as 'a feeble old man' – he died of an epileptic seizure in Maryborough Prison in August 1895. John Casey, Michael Casey's nephew, emphatically denied 'having participated in the horrible tragedy' and claimed to have been in bed at the time. He died of pulmonary consumption in Mountjoy in 1900. He was 54 years old.[40]

The last three prisoners, Martin Joyce, Patrick Joyce and his son Thomas were released from prison on 24 October 1902. *Maamtrasna: The Murders and the Mystery*, ends with the three making their journey home after serving twenty years in prison for a crime they did not commit. In the words of Waldron, 'the withering nightmare of Maamtrasna had run its course'.[41]

FRANK DU BEDAT

One of the more unusual prisoners to have been held in Mountjoy was Frank Du Bedat. He was a member of a long-standing and well-respected Huguenot family whose solid reputation was epitomised by its motto, *Sans Tache* – 'Without Stain'. In 1872 Frank, the youngest of seven children, married the eminently respectable Mary Rosa Waterhouse. Employed in his father's financial firm, William George Du Bedat & Sons, he became Trustee and later Treasurer of the French Huguenot Fund. When his father died he took over the business. In October 1890 he reached the height of his career when he was elected President of the Dublin Stock Exchange. Known as 'The Baron' to his friends and 'The Actor' to his family he was an important man about town. Twenty-four stone in weight, he was what we would now call the stereotypical 'fat cat'. He was a man who apparently had everything. However, he had a fatal flaw. In 1889 Du Bedat purchased Stoneleigh, a granite mansion with spectacular sea views, in Killiney, County Dublin. Rather immodestly, he renamed it Frankfort and immediately began its spectacular renovation. To finance the project Du Bedat used his clients' funds. Du Bedat gambled on a stock market boom to keep him out of trouble. He lost. Two months after being elected President of the Exchange Du Bedat fled the country leaving debts in excess of £100,000. Subsequently arrested in South Africa, he was brought back to Ireland by James Smith, Superintendent of the Dublin Metropolitan Police. At his trial he pleaded guilty to charges of breach of the bankruptcy laws and misappropriation of property. On 20 October 1891 Du Bedat was sentenced to twelve months hard labour and a total of fourteen years penal servitude.

Within three months of the beginning of Du Bedat's sentence, Mountjoy's medical officer, Dr George White, expressed grave concern about Du Bedat's health. The prisoner had a ruptured hernia caused when he slipped getting out of a cab outside court. The hernia was described as very tender and 'quite irreducible'. Because of it he was unable to keep his food down. Dr White described his condition as being one of 'grave risk'. In February Du Bedat was being fed artificially through the rectum which, according to the medical officer, 'will not sustain life for any prolonged period'. Dr White felt that the prisoner should be released because of his condition. However, the Lord Lieutenant decided that the prisoner was as well cared for in Mountjoy as he would be anywhere else. In May 1892, by which time the hernia condition had eased, his general condition had declined alarmingly. Du Bedat remained confined to bed in the Infirmary. He was wasting away. Since January he had lost eight stone, he was unable to stand and, it was reported, 'his colour had faded and his skin has become loose, sallow and pendulous'. He consumed little

Frank Du Bedat – on his committal to Mountjoy Prison (left) and on his release from prison (right). Note the marked change in the prisoner's weight.

food and what he did manage to eat was often vomited.

Du Bedat presented the authorities with a dilemma. The Chief Secretary, John Morley, responded to one call for Du Bedat's release by writing, 'If he is released we may expect the usual howl from the public and the charge of differential treatment in consequence of social class. At the same time we are not justified in keeping a man in prison if by so doing we are killing him'. In the face of calls by the Mountjoy medical staff to release Du Bedat the Lord Lieutenant appointed the President of the College of Physicians, Dr Finny, and the senior medical officer at the Mater Hospital, Dr Nixon, to definitively answer the question, 'is imprisonment killing the man, or is he dying from other causes?' They concluded 'imprisonment is not killing this man'. In fact, the two reported that they found no evidence of 'organic disease' and believed Du Bedat was feigning illness in order to gain early release. Despite this diagnosis Du Bedat's condition continued to deteriorate. The GPB continued to refuse to release him on the grounds that his refusal to eat was due 'either to apathy on his part with regard to life under existing conditions, or, what is more probable, to a desire to be relieved from the irksomeness of prison life'. On another occasion the GPB medical advisor Dr Stewart Woodhouse wrote, 'there has been nothing in his imprisonment to cause or aggravate his condition except that the circumstances of being kept in prison, and without the solace of wife and family, bring home to him more acutely than to the average prisoner the realization of his downfall and his crime'.

By March 1894 Du Bedat's weight had fallen to just over nine stone but he still remained in prison. In 1896 a number of petitions and correspondences were written on his behalf. Among them was a letter from S.S. Waterhouse who was not only his father-in-law but also one of his largest creditors. He wrote that he would like to see the prisoner released so that he could look after his family. His wife wrote that she was willing to receive him. In one petition 'the workingmen of Killiney' asked for his release. In another, written in June 1896, some of the most respected members of Irish society, many of whom had lost money due to their friend's fraud, asked for Du Bedat's release. Included in the list were several Justices of the Peace, Tim Harrington, MP, Horace Plunkett, MP, Viscount Plunkett, John Wyse Power, editor of the *Evening Herald*, and Richard McCoy, Lord Mayor of Dublin. Their petition drew particular attention to the prisoner's dramatic weight loss. They also reminded the Lord Lieutenant that he had reduced the prison terms of some 'Dynamiters' who had been convicted of far more serious crimes than Du Bedat. Under the weight of pleas and in light of the fact that his hernia had returned causing swelling 'as large as an infant's head', Du Bedat was discharged on licence in November 1896 (he was discharged from Maryborough Prison where he had been transferred in August).

After his release from prison Du Bedat tried to re-establish himself in the world of finance. However, he soon found himself on the wrong side of the law for a second time when a Mozambique capital venture went wrong. In 1903 he was again convicted of fraud. On this occasion Du Bedat had protested his innocence throughout, but to no avail. When sentencing him the judge addressed the prisoner:

> Francis E. Du Bedat, the jury who tried you have discharged their duty, a very painful and a very onerous one, with great fairness and courage and in my opinion with resolute justice ... I cannot shut my eyes to the fact that this is not the first time you have stood in the dock ... One would have thought that would have been a warning and a lesson, and that you would have employed your great ability honestly. The one thing that has been vouchsafed to you is great ability, common honesty you have not. I must protect society as far as I can from men like you. As I said before men like you will always find dupes. In performing the duty I owe to Society I cannot impose upon you a less sentence than four years penal servitude.

After remaining in Mountjoy throughout his trial Du Bedat was sent to the convict prison at Maryborough after conviction. During this imprisonment he experienced a similar decline in weight to the first time. However, his stay was short. New evidence relating to the case came to light and Du Bedat's claim of innocence was upheld. He was released in August 1904.

Maria Wooton, in her booklet, *The Du Bedat Story: From Killiney to Kommitje*, traces this remarkable story from its lofty and respectable beginnings to its almost anonymous end. After release from prison Du Bedat went to South Africa to start a new life. His family in Ireland either left the country or changed their name – the name Du Bedat virtually disappeared from Ireland after the scandal. Meanwhile in South Africa, Du Bedat was anxious to obliterate his own past. He told his son from his second marriage that he had left Ireland because he had thrown a man who had insulted his wife into the Liffey. He told his neighbours that he had fled Europe because he had campaigned on behalf of the French Jew Dreyfus. He rarely left his house. He died in 1919, virtually penniless.[42]

JOHN LOGUE

On 26 June 1861 seventeen-year-old John Logue was tried at the Hillsborough Quarter Sessions, County Down, for stealing a sheep from one James Wilson. He was convicted on the evidence of a neighbour called Graham (against whom he swore revenge) and was given four years penal servitude. According to a report in *The Irish Times* the warders, while not thinking him insane, felt he 'lacked something'. Indeed, some thought that his mind had been affected by his term of penal servitude. Logue earned no remission and a petition for release was turned down in 1863 – the judge reported the prisoner was a 'decidedly bad character'. After finishing his sentence in June 1865 he stayed in Dublin for a time. During this period he witnessed the city's last public execution when he watched Patrick Kilkenny – convicted of murdering his ex-girlfriend – being hanged over the front door of Kilmainham Gaol on 22 July 1865. Afterwards he returned to Down where, in March 1866, he attempted to carry out his courtroom threat. He went to Graham's house and told him that his pigs had strayed out onto the road. When Graham investigated, Logue shot into the dark night. However, the shot did not kill the man who gave evidence against him, it killed his ten-year-old son Thomas. Logue was sentenced to death for the murder.

While he awaited his execution in Downpatrick Gaol, Logue continuously protested his innocence – such was the vehemence of these protests, 'his levity and callous disposition' shocked the staff of the prison. Vain attempts were made by the Dean of Down and other clergymen (Logue pretended to have converted) to get him to confess. In the meantime they had sent a petition to the Lord Lieutenant appealing for clemency. The petition stated that those who put their names to it:

> ... believe under the Christian Dispensation it is forbidden to take away the life of a human being, that life having been the creation of the Deity who alone has given and who alone ought to take away.

That your Petitioners believe the punishment by Death so far from securing the sacredness of life, by familiarisation, the Public with its deliberate destruction, prepare for and prompts to social insecurity.

That all experience goes to prove the more sanguinary the Criminal code of a People may be, the greater and more frequent the crimes of society, and whoever and whenever punishment has become milder the more serious offences have been found to diminish.

When the plea was turned down Logue wrote a note to the Viceroy on the back of the religious tract 'Come to Jesus, to be reconciled with God'. In the note Logue addressed the Lord Lieutenant as the 'Blood Thundering Swine that you are' and expressed the wish that His Excellency would be 'hurried to the judgement seat of God by some untimely death'. He also hoped that God would send both His Excellency and the jury 'into everlasting torment for in a few days I'll either go to heaven or hell. And My last prayer on this earth will be that you shall be taken and hired up by the two big toes in hell'. He finished off by writing 'may the devil take you before the 19th'.

On the morning of 19 April a crowd of between 300 and 400 assembled in the wind and rain outside Downpatrick Gaol. A constabulary force 50 strong formed a guard in front of the prison but there were no disturbances. Logue ascended the gallows and met the hangman who was dressed in prison clothes and had a black veil over his face. When Logue declined to make a last statement to the crowd 'the cap was then drawn over his face and the bolt having been withdrawn, the unhappy culprit ceased to exist. The fall was fully twelve feet, and he died without a struggle'. Much was made in the paper that it was the first execution in County Down for 30 years but the real significance of the hanging was not apparent until the passing of the 1868 Capital Punishment Act. Logue, having witnessed the last public execution in Dublin after his release from Mountjoy, became the last person publicly executed in Ireland.[43]

JOHN TOOLE

On 7 March 1901 at 8am the first person executed in Mountjoy was hanged. For the hanging there was no hangman's noose of the movies, which would cause strangulation. The rope used was made from Italian hemp and was slipped through a metal eye placed under the jaw. As the body fell, the rope tightened, the eye moved under the chin and the head was snapped back. When hangman T.H. Scott pulled the lever, John Toole, convicted of murder, dropped seven feet nine inches. His fourth, fifth and sixth vertebrae were fractured. Although a four-inch wound opened up in Toole's neck exposing the larynx, Mountjoy's Governor, Captain Mac Murray, reported that Scott had performed his job 'quite satisfactorily'.

Toole was a 62-year-old cab driver 'of powerful build and coarse expression'. A married man with three children, he had left his family and for three years had lived with and supported Elizabeth Brennan, a.k.a. Toole. In November 1900 the cab business became so bad he had to sell his horse and car. With the proceeds the two went on a three-week drinking spree. It finished on the night of 2 December when, after visiting various public houses in the city, they returned to 45 Charlemont Street. There Brennan, of whom it was written 'was of a quiet, inoffensive character', had her throat slit from ear to ear as she slept. Toole then put the knife to his own throat and cut it (it was this wound that opened during his execution).[44] Tried before Justice Kenny, Toole's actions were deemed to be premeditated and not made in 'a sudden frenzy or ebullition of temper'. When sentencing him, the judge told Toole that he would be taken to Mountjoy Prison, 'and there be hanged by the neck until you be dead, and that your body be buried within the walls of the prison in which the aforesaid Judgement shall be executed upon you, and may God in His mercy, have mercy on your soul'.

As Toole awaited his death in Mountjoy an official interview was held with him on 19 February. The notes of the meeting

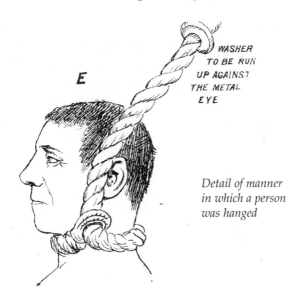

WASHER
TO BE RUN
UP AGAINST
THE METAL
EYE

E

*Detail of manner
in which a person
was hanged*

described him as being in sound mental condition – for the first few days he had looked 'callously' on his situation but, 'since then he has realized its gravity'. Toole, it was reported, 'is doing his best to attend to the Chaplain and his religious duties. He spends much of his time reading. He does not converse much but what he does say is to the point'. Four days after the interview a petition was sent to the Lord Lieutenant on behalf of the condemned. It ended '... your Petitioner prays your Excellency to exercise the first act of clemency in the reign of His Majesty King Edward VII in the case of John Toole by reprieving him'. On 28 February Governor Mac Murray informed Toole that his petition had been unsuccessful. The execution would go ahead, as planned, on 7 March.

Hangman Scott travelled from Halifax on a second-class ticket. It was a familiar journey across the Irish Sea – he had carried out most of the executions in Ireland since 1888 – but this was his first trip to Mountjoy. Arriving at the prison the night before the execution, he discreetly spied Toole to gauge his weight. Judged at 172 pounds, he took into account Toole's 'short and thick' neck and calculated a drop of seven feet nine inches. Preparing the scaffold he tied a bag of sand the same weight as Toole to the end of the rope. The lifeless sack was dropped the same distance that Toole would fall in order to 'exert a force of about 900 foot-pounds'. Once he was satisfied with the preparations, the door to the scaffold was locked and all his appliances were securely stored away. Meanwhile the bag of sand hung silently through the night 'so as to take the stretch out of the rope'. At 6am the bag was raised from the pit and dropped again. It was then taken off, the trap door was closed and a chalk mark made on the spot where Toole would stand.

Toole passed the night in the condemned cell, perhaps reading, maybe playing cards with the two prison officers who had stayed with him to prevent him from killing himself and cheating the hangman. At 7:00am he went to mass and afterwards returned to his room. As 8:00am approached the door of his cell was opened briskly. Toole's last terrifying minute had begun. His arms were pinioned by the hangman and he was led to the execution chamber in a procession that included the governor, the medical officer, the Catholic chaplain, the under sheriff for Dublin and six prison officers. Toole was placed on the chalk-mark, his legs were strapped tightly, a white linen cap was put over his head and the rope was put round his neck with the cap between the rope and the neck. Once everything was satisfactory and all but Toole's feet were clear of the trap door the lever was pulled. Toole dropped, the rope tightened and he was dead. Outside Mountjoy a crowd of around 500 heard the prison bell toll. A black flag rose slowly to signal the passing of the prisoner. One hour later Toole was pulled out of the pit, the body was examined and then buried.[45]

Chapter Eight

Bastille I – 1865-1914

So amidst all the pride and strength of the Royal Irish of the town, I was conveyed to the railway station, thence to Dublin, and emerged from the dark prison-van into the institute for making Irish rebels – to wit, Mountjoy prison.

John K. Casey, Fenian prisoner, Mountjoy Prison

To understand the history of some countries one should visit their most important palaces and learn of their kings and queens, their nobility and dynasties. To understand the history of Ireland one should visit its prisons. There are few countries, other than Ireland, that can so minutely trace its political development through the yards and cells of its prisons. If the level of imprisonment of ordinary prisoners was a barometer of social conditions, the imprisonment of political figures almost perfectly reflected the ebb and flow of mainly nationalist agitation. From the late eighteenth century until the Civil War hardly a year, month or week passed when there was not someone in an Irish prison for a political offence – at times many of Ireland's prisons were full of political prisoners. Looking at a 'who's who' of nationalist leaders, it would be difficult to find one who did not end up behind bars for Ireland. Many were confined in the 'doomed palace' of Mountjoy.

The government intended that imprisonment would, of

course, suppress political movements. But their instrument of oppression often became a powerful tool for rebellion. Imprisonment offered many advantages to those confined within prison walls – this was a stage for direct confrontation with authority, a vehicle for disobedience and a focal point for publicity associated with exposés of harsh conditions, sensational escapes and hunger strikes. The benefits of imprisonment led some to court imprisonment. After release many wrote of their experiences in 'jail journals' – one of the most potent genres of Irish political literature.

The close association between prisons and politics in Ireland has resulted in its prisons being seen as almost completely political structures. Kilmainham Gaol is etched in the Irish psyche as the ultimate political prison. Here, each year, tens of thousands of visitors experience a confrontation with history that ends in the 1916 Execution Yard. However, like all other prisons in Ireland, Kilmainham was a general prison and acted as such for most of its existence. Even in its broadest sense, only a fraction of Irish prisoners could be described as political prisoners. The vast majority of prisoners were ordinary criminals – they did not rape, steal from a church, forge a postal order, murder their child or steal a bicycle in order to create a republic or any other form of government.

When Mountjoy opened in 1850 political Ireland was relatively quiet. The Young Ireland Rebellion of 1848, the first rebellion since 1803, had been quashed. There was no organised political agitation in Ireland until the Fenian movement was established in 1858 in the form of the Irish Republican Brotherhood (IRB). In parliament the Independent Irish Political Party had a short-lived existence (the party was undermined when two of its most prominent figures, William Keogh and John Sadlier, took up government appointments). However, in Ireland politics was not always clear-cut or organised. Secret societies lacking any political structure were widespread. Commonly called 'Ribbonmen' and 'Moonlighters', many members of these societies were imprisoned in Mountjoy for sending threatening letters, intimidation, maiming cattle, etc. Among them was James Hagan from Belfast who was sentenced to four years penal servitude for Ribbonism in 1854 (he was apprehended in possession of the passwords of a secret society). During each year of his imprisonment Hagan wrote to the Lord Lieutenant promising to change his ways and asking to be released. In one year he wrote to His Excellency that his wife had died thus 'leaving his child to the mercy of the world'. In another he stated, somewhat humorously, that as far as he was aware the Belfast Ribbon Society had ceased to exist, 'and that the only society of a secret character having signs and passwords now supposed to exist is the Orange Society with which Memorialist never had and does not intend to have any connexion'.[1]

The real beginning of Mountjoy as a political prison came with the large-scale imprisonment of Fenians in 1865. Between 1865 and June 1868 over 60 Fenians convicted of Treason Felony and sentenced to penal servitude passed through Mountjoy. For security reasons Fenians sentenced to penal servitude were forced to serve their time in England, with Mountjoy acting as a clearing-house after sentencing. One group, when arriving at Kingsbridge station, 'presented a wretched appearance. Clothed in the convict uniform, their beards and moustaches shaven off, and their hair closely cropped, it was impossible to distinguish them from felons of the lowest class'.[2] In addition to these convicts were hundreds held without trial under the suspension of the Habeas Corpus Act. The Fenians were classed as ordinary criminals, what one called 'all the scum of ruffianly society',[3] but the arrangements made for their confinement were far from ordinary. In anticipation of the arrival of the first Treason Felony convicts a stock check of weapons at Mountjoy was carried out (there were 52 carbines, 52 pistols, 52 bayonets and 33 cutlasses[4]) and an order was made for 450 rounds of carbine cartridge balls, 675 percussion caps, 15 muskets, 7 bayonets and 8 swords.[5] When the Fenian Rising broke in March 1867 the

Drawing of Fenian prisoners exercising in Mountjoy, from Le Monde *newspaper.*

armed police guard was removed from outside the prison and military pensioners from the Royal Hospital Kilmainham were drafted in to patrol the perimeter during the hours of darkness.[6] In order to frustrate any escape attempts the most important of the convicted Fenians were exercised alone, while at night the convicts were kept in different cells from where they had spent the day, their clothes were taken from them and they were inspected every half an hour.[7] Warder Finnimore, whose Protestantism and loyalty to the Crown were thought to make him incorruptible, superintended visits to the Fenians.[8] The prisoners were not the only ones closely watched. While the Fenians were incarcerated staff indiscretions became serious offences. Every lock not double-locked became the subject of a written report. In 1866 night watchman Patrick Byrne fell foul of the rigorous regime when he was dismissed for being under the influence of alcohol while on duty – he was married on the day in question and, he futilely explained, had 'resorted to a couple of drinks'.[9]

The first Fenians committed to Mountjoy included Thomas

Clarke Luby, Jeremiah O'Donovan Rossa, John O'Leary (the lamented figure of romantic Ireland in W.B. Yeats' poem *September 1913*), John Murphy, Michael Moore and John Haltigan, all arrested when the offices of the Fenian newspaper the *Irish People* were raided in September 1865. Held in Richmond Prison, they were tried in front of Justice Keogh (former leader of the Independent Irish Party) at Kilmainham courthouse. After being sentenced to penal servitude for terms ranging from seven years to life they were transferred to Mountjoy Prison. Jeremiah O'Donovan Rossa, in his famous jail journal *My Years in English Jails*, wrote of this first journey as a convict: 'the van rattled through the streets, the soldiers galloped at each side of it with sabres drawn, and in less than half an hour the world closed upon me, and the first light of a very dark life dawned on me inside the portals of Mountjoy'.[10] Inside Mountjoy his hair was cut by one warder while another held a candle. Noticing sympathetic tears in the eyes of the warder holding the candle the Fenian too began to cry. It was the first time, he later declared, that he became 'soft' during his imprisonment.[11] Of another occasion when a Mountjoy warder's tears betrayed his true sentiments, O'Donovan Rossa wrote, 'that a red coat, a green jacket, or a jailer's livery may cover as Irish a heart as any in Ireland'.[12]

On 23 December 1865 at 5:15am some of the *Irish People* convicts, joined by Jeremiah O'Donovan (not to be confused with O'Donovan Rossa) and 'Pagan' O'Leary (convicted earlier in the year of Fenian activities), were loaded into a prison van and escorted by warders and a company of marines to a steamer at Kingstown harbour. They were the first batch of Treason Felony convicts to be transferred to England. During the next two years nearly 60 Fenians – including Charles J. Kickham, James Flood, Dennis Mulcahy, Thomas Duggan and John Devoy – were transferred from Mountjoy. In England some took up the government offer of transportation to Western Australia for the remainder of their sentence (in 1867 Michael Moore and

Jeremiah O'Donovan were part of the last human cargo to be transported to a penal colony from England). Those who remained in the English convict prisons of Pentonville, Millbank, Portland and Dartmoor became the focus of agitation by the Amnesty Association – a pressure group calling for the release of Fenian prisoners. In 1870 the Association, under its President Isaac Butt (later founder and leader of the Home Rule Party), succeeded in forcing the government to establish the Devon Commission of Inquiry into the conditions in which the Fenians were held. Reports of brutal treatment meted out to the Treason Felony convicts indicted the prison system. As a result of the widespread indignation caused by the findings of the Devon Commission, the Fenians were given the option of exile. Among those who went to America was O'Donovan Rossa where he helped organise a 'Skirmishing Fund' to support a dynamiting campaign in England.

When O'Donovan Rossa died in 1915 his body was returned to Ireland for burial. At Glasnevin his funeral became a powerful public display of nationalist sentiment. At the cemetery Patrick Pearse emerged from the shadows of the nationalist world to give his landmark oration over the grave of the indomitable Fenian, 'life springs from death; and from the graves of patriot men and women spring living nations. The Defenders of this Realm ... think they have pacified Ireland ... but the fools, the fools, the fools! – they have left us our Fenian dead, and while Ireland holds these graves, Ireland unfree shall never be at peace'. On its way to Glasnevin the cortege had passed Mountjoy Prison. Inside were republicans Sean Milroy, Sean MacDermott (a signatory of the 1916 Proclamation executed at Kilmainham Gaol in May 1916) and Liam Mellows (a republican executed in Mountjoy during the Civil War). In the exercise yard that day Milroy was overcome with the vision that the other prisoners, dressed in their ridiculously ill-fitting prison garb, were no longer mere criminals. They were Wolfe Tone, Robert Emmet, the Sheares brothers, Thomas Francis

Funeral cortege of Jeremiah O'Donovan Rossa leaving the City Hall, Dublin.

Meagher, Charles J. Kickham, the Manchester Martyrs and Jeremiah O'Donovan Rossa. 'Yes,' Milroy thought, 'the path I am treading is no longer the ring of Mountjoy merely. It is the pathway of Irish history, and we three – Mellows, MacDermott and I, felons of 1915 – are marching with the men who suffered for the same cause and stood against the same power as that which deprived us of liberty, and which holds us in its tenacious grip.'[13]

Apart from the Treason Felony convicts, hundreds of Fenians were held in Mountjoy without trial under the suspension of the Habeas Corpus Act (at times there were over 200 Fenians held there without trial). Mindful of the effects of revelations about any ill-treatment of political prisoners, all letters from Fenians that praised their prison conditions were copied by the authorities. In one letter prisoner James O'Mahony wrote to his sister, 'now that I find myself comfortable here I don't see why I should be in a hurry, we have pretty good attendants and the food tolerably fair, and nothing to do, who would think to go out to a world of want and scarcity'. Another prisoner wrote to his mother in May 1867, 'I am getting used to the imprisonment and do not find it near so hard as at first ... I am getting along first rate'. Maurice Syttleton, obviously concerned at the impact of media reports of prison conditions, wrote to his wife, 'it may not be uninteresting to you to know that we Prisoners in Mountjoy receive far different treatment to what ignorant prejudice and narrow minded letter writers would have you believe. The trumpeted reports, slanderous rigmaroles and frantic rhapsodies of some Irish Pot house philanthropists in England, magnify trivial chastisements for some breach of discipline or misdemeanor into Herculean punishments and gross cruelties'.[14]

The untried Fenians held in Ireland were not subjected to the same treatment as the English Fenian convicts. They could get food from outside prison (if they could afford to pay for it), they were allowed to smoke and books could be sent in to them. However, life was by no means as comfortable as letters to loved ones indicated. In 1868 the treatment of Fenian prisoners reached the public arena in the 'Mysteries of Mountjoy' libel case between Coroner William White and the *Nation* and *The Weekly News* (Isaac Butt defended the newspapers). During the case reports written by Mountjoy's Dr McDonnell, which had been suppressed by the Directors of Convict Prisons, were released. In one, dated 24 February 1867, Dr McDonnell wrote of the changes wrought by confinement on the political prisoners. 'Anyone can perceive that they are emaciated and worn looking, and their muscles are soft and flabby; some have shown unmistakable signs of mental disturbances.'[15] Three days later he drew the Governor's attention to 'the present state of things, which is, in my opinion becoming serious':

> Thomas Bourke is showing undoubted symptoms of insanity; Finnegan has latterly given way to one of those paroxysms brought on by long confinement; *Sweeny is very unsettled in his mind* ... Whyte *(latterly discharged)* was considered unfit for cellular discipline; Barry *(also latterly discharged)* was considered unfit from

his mental state to go away from the prison without someone in charge of him. *I have not the slightest doubt that the* prolonged confinement and severe discipline is the chief cause of all this. *Apart from considerations of humanity; it would be a very grave matter if any of the untried prisoners (particularly anyone like Bourke or Sweeney) the former of whom has been twelve, the latter seventeen months in confinement, should commit suicide.*[16]

Fenian John K. Casey, alias 'Leo' the poet.

Many Fenians were released on the condition that they emigrated. Escorted by the military to boats in the harbours at Kingstown or Queenstown they sailed into exile. Among those ordered to go to America was the young poet John Keegan Casey, alias 'Leo', best known for penning the ballad, *The Rising of the Moon*. Prior to release from Mountjoy (after his release his order to emigrate was rescinded), Casey penned an exile's thoughts in his Mountjoy cell:

Farewell! The brown moon rises high
Above the dun grey sea
While by the lone beach now I sigh
My last farewell to thee:
Land of my race! Sad land of tears!
Pride of my youthful song!
Farewell – the dreams of coming years
Upon my bosom throng.

I've sung erewhile the exile's fate,
Nor dreamt it would be mine,
Not all the storms of guile and hate
Could tear my heart from thine – ah no!
Its pulses still shall dwell,
Where now with saddened voice and low
I murmur thee, farewell![17]

In June 1868 the last of the Fenian prisoners left Mountjoy. As part of getting the prison back in order the Governor ordered the cells to be repainted to obliterate the Fenian graffiti.[18] Mountjoy's first political phase had come to an end and the prison could fall back into the comfort of routine.

However, there did not need to be a mass movement or revolutionary organisation for Mountjoy to have political prisoners. In 1891 the Governor reported that there were 31 agrarian and political offenders in Mountjoy.[19] Charles Cook, author of *The Prisons of the World*, visited Mountjoy and noted the prevalence of 'Moonlighters'. According to Cook they were 'not the usual type of criminals', but 'had been led astray by political agitators and are now reaping the sad results'.[20] Some of these were associated with the most important cases of the time.

Pat Nally was a leading figure in the Irish Republican Brotherhood and a founder member and secretary of the Land League. He was also a legendary athlete (a discussion he held with Michael Cusack in the Phoenix Park bemoaning the lack of a native athletics organisation led to the founding of the Gaelic Athletic Association – today a stand at Croke Park bears his name). In 1884 Nally was convicted of taking part in what was known as the 'Mayo' or 'Crossmolina Conspiracy' – the attempted murder of two land agents – and was sentenced to ten years penal servitude. He was 26 years old. Kept in Mountjoy for the first two years he was then transferred to Downpatrick Convict Prison for five years. During that time he was called as a witness to *The Times* Commission in London. While at Downpatrick train station on his way to Millbank Prison he took off his convict cap and shouted 'God save Ireland and to hell with her enemies'. In London Nally refused to give evidence to the Commission. Back in Downpatrick, apparently in punishment for the outburst at the station and his refusal to give evidence at the Commission, he was kept in his cell 22 out of every 24 hours. As a result his health deteriorated dramatically – he was seen by the doctor 103 times. When Nally was transferred back to Mountjoy in April 1891 (Downpatrick Prison closed in May) the staff at the prison immediately noted the marked decline in his physical health. Once one of the greatest athletes in the country, Nally was a shadow of his former self. In October, while he was working in the prison piggery, he complained of feeling ill but his complaints went unheeded. According to fellow prisoner Thomas MacAwley, Nally 'from sheer exhaustion ... left work one day and lay down in his cell'. A couple of days later he was admitted to the Infirmary but it was too late. Nally died on 9 November. The coroner's jury found that Nally had died of typhoid fever arising out of 'harsh and cruel treatment to which deceased was subjected in Millbank Prison for refusing to give evidence on behalf of *The Times* at the Special Commission, and that the same cause on his return to Downpatrick so shattered his mentally strong constitution as to leave him susceptible to the disease to which he succumbed'. The jury condemned 'the prison system generally as harsh and cruel, especially in relation to political prisoners'.[21]

Pat Nally, who died in Mountjoy Prison.

In 1883 members of the Invincibles – a splinter group of the Fenians – were convicted of the assassinations of the Chief Secretary, Lord Frederick Cavendish and Under-Secretary T.H. Burke in the Phoenix Park in May 1882. The 'Phoenix Park Murders', as they were called in the press, caused the most sensational outrage in Ireland for years. Over 30 Invincibles were arrested. The trial hinged on the word of informer, James Carey. Five of his fellow Invincibles were sentenced to death and executed in Kilmainham Gaol (they were hanged from a scaffold erected by convict labour from Mountjoy for which the convicts

Mugshot of 'Invincible' James Fitzharris, alias 'Skin the Goat', on release from prison.

were paid a special gratuity). The other Invincibles found guilty were sentenced to penal servitude. Most were released from Mountjoy in 1891. The last of the group to remain in prison was cab driver James Fitzharris, alias 'Skin the Goat'. He was released from Maryborough Prison on 23 August 1899 with another Invincible, Laurence Hanlon (sentenced to penal servitude for life in 1883 for the attempted murder of juryman Dennis J. Field). Accompanied by a warder and followed by a policeman, the two arrived in Dublin's Kingsbridge train station at 10:45pm and took a cab to a public house in Lower Bridge St owned by James Mullet (an Invincible released from Mountjoy in 1891). At 1:00am the policeman left the two who, he reported, 'had no appearance of leaving'.[22]

The land and national questions had traditionally dominated politics in Ireland. However, legislation culminating in the 1903 Wyndham Land Act largely removed the agrarian question from the political agenda and Parnell's death in 1891 robbed the Irish Parliamentary Party of much of its drive and focus. The next political phase in Mountjoy came from the very different sources of the labour and suffragette movements. Dublin was a city infamous for its poverty. The slums of the 'Strumpet City' filled Mountjoy with ordinary prisoners. After Jim Larkin's arrival in Ireland in 1907 labour was in ferment. Many labour activists, attempting to improve conditions, were imprisoned in Mountjoy. In 1910, the year after the founding of the Irish Transport and General Workers' Union, Larkin was sentenced to twelve months hard labour in Mountjoy for 'attempting to defraud a number of quay labourers in the City of Cork'. Larkin, innocent of the charge, had served just four months of the sentence before he was released by order of the Lord Lieutenant, Lord Aberdeen. During the next two years Larkin achieved many 'peaceful' victories. In August 1913 he called out the Dublin workers from William Martin Murphy's Dublin Tramways Company. The Great Lockout had begun.

During the Lockout Mountjoy received scores of trade union prisoners. Larkin himself was imprisoned in Mountjoy after appearing on the balcony of William Martin Murphy's Imperial Hotel on O'Connell Street in defiance of a police ban (this was the occasion of great violence which left two strikers dead and hundreds injured). In September 1913 James Connolly was released after a week on hunger strike in Mountjoy (from Mountjoy he wrote to his wife, 'At least while I am here there is not much chance of getting my head broken, as many poor fellows are getting outside'.[23]). Another, Frank Moss, went on a 32-day hunger strike. Scores of others were committed to Mountjoy for riot, wilful damage to tramway glass, assault, intimidation, etc. One Mountjoy warder reported that with 25,000 locked out, 'whatever may be the condition of other businesses in the city ours has been booming during the dispute'. Indeed, he was quoted, they were, 'overworked and underpaid before the labour trouble started in Dublin: now we are absolutely sweated'.[24] By the end of January 1914 the strike was over and most of the strikers had been released. The workers were beaten and, in the words of Connolly, had to 'eat the dust of defeat and betrayal'.[25]

During the dispute the strikers did not end up in prison by design. The labour movement's battlegrounds were the city's streets and quays. The cells of Mountjoy were a distraction. Nevertheless they demonstrated outside Mountjoy for the release of the lockout prisoners. A labour march banned from going to the High Park Convent (where one young female striker was being held) was detoured past Mountjoy. Opposite Mountjoy, 'a short halt was called and a spirited cheer was raised along the line of processionists'. In November 1913, when they assembled for a demonstration on the west side of the prison, a separate group was assembling on the female side. This second group was made up of suffragettes trying to cheer one of their number held in Mountjoy.[26] For them the prison was no mere side show – it was centre stage.

Since Charles Stewart Parnell disbanded the embarrassingly radical Ladies Land League in the early 1880s, Ireland's mainstream politicians had increasingly marginalised the women of Ireland. In the specific area of votes for women the only advance had been the granting in 1898 of the vote in local elections for women with property. In April 1912 the Third Home Rule Bill was introduced into Parliament. It made no provision for the vote for women in the new Ireland. Frustrated at once again being ignored, some of the more radical suffragettes, members of the Irish Women's Franchise League (IWFL), decided on direct confrontation with authority. Between the summer of 1912 and the outbreak of the First World War, nearly two dozen suffragettes were imprisoned in Mountjoy as part of the 'breaking windows' campaign. It was a campaign designed to ensure arrest, imprisonment and, according to one of their leading figures, to clear the cobwebs away from more than one male intellect. A poem by Samuel Kingston sets the scene:

A cartoon from the 1913 pamphlet 'Votes for Women' lampooning the attitude of John Redmond and the Irish Party to the Irish suffragette movement.

Hurro ! For Liberty !!!
No Irish Woman need Apply

No Votes For Women By order The New Liberator — M —

The Irish Citizen Equal Rights & Duties for Men & Women

A crash of breaking glass, a rush of feet
A muttered imprecation, cheers, a scream
A burst of mocking laughter – and the streets
Seethe with a surging, struggling crowd who stream
Fast to the scene to see the latest fun –
A raid of Suffragettes has just begun.[27]

The first suffragette attacks took place on 13 June 1912 when windows of the General Post Office, Customs House, Land Commission Offices and Ship St Barracks in Dublin were broken by Kathleen Houston, Margaret Hasler, Hilda Webb and Maud Lloyd. Each of the women was sentenced to six months in Mountjoy. In November, when an amendment to the Home Rule

Bill proposing the vote for women with property in Ireland was being debated, the women wrote to the leader of the Home Rule Party, John Redmond and T.M. Healy from Mountjoy. They reminded them that 'Irishwomen in prison for the vote look to you to see that their countrywomen are not excluded from the Franchise under Home Rule'.[28] The letters were never sent by the prison officials and remain in the prison files to this day.

To heighten interest in their cause and to show that they were not merely 'silly women', the suffragettes frequently embarked on hunger strikes in Mountjoy. The suffragettes were the first to widely use the potent moral weapon of the hunger strike in Irish prisons. The authorities, in order to avoid bad publicity, often released the suffragettes well before the end of their sentence. The attention attracted by the suffragette's attacks, imprisonment and hunger striking was heightened by demonstrations in support of the defiant women held outside the walls of Mountjoy (the first demonstrations to take place outside the prison). In November 1913 Hanna Sheehy Skeffington was sentenced to one month for assaulting policeman William Thomas outside Lord Iveagh's house on St Stephen's Green while she was waiting for the arrival of Bonar Law and Sir Edward Carson. At Mountjoy she immediately went on hunger strike. On 30 November a meeting planned for outside the prison was banned (egged on by a crowd returning from a football match at Dalymount Park, her husband Francis Sheehy Skeffington tried unsuccessfully to break through the strong police cordon). The next day the IWFL held a demonstration in support of their suffragette sister – the hunger striker waved a handkerchief in gratitude through the bars of her cell window. On 3 December, the fifth day of her hunger strike, she was released.[29]

On 19 June 1912, the night before Prime Minister Asquith and John Redmond were due to address a Home Rule meeting at the Theatre Royal, two English suffragettes tried to burn it down (many of the most active suffragettes were not Irish but had come to Ireland in the spirit of international co-operation to help their sisters). Gladys Evans tried to set fire to one part of the theatre, while Mary Leigh, who was in a box, poured petrol on the curtain and chairs and set them alight. Most suffragettes had been arrested for the relatively minor offence of wilfully breaking glass and normally received short sentences. The prison authorities were faced with a much more difficult and serious situation when Evans and Leigh were convicted of arson and sentenced to five years penal servitude on 6 August. Leigh was one of the most ardent and radical of the suffragettes. She had gone on hunger strike in England's Birmingham Prison in 1909.[30] Violently refusing to be force fed she brought a case against the then Home Secretary, Winston Churchill, questioning the legality of the practice. However, the court ruled that a prison medical officer had the right to force-feed a sane prisoner in order to preserve life. In Dublin, when Leigh was sentenced, she announced she would fight the government in prison, 'while there was breath in her body'.

On 14 August Evans and Leigh went on hunger strike in Mountjoy to gain political status. However, as the strike progressed the women's demand increased to the vote for women, or a pledge that it would be introduced. The two were force fed twice a day until the end of August, then three times a day. By the end of August Leigh had vomited over half the food. After five weeks of forced feeding she had lost nearly two stone and was reported to be near death. At this stage Medical Officer Dowdall wrote to the Chairman of the General Prisons Board detailing Leigh's treatment:

> I beg to report that yesterday this woman was fed as follows – 9am Milk, Benger's food and one egg. Total 8 oz. Vomit 9 oz. 12:30pm. Beef Juice, Brand's, chicken and milk. Total 8 oz. Vomit 4 $^1/2$ oz. 6:30pm. Milk, Benger's food, egg. Total 10 oz. Vomit 9 $^1/2$ oz.
> The stomach was washed out before the first meal. [The stomach was washed out with $1^1/2$ pints of water containing 30 grains of bread soda.] ... I find there is a marked loss of vital power and

the case has in my opinion become one of urgency. The woman was assisted this morning while walking from her cell, and it was necessary to lift her and place her on the couch before feeding. The pulse is weak, the urine is high coloured, acid and contains albumen.

The manner of her forced feeding was outlined in disturbing detail:

The appliances used were a funnel, and a fine soft rubber tube of special manufacture for nasal feeding. The tube was new. The patient was placed in the chair, her wrists and ankles loosely strapped thereto, in view of violent resistance in Birmingham prison. She however made no resistance, and the strapping was discontinued after a few days.

The chair used is specially designed for artificial feeding. The patient is enveloped in blankets and a hot jar placed at her feet. She was at first kept one hour in the chair after food, but proved ineffective to control the vomiting; two hours was then tried but without success, and the period of one hour has been reverted to. A special couch was obtained from Messrs. Carter of London, so as to retain the patient on her back after feeding, but this has not reduced the vomiting. Two matrons remain with the patient during the time she reclines on the couch.

The act of evacuating the contents of the stomach cannot in this woman's case properly be described as vomiting. The liquid wells up in the mouth and is expelled by her. There is no tendency to retching, nor any muscular movement such as one observes in ordinary sickness. It is more akin to the vomiting of Hysteria ...

On three occasions, i.e. 29th August, 4th September, and 8th September after she had been artificially fed, the patient had convulsive seizures. The first of these resembled Tetany, the other two were typical of the convulsions associated with Hysteria. The arms and legs only were affected, the arms being flexed at the elbow, the hands clenched, and both feet extended in a state of tonic spasm. This continued for about five minutes.

Fearing that Leigh's death was imminent she was released on licence on 20 September. Shortly after her release Evans, who had been more co-operative and had lost just five pounds since her committal to Mountjoy, reached breaking point. On 2 October the medical officer reported that Evans had barricaded herself into her cell the previous day in protest at the forced feeding. She was 'restless at night, has become much weaker and shows clear evidence of great nervous tension and general breakdown'. The medical officer wrote an emergency memo in which he stated that continued forced feeding might kill her. She was released that morning by order of the Chief Secretary, Augustine Birrel.[31]

To frustrate the suffragettes the Government passed the 'Cat and Mouse Act' which allowed the release of a prisoner on medical grounds but also allowed for re-arrest at any time. On 1 May 1914, in protest at the re-arrest of Mabel Small in Belfast – the first to be arrested under that act – Kathleen Houston stood outside College Green post office and 'at once set to work in the most matter of fact manner to break the windows with a walking stick'. The next day Hanna Sheehy Skeffington addressed a demonstration outside Mountjoy where Houston had been brought. The *Daily Sketch* headline read 'Rebellion Through a Megaphone: How a Suffrage Mouse was cheered in her Prison cell' (according to Mountjoy's Governor Munro Houston was in the hospital at the time and was unaware of the demonstration). After four days hunger strike the order was given for Houston's release (when leaving prison she declined the medical officer's offer of milk and brandy and was whisked away by her supporters to a private hospital).[32] Houston was the last suffragette to be imprisoned in Ireland (women were given the vote in the 1918 General Election). She was also the last political prisoner in Mountjoy before the outbreak of the First World War.

Chapter Nine

BASTILLE II – 1914-1924

... the rise and fall of the wind is like somebody keening for us, like everybody in Ireland keening for us.

Frank Gallagher, Mountjoy prisoner, War of Independence and Civil War

When the Great War began in 1914 life in His Majesty's Prison Mountjoy changed. Prisoners were released to join up and fight in the trenches of Europe, warders who were reservists in the army or navy left the prison to join their regiments and sandbag-making was introduced as a new form of prison labour. The war also brought new types of prisoners. English conscientious objectors, conscripted into the army and stationed in Ireland, were tried at Arbour Hill for disobeying lawful commands while on active service. Several were imprisoned in Mountjoy. One conscientious objector was Archibald Fletcher. In 1917 Fletcher wrote a letter from his cell in Mountjoy explaining his beliefs. 'I am and have been for upwardly of 16 years opposed to all forms of Militarism. I have consistently in and out of season striven toward the ideal of Internationalism and universal brotherhood by which I mean the absolute negation of war and destruction of human life. In pursuance of this ideal I have made sacrifices quite within my power to avoid.'[1] In 1915 Francis Sheehy Skeffingon (husband of suffragette Hanna) was sentenced to six months hard labour for making an anti-war speech at Beresford Place. Imprisoned in Mountjoy he went on hunger-strike and was released after one week.

While the conscientious objectors opposed all wars, Mountjoy also began to receive prisoners who were not opposed to war *per se*, just a war that was not aimed at achieving independence for Ireland. They were members of the Irish Volunteers arrested under the provisions of the Defence of the Realm Act (DORA). Among the first Volunteers committed to Mountjoy were Desmond Fitzgerald, Sean Milroy, Liam Mellows and Sean MacDermott. All were arrested for making statements, 'likely to prejudice the recruiting of one of HM Forces'. At Desmond Fitzgerald's trial lines from a speech he made in Wicklow were quoted. 'Your place is here in Ireland; you are not to join the army, because if you do you will have to fight elsewhere than in Ireland.' Fitzgerald told the court, 'I made that speech as an Irish Nationalist. I did my best to explain what I understood was Irish Nationalism to Nation-alists of Bray'.² Next April each of these men took part in the 1916 Rising.

In the weeks following the Easter Rising hundreds of those who took part were tried by court martial. Between 3 May and 12 May fourteen were executed at Kilmainham Gaol (Thomas Kent was executed in Cork and Roger Casement was tried in London and hanged in Pentonville Prison). The shots that killed Pearse, Connolly, McDonagh, McBride and the other leaders not only rang around the prison's old stonebreakers' yard, they resounded throughout the country. Even as the bodies were being deposited in a mass grave at Arbour Hill military prison, popular sentiment was turning in favour of the rebels and their republican ideal. In the words of poet W.B. Yeats, 'Now and in time to be,/Wherever green is worn,/Are changed, changed utterly:/A terrible beauty is born.'

During the last years of British rule in Ireland the Chairman of the General Prisons Board was Max S. Green. Born in Air Hill, County Cork, he studied engineering at Trinity College Dublin. Between 1885 and 1897 he was employed by the Congested Districts Board in harbour and railway construction. Dabbling

Mountjoy mugshots of Peadar Clancy after the 1916 Rising. Clancy was later killed by the British during the War of Independence.

in writing he had two articles published in the *New Ireland Review* in the mid-1890s. One was on railway administration. In the other, entitled 'Our Ideals and Methods', he castigated both the Irish middle class for not buying Irish goods and the Irish workman for his evident definition of excellence – 'it will do well enough'.[3] In 1897 he was appointed engineer to the Prison Service (he was responsible for the structures and maintenance of prisons) and in 1907 he was made Private Secretary to the Lord Lieutenant, the first Marquess of Aberdeen.[4] During this period he became engaged to playwright Johanna Redmond (her plays, including *Falsely True* dealing with the aftermath of Emmet's Rebellion, were staged at Dublin's Court, Palace and Gaiety theatres). Johanna was youngest daughter of Irish Parliamentary Party leader John Redmond and acted as his private secretary until she married Green in 1913.[5] The year before their marriage, as a concession to the Irish party leader, the Liberal Government appointed Green Chairman of the GPB. During his time in office (which ended tragically in April 1922 when he was shot while making a 'plucky attempt' to stop an armed robber at the Dawson St gate to St Stephen's Green) Green saw political developments from an awkward perspective. While his father-in-law urged Irishmen to join the British Army to fight in the Great War and told Parliament that Ireland was pacified, Green's prisons were receiving individuals of a very different persuasion.

In the aftermath of the 1916 Rising, Mountjoy again acted as a clearing-house for sentenced political prisoners before they were transferred to prisons in Britain. On 4 May the first of over

100 prisoners sentenced to penal servitude were transferred from Kilmainham to Mountjoy – the volleys that killed Joseph Plunkett, Edward Daly, Michael O'Hanrahan and Willie Pearse at dawn that morning still ringing in their ears. Among the political convicts who passed through

Mountjoy mugshots of John Plunkett (brother of Joseph Plunkett) after the 1916 Rising.

Mountjoy were Austin Stack, Eamon de Valera, Constance de Markievicz and Eoin MacNeill (the leader of the Irish Volunteers who countermanded Pearse's order for the Rising).[6]

By the summer of 1917 most of the Sinn Féin convicts and internees were back in Ireland. Here they set out to harness their new-found popular support. The republicans fought their campaign on a number of fronts. In the 1918 General Election they won a resounding victory over the Irish Parliamentary Party. In January 1919 the first shots of the War of Independence were fired. For people who saw Ireland under British rule as one large prison, Mountjoy held little terror. When republicans began to be arrested on a massive scale the prisons became almost a third front in the campaign for hearts and minds.

On 20 September 1917 the first hunger strike by Sinn Féin prisoners in Mountjoy began. On the fifth day of the strike Thomas Ashe (the leader of the Volunteers at Ashbourne in County Meath in Easter Week) died while being forcibly fed. The official cause of death was given as 'heart failure and congestion of the lungs', but the inquest into his death indicted the government in Ireland and its cruel and inhumane treatment of Ashe. The Lord Mayor of Dublin, who had visited Ashe prior to his death, told the inquest 'I left poor Ashe. He died – well, it is for his country to decide whether it is a good cause or not'.[7] For a public that had been unable to mark the deaths of the 1916 leaders the Ashe funeral was not just a focus for nationalist sentiment – it was a key moment in the history of the independence movement. At the graveside, after a volley of shots was fired over the coffin, Michael Collins stepped forward in Volunteer uniform and declared, with ominous and chilling brevity, 'nothing remains to be said. That volley which we have just heard is the only speech which it is proper to make over the grave of a dead Fenian'. The *Daily Mail* reported that the funeral of 'Sinn Féin's New Martyr' had 'set the eddy of unrest and emotion spinning again in Ireland'.[8]

It is a strange fact but prison life is based on a high level of tacit co-operation between prisoners and staff. Without this co-operation normal prison administration becomes impossible. In January 1919, Patrick Fleming, who had waged a personal campaign for political status in Maryborough Prison, was transferred to Mountjoy. Fleming was determined that there would be no co-operation and he led a fight against the Mountjoy regime. With just a handful of prisoners in C and D wings Fleming virtually brought the prison to its knees with 'open and concerted misconduct'. Each night they smashed their cell furniture, broke up floorboards, shouted political slogans, sang rebel songs and banged on doors. During the day they slept in order to be well rested for another night of disturbance. They were periodically kept in handcuffs but, once released, merely picked up where they had left off. Every opportunity for confrontation was seized.

On one occasion when the Prison's Visiting Justices Committee was inspecting the prison, Fleming approached its Chairman, John Irwin, and asked for the Sinn Féin prisoners to be allowed out to exercise. Irwin replied that he would grant permission if they would promise to behave, like they had promised the day before. When Fleming denied they ever gave such a promise Alderman Kelly, another member of the Committee, excitedly removed his hat and waved it in the air exclaiming, 'And I believe you!' The prisoners, encouraged at this unlikely source of support, refused to go back to their cells. According to Munro, 'a scene of almost indescribable excitement and disturbance ensued' and for the next two hours the prison staff struggled to get the dozen prisoners back in their cells – eventually the water hose was used.[9] In March Fleming finally called off his campaign. If the prison staff took any solace from this apparent victory it was quickly shattered. He had merely dropped the campaign to put the prison staff 'to sleep' so he could escape (see below).

The Ashe case had shown just how vulnerable the government was in relation to prison issues. After Ashe's death force feeding was never again resorted to in Mountjoy and most Sinn Féin prisoners (not convicted of serious crimes) were granted 'ameliorations' which recognised, at least to some degree, their political status. However, the fight continued and on 5 April 1920 another concerted challenge to the authorities was launched when 36 untried Sinn Féin prisoners went on hunger strike for prisoner-of-war status. Convicted Sinn Féin prisoners who had been excluded from extra privileges soon

British troops outside Mountjoy Prison during the hunger strike in 1920.

joined them and by 14 April there were 92 men on hunger strike in Mountjoy.[10] The impact of the hunger strike outside the prison was enormous. Mountjoy once again became the focus of the independence movement. A general strike called in support of the Mountjoy prisoners brought the country (outside of Belfast) to a standstill. The strains created by the strike were again reflected in the Visiting Committee when Thomas Clarke resigned. He later explained:

> I resigned my position as a protest and in condemnation of the Monstrous injustice of British rule in this Country in seizing and casting into Prison men of the highest Character and reputation without trial or charge being made against them and thus driving our fellow-Countrymen to resort to such desperate and revolting remedies as hunger-striking endangering their lives and permanently injuring their health. The agonising scenes of inhumanity and torture which I have witnessed in Mountjoy Prison will never be effaced from my memory.[11]

After Ashe's death a policy of 'no feeding, no release' had been tried but proved unworkable. The government was now in an

Mountjoy Prison staff during the War of Independence.

impossible position. They could not force feed the prisoners but equally they could not let the strike continue and reach its ultimate, logical and fatal conclusion. On 14 April Governor Munro met the Lord Lieutenant and Lord Mayor of Dublin in the Vice-Regal lodge in the Phoenix Park where the three agreed that the only solution was to release the prisoners.[12] Once again the normal tools of prison control were rendered impotent in the face of politically-motivated and highly-organised prisoners. While the War of Independence was being waged outside the independence movement had won another battle in the prisons.

The prison staff was at the uncomfortable coalface of the government's prison policy. According to Max Green the staff were 'charged with enforcing an extremely unpopular political policy of the Executive, which enforcement places individual members of the prison service in active conflict with the political wishes and ideas of the majority of the Irish people'. After Sinn Féin's stunning electoral successes Green was aware that his current masters might soon depart and be replaced by the very people he was holding in his prisons. As a result of the politicisation of the prisons, Green wrote, 'the greatest uneasiness exists throughout the service – this uneasiness is still further accentuated when each of us in our own persons has experienced the atmosphere of social ostracision [sic] incurred because we are and have been loyally carrying out the policy of the Executive for the time being'.[13] In another report it was stated that the staff of Mountjoy were, not surprisingly, 'very worn and harassed, and very much inclined to avoid conflict with the Sinn Féin prisoners at all costs'.[14]

In the circumstances Governor Munro seems to have suffered more than most. In his mid-forties, Munro was described by Sean Milroy as 'a diminutive, shrivelled, ill-tempered shrew, trying to look severe and stern, but only succeeding in giving an impression of waspish insolence'.[15] Munro was appointed Governor of Mountjoy in 1911 (he held a post in the Indian Police prior to joining the Irish prison service in 1902 as Governor of

Derry Prison)[16]. Before the War of Independence Munro had dealt with many difficult prisoners in Mountjoy but the large-scale confinement of republicans strained his abilities to near breaking point. Apparently incapable of delegating authority and intent on running the prison as if everything were normal, Munro suffered from nervous tension and exhaustion.[17] Shortly before the Anglo-Irish Treaty was signed in London Munro, in what was yet another plea to the GPB in Dublin Castle for assistance, expressed his worry that with the Sinn Féin prisoners, 'proper supervision is impossible without resorting to drastic measures'. On the verge of losing patience with Munro's neurotic concerns, Green wrote that in the prevailing circumstances, 'we must use all our ingenuity to cope with dissatisfaction since we cannot transfer it elsewhere, or put an end to it'. Recognising the impossibility of the situation the Chairman asked Munro to 'please do your best'.[18] Indeed Green may have considered finishing the letter by quoting one of his own articles written in more peaceful times – 'it will do well enough'.

Until the large-scale imprisonment of republicans escapes from Mountjoy were rare. But during the War of Independence there were times when the prison seemed like a penal sieve. The republicans' massive network of supporters outside prison smuggled escape material in to prisoners and facilitated the disappearance of escaped prisoners into the little streets of Dublin – as one paper commented in 1919, 'a burglar who should escape from Mountjoy would be recaptured within a few hours, but the recapture of a political prisoner is a very different matter'.[19] The staff of the prison presented a further problem. Despite being compelled, in the face of rising nationalist sentiment, to take an oath of allegiance to the Crown, at least some prison officers were sympathetic to the cause of their political prisoners. Others, acutely aware that their political prisoners were dangerous and potentially lethal enemies, were no doubt reluctant to blow the whistle on Sinn Féin escape attempts. By 1 January 1919 over 30 republicans had escaped from various Irish prisons.[21]

The first escape from Mountjoy during the War of Independence was in March 1919 when Robert Barton TD (later a signatory of the Anglo-Irish Treaty) climbed over the back wall of the prison. Barton had been held in the relative comfort of the Infirmary with Piaras Beaslaí, William Sear and J.J. Walsh – fellow TDs from the 'Parliament of Felons'. For three nights he studiously cut through the bars of the window with a hacksaw. On the night of 16 March he made his bid for freedom. Climbing through the window and making his way to the outer wall of the prison, he threw a piece of soap over the wall. From the other side his rescuers threw a rope ladder. Barton was on his way. The escape was not discovered until 8:00am the next day (to buy extra time he had put a dummy figure in his bed). When his cell was searched a note was found addressed 'To the Governor'. In it Barton wrote, 'I am about to make an escape from your hospitality. If I escape well and good, if not I am prepared to suffer the consequences'. Ironically praising the loyalty of the warders to the prison regime (which immediately put them under suspicion) he finished the letter, 'I hope that we may shortly turn your prison to a useful national purpose'.[22]

While Governor Munro and his staff were still recovering from the shock of Barton's departure, the most sensational escape of the War of Independence took place. Organised by Michael Collins, the plan was to free Patrick Fleming, Piaras Beaslaí and J.J. Walsh on Saturday 29 March. It was a simple arrangement with a rope ladder again being used. But this time the escape bid was to be made in broad daylight. At the appointed time a rope ladder was thrown over the wall of an exercise yard and the three intended escapees climbed over. The other prisoners in the exercise yard could not resist the sight of the dangling rope ladder. In the end twenty prisoners got away. Just seven republicans were left inside to greet the military when they arrived. It was one of the greatest publicity coups of the war. A republican propaganda cartoon postcard of the time brilliantly exploited the opportunity. It showed Mountjoy prison flying the Union Jack. Troops, machine guns, artillery and air-planes cover the front gate. An inset entitled 'The Back Way' shows a procession of men climbing down a rope at the back of the prison. A burly armed guard stands dauntingly at the entrance with a young boy at his feet. The boy says to the guard, 'Hey! Mister, d'ye know there's a back way in your place'.[23]

On 14 May 1921 there was an audacious but unsuccessful attempt to rescue a prisoner from Mountjoy. At 9:30am a 'Peerless' armoured car was captured by Volunteers while on ration duty at an abattoir off the North Circular Road and driven to Mountjoy. Arriving at the gate the leader of the escape party, sporting pince-nez glasses and dressed in the uniform of an Auxiliary officer, announced himself in a cockney accent as Captain Dawson looking for prisoner John McKeown. Waiting at the gate were several armed volunteers dressed in civilian clothes pretending to be delivering parcels to prisoners. When the gate opened the guard was rushed and disarmed. Two of the 'officers' from the Peerless went into the prison offices and began to tie up Munro and his office staff. Shortly afterwards a sentry happened upon the scene and fired on the raiding party – taking cover behind what he saw as a 'friendly' armoured car, he was captured. Inside the office the raiding party heard the shot and, fearing the attempt was being abandoned, left the governor and his men. Munro, on the other hand, thought the shot signalled a general attack on the prison. According to the official report the incident closed 'with something approaching internecine warfare at the Governor's office door, the Governor holding it against what he thinks are rebels, and the party in the passage actually consisting of soldiers and warders battering in the door under the impression that the Governor and Staff are still at the point of revolver inside'. The 'Peerless' was later found abandoned on the Malahide Road in Clontarf. It had run out of petrol.[24]

The last escapes from Mountjoy were made in the weeks leading up to the signing of the Anglo-Irish Treaty. On 30

Page from an auto-graph book belonging to prisoner Kathleen Kavanagh Merrigan, 1920-4.

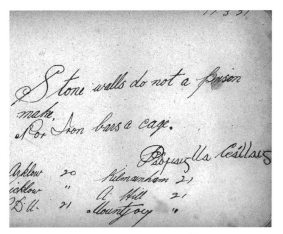

October 1921, Linda Kearns, Annie Coyle, Aileen Keogh and May Burke, serving sentences ranging from two to ten years, escaped from the women's prison. They smuggled a key in a birthday cake for Linda Kearns and under cover of a football match, 'Sligo vs. the Rest of Ireland', in one of the wings, the women got out of the prison building. At the wall they threw over the distinctly feminine signal of a perfume bottle and then climbed the rope ladder. In the following month seven of the male prisoners escaped through the front gate, some dressed in home-made Auxiliary uniforms.

For a government that tries to retain a semblance of legitimacy in the face of a hostile population, the prison offers few benefits. It becomes almost exclusively the tool of the prisoners. The executions of Republicans during the War of Independence was a case in point. While hardly acting as a deterrent, they provided an emotional focal point for nationalist feeling. The largest single day of executions in Mountjoy's history was on 14 March 1921 when six men were hanged. Four of the men – Frank Flood, Patrick Doyle, Thomas Bryan and Bernard Ryan – were condemned for being 'armed with firearms and explosives' in Drumcondra. The other two were Thomas Whelan and Patrick

Moran, both convicted of taking part in the Bloody Sunday attacks of 21 November 1920. On that morning eleven British intelligence agents, members of the 'Cairo Gang', were killed by Michael Collins' 'Squad'. Finally undermining Dublin Castle's network of spies it was one of the decisive attacks of the War of Independence. Later that day the Black and Tans fired into a crowd at Croke Park killing eleven innocent civilians.

Patrick Moran (left) and Thomas Whelan (right) shaking hands in Mountjoy Prison in the days before their executions on 14 March 1921.

The story of Patrick Moran is one of the more tragic of the War of Independence. In February 1921 Moran was held in Kilmainham Gaol awaiting his trial. Ernie O'Malley and Frank Teeling were confined in the same corridor (they were also awaiting trial in connection with the Bloody Sunday attacks). With the assistance of two of their British soldier guards, Privates Roper and Holland, the three unsuccessfully tried to escape on 13 February. The next day O'Malley and Teeling resolved to try again but Moran had second thoughts. Innocent of the attack he was accused of taking part in, and believing he could prove this, he declined to go on the second attempt. That night as he lay in his cell his replacement, Simon Donnelly, walked out a side gate with O'Malley and Teeling. Going out onto the main road they caught a tram into the city centre. They were never recaptured.

In an atmosphere hardly conducive to good justice, Moran's court martial began in City Hall the day after the escape. During the trial great weight was given to the evidence of one British officer who thought, but could not swear, that Moran was the man who killed Lieutenant Aimes. The second dubious point in the case was the sheer logistics of Moran getting to the scene of the killing at 36 Upper Mount Street by 9:30 on the Sunday morning. Moran, a grocer's assistant, lived on the main street in Blackrock, about six miles from Merrion Square. After going to 8:00 mass Moran was seen by a policeman in Blackrock at 9:00 and was, according to his landlady, eating breakfast at 9:30. The prosecution alleged that Moran must have taken a tram to the scene of the murder. But the first tram did not leave Blackrock on a Sunday morning until 10:00. It was virtually impossible for Moran to have killed Aimes. Moran's defence counsel, aware of his client's difficult position, reminded the six British army officers who formed the jury, that 'there is one thing of more importance than the shortening of a period of temporary insurrection. It is that the eternal principles of truth and justice shall not be violated by those in authority'. Concluding his presentation he urged the soldiers to show real courage, to put their hands on their hearts and say 'no matter what I may think about this man's political feelings, no matter what I think I may have heard upon the evidence. Upon the evidence I have sworn to consider the case. On the evidence I say he is not guilty of the charge brought against him'. It was a futile plea. Moran was found guilty of killing Lieutenant Aimes on Bloody Sunday and was sentenced to death.[25]

Hopes for a reprieve proved ill-founded and the clock inexorably counted down to the fatal day. Nuns began to visit the prisoners to offer them solace while they contemplated their own deaths. Hangman John Ellis and two assistants began their journeys from England. Around this time a remarkable set of photographs was taken in Mountjoy of Moran and Whelan (who also claimed to be innocent). The two are seen to be in fine form, amiably chatting with Auxiliaries. Whelan, a deeply religious man, had told his mother, 'that as a priest at the time of his Ordination starts a new life, so on Monday I shall start a new life which shall never end'. The Saturday before the executions the six men were allowed to congregate together. Friends brought them in cakes and oranges. According to the nuns who visited them during their last days they 'met together in one of the cells and made merry – Whelan and Bryan, with their fine voices, contributed musical items. Bryan also entertained the others by dressing himself up in part of the Black and Tan's uniform'. Inside the prison, the night before their executions, the condemned men talked playfully 'of their places in Heaven. All seemed to agree that Whelan would be highest'.[26] A note signed by Arthur Griffith and Eoin MacNeill was passed to Moran in his condemned cell; it read 'all recognise that the death to which you are doomed by the tyrant and oppressor of our nation is an honour to you. We know that you are going to that death in the spirit of the best and bravest of your race'.[27] Thomas Bryan, in a last letter to a friend, wrote, '... at eight o'clock in the morning I go over the top and I feel assured of a good reception, it will be fine to See P.H. Pearce [sic] and the Rest of the men'.[28] Outside a crowd assembled in the shadow of Mountjoy. Muted prayers were recited and *The Soldiers Song* and *Wrap the Green Flag Around Me Boys* were sung before they dispersed at the approach of curfew.[29]

A general strike was called for the morning of the executions. The streets of Dublin, under a light fog, were eerily quiet. But outside Mountjoy, thousands joined the families of the condemned and 'surged up the lonely avenue along which so many Irish heroes and patriots have been drawn'. According to a reporter 'all classes of Dublin people were there, from newsboyto merchant, from peasant to priest, from young girls to aged women; subdued, calm, undaunted before the mute granite temple of death'. The men were hanged in pairs starting at 6:00am. By 8:00 'the souls of six young Irishmen had passed into heaven and their heritage into the keeping of their people'.[30] Five of the families gave in written requests for the bodies of the dead but they were buried in the grounds of Mountjoy.[31]

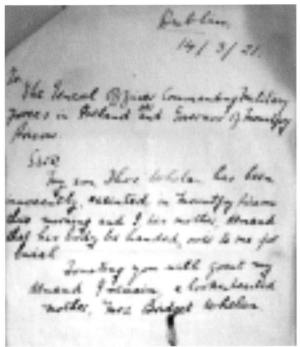

Letter from Bridget Whelan to Governor Munro asking for the body of her executed son, Thomas.

The youngest person to be executed in Mountjoy was eighteen-year-old Kevin Barry, a medical student at University College Dublin. He was convicted at court martial in Marlborough Barracks of killing Private Matthew Whitehead (a British soldier the same age as Barry) in a raid on an army bread lorry at Church Street on 20 September 1920.[32] While awaiting execution in Mountjoy he gave a sworn statement in which he alleged that during questioning he was tortured to give information about his comrades (he refused). Executed on 1 November Barry's case was trumpeted to the world by the Sinn Féin publicity machine. A famous ballad commemorating his death begins:

> In Mountjoy one Monday morning
> High upon the gallows tree

Kevin Barry gave his own life
For the cause of liberty
But a lad of eighteen summers
Yet no one can deny
As he walked to death that morning
He proudly held his head up high.

On 7 June 1921 Edward Foley, Patrick Maher and William Mitchell were hanged. Foley and Maher had been convicted of killing Sergeant Wallace of the RIC at Knocklong train station on 14 May 1919. Mitchell was a police constable hanged for the murder of Robert Dixon, a Justice of the Peace, in Dunlavin, County Wicklow in

Kevin Barry, the youngest person executed in Mountjoy.

February 1921 (he had gone to Dixon's house to extort money). A fellow RIC man who had taken part in the raid committed suicide shortly after his arrest.[33] The crowd assembled outside the prison in sympathy with Foley and Maher 'offered prayers for the doomed man Mitchell as well'.[34] They were the last executions in Mountjoy during the War of Independence. In July a truce was called and negotiations began.

After the Anglo-Irish Treaty was signed in London on 6 December 1921 by Michael Collins and Arthur Griffith (Griffith had been committed to Mountjoy in December 1920 but was released when the Truce was called) nearly 200 republicans were released from Mountjoy. On 7 January 1922 the Treaty was approved by 64 votes to 57 in Dáil Éireann. The War of Independence was officially over. But the Treaty had within its articles the seeds of a further conflict. Mirroring the division in the Dáil the country split into pro- and anti-Treaty camps. Families divided and comrades who had fought side by side during the War of Independence became bitter enemies. Those who supported the Treaty felt it offered enough independence or would act as a stepping stone to a complete independent republic.

Prisoners released from Mountjoy at the end of the War of Independence.

Those who opposed the Treaty felt it was a betrayal of the Republic for which people had previously fought and died. Ireland remained part of the British Commonwealth and owed an oath of allegiance to the British Crown. For six months the country witnessed an uneasy coexistence of armed and hostile pro- and anti-Treaty forces. In Dublin the anti-Treaty Republicans, or 'Irregulars' as their opponents dubbed them, occupied important buildings and established their headquarters at the Four Courts. When Sir Henry Wilson, ultra-Unionist military advisor to the Northern Ireland government, was assassinated in London on 22 June the fuse of this explosive mix was lit. The British government, believing anti-Treaty forces were responsible, called on the fledgling government in Dublin to deal at last with its armed opposition or consider the Treaty null and void. As the provisional government debated the demand the situation quickly deteriorated when republican Leo Henderson was caught commandeering cars from a garage in the city and was imprisoned in Mountjoy. In reprisal the republicans captured the government's Deputy Chief of Staff 'Ginger' O'Connell. On 28

197

June the Four Courts garrison ignored a call to surrender. A short time later James Gandon's architectural landmark was fired on by government forces. The Irish Civil War had begun.

On 29 June Mountjoy received its first Civil War prisoner. It was the legendary Tom Barry, leader of the West Cork flying column of the IRA during the War of Independence, captured trying to join his comrades in the Four Courts. In Mountjoy Barry and Henderson could hear the booming guns and crack of rifle fire that eventually forced the republicans to surrender. The Four Courts fell at 9:00pm on 30 June and the bulk of the prisoners began to arrive. On 2 July the male prison was made into a military prison under Colm O'Murchadha and Diarmaid O'Hegarty. Governor Munro, no doubt to his great relief, was not put in charge of the anti-Treaty prisoners but looked after the criminal prisoners who were transferred to the female prison. As soon as the anti-Treaty forces were admitted to Mountjoy they began the systematic destruction of the prison. Cell walls were hacked through, doors were broken and windows smashed. Each day their supporters gathered outside the prison walls to shout messages. On 14 July, concerned at the growing size of the crowds, an ultimatum was issued to the prisoners – they must stop communicating through the windows by 3:00pm or they will be fired upon. When the prisoners refused, the military guard opened fire. Two prisoners were injured including Count Plunkett (father of Joseph Plunkett, executed at Kilmainham Gaol in 1916). Thirty soldiers on duty at the prison refused to take part in the action and were removed to barracks under armed guard and O'Murchadha, 'reported to be feeling the strain of his responsibilities', was transferred from the prison – he resigned from the army in August. By this point there were over 300 military prisoners in Mountjoy. In the Civil War Mountjoy received some of the leading figures of the anti-Treaty side – Sean MacBride, Ernie O'Malley (committed to Mountjoy in October 1923 he began the notes which would eventually turn into his classics of Irish historical literature, *The Singing Flame* and *On Another Man's Wound*),

Supporters communicating with prisoners at the start of the Civil War

Austin Stack, Dan Breen, Frank Gallagher, Oscar Traynor, Joe McKelvey, Joseph McDonagh, Peadar O'Donnell, Robert Duggan and Seán Lemass.

After the initial excitement, prison life settled down into a semblance of routine, bizarre though it was. Imprisoned by men who had once fought with them for prisoner of war status the Civil War internees were denied this recognition. However, they were allowed a great degree of freedom. In Mountjoy some prisoners learned Irish, others read the classics of literature. A chess club was set up and cards became a favourite pastime. Regular sports events were held in the exercise yard. Prison magazines were produced including *C-Weed* and *The Trumpeter: When Gabriel Sounds the Last Rally*. Discipline though, when it was enforced, was often blunt. The gas supply was turned off to punish prisoners. Each night at 11:00 they were told to go to their cells. If they failed to do so the four soldiers stationed in the circle would fire down the wing, the bullets ricocheting.

No history of Mountjoy would be complete without Paudeen O'Keefe who was appointed Deputy Military Governor of

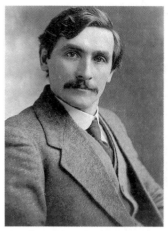

Paudeen O'Keefe, deputy military governor of Mountjoy during the Civil War.

Mountjoy after the transfer of O'Murchadha. In August 1922 Phil Cosgrave, brother of Chairman of the Provisional Government, William Cosgrave, replaced O'Hegarty. Because Cosgrave was seriously ill, O'Keefe assumed most of the duties of Military Governor. In the midst of a bitter Civil War and in an institution that had often destroyed the better human qualities, O'Keefe stands out for his humanity and humour. Paudeen, as the prisoners knew him (unless they wanted a cigarette or some other favour when they would refer to him as 'Captain' or 'Commandant') had fought in an outpost of the GPO in 1916 and was interned in Frongoch. In 1917 he became Secretary of Sinn Féin and played a key role in its reorganisation before the 1918 General Election (he was also elected TD). Once asked the policy of Sinn Féin he replied, 'Revenge, by Jaysus, revenge!'[35] In September 1919 he was given eighteen months in Mountjoy but was released the next month after going on hunger strike.[36]

Described by Peadar O'Donnell as 'a restless little man with a fine pair of eyes and a waspish tongue', he did not command much respect (at night the prisoners would screech Paudeen's name like a pack of cats) but he was liked by almost all the prisoners (a notable exception was Mary MacSwiney who could not see through the colour of her own politics[37]). Generous to the prisoners when his situation allowed him, he tried to calm what was an often bitter atmosphere. Above everything else Paudeen's comments were legendary. After an escape tunnel was discovered Paudeen gleefully announced 'nothing escapes from here, only gas'.[38] When the interned prisoners were fed up

Maud Gonne and Charlotte Despard holding vigil outside Mountjoy during the Civil War hunger strike.

keeping two prisoners hidden in the cells, the count of prisoners was curiously two up. Double-checking the numbers Paudeen approached their representative, Andy Cooney, and asked, 'Jaysus, Cooney, which of you had the twins?' One May day Paudeen was seen standing at a window with his legs apart, hands holding a gun behind his back. Looking out at the inclement weather he remarked, 'Christ, such a country to be in jail for, snow in the middle of May'.[39] In the second week of June 1923 the last of the women prisoners were transferred to the North Dublin Union. It was a night of violence in which many women were injured by forces not under Paudeen's control. From the back of the lorry Margaret Buckley turned to see Paudeen at the gates of Mountjoy and thought, 'we shall never look upon his like again'.[40]

In November 1922 the black heart of Civil War was brought into the prisons when the government began executing republicans. On 17 November the first of 77 were shot by firing squad in Kilmainham Gaol. One week later Erskine Childers, author of *The Riddle of the Sands*, was shot in Beggars Bush barracks. One of Mountjoy's prisoners wrote that news of the executions sounded like 'the thud of falling bodies' and that 'the constant state of misery, tension and nervous terror, had its visible effects on many faces. Cheeks once crimson with the glow of health were now a dirty white or green pallid'.[41] When republican assassins gunned down Seán Hales T.D. on 7 December the grim shadow of execution shrouded Mountjoy. In reprisal Kevin O'Higgins, Minister of Home Affairs, ordered the execution of four of Mountjoy's leading prisoners – Dick Barrett, Joe McKelvey, Liam Mellows and Rory O'Connor (O'Connor had been O'Higgins' best man at his wedding in 1921). On the morning of 8 December the four were taken from their cells and shot. Half an hour before his death Mellows wrote to his 'dear comrades in Mountjoy! God Bless you boys, and May He give you fortitude, courage and wisdom to suffer and endure all for Ireland's sake. *An Poblact Abú'*. A government statement described the executions as 'a solemn warning to those associated with them who engaged in a conspiracy of assassination against the representatives of the Irish people'.[42]

In April 1923 the anti-Treaty forces called a 'permanent cessation of hostilities'. Two months later the first stage in getting the prison back in order came in Mountjoy when two wings began to be handed back to the civilian authorities for maintenance. The damage caused by the political prisoners was assessed. While D wing would cost over £1,000 to repair, the list of damage to C wing was impressive. Nearly all the cell fittings were broken, the cell bell wires, indicators and handles were pulled out of the walls, twelve gongs were missing, 30 shelves were destroyed, 105 cell-door locks were missing, a large number of spy holes were smashed, three cell doors were badly damaged, three floors were torn up and a large hole was broken through the outer wall of cell C.1.10 and camouflaged with a piece of lime-washed canvas.[43]

In October 1923 the last act in the drama of Civil War began in Mountjoy. As part of their policy of normalisation the Free State reviewed the situation in Mountjoy in September. What they found was a laxity in the discipline of both prisoners and staff. As a result Paudeen left Mountjoy (he later became senior clerk in Dáil Éireann) and a new governor, Commandant Fitzpatrick, was appointed to implement a new regime. The prisoners' representatives were no longer recognised, exercise hours were reduced, no clean linen or underwear was issued and bullets fizzed down the wings with greater frequency. The prisoners issued a statement declaring that 'the terrorist is still in his element here'. The representative of B wing wrote to Commandant MacManus that 'the object of this cowardly ill-treatment is apparently to break us into submitting to your design to class us and treat us as criminals'.[44] After a month of 'the baton, the bullet, the hose-pipe, starvation and exposure'[45] meeting prisoners' resistance, a crisis point was reached. On the night of 12 October the prisoners in Mountjoy resolved that 'in the face of all these facts the prisoners now feel that there is but one alternative left to them – the hunger strike, the ultimate weapon of passive resistance'.[46] That night Frank Gallagher, who had been part of the hunger strike in Mountjoy in April 1920, wrote in his diary, 'tonight we had our last meal. It was a bumper one ... luscious to the eye and taste. We ate it with sinking hearts, however, feeling that each mouthful went much too quickly into the deeps'.[47] The strike spread quickly from the wings of Mountjoy to the other prisons and internment camps (the largest of these were Tintown A and B, Hare Park, Gormanstown Camp and Newbridge Barracks). Soon nearly 8,000 internees were refusing food. However, its very size ensured its failure. There are few people who can withstand such deprivation to the end and mass defections from the strike weakened it. It was finally abandoned at 1:00am on 23 November 1923.

During the next months the republicans were gradually released from prison. In January 1924 Mountjoy was handed back to the civilian authorities. The Civil War was over and a most extraordinary episode in Mountjoy's history had come to an end. Almost breathless at what it had witnessed, Mountjoy reverted back to being a 'normal' prison.

Chapter Ten

1924-1962: THE QUIET YEARS

It is unlike any other prison in Ireland. It is more like an old-time work-house than a jail. About 500 prisoners, all ages and types; the old-timers, the jetsam of Dublin, incorrigible petty thieves and drunkards who have huge numbers of convictions, all for short periods of from seven days to six months; a large number of juvenile offenders who are kept absolutely separate from adults, and who mostly work in the open air at wood-cutting and gardening; many sexual offenders; and a number of first offenders who, because they are only learning prison rules and routine, and are weighed down with scorching worry and sorrow, are often a nuisance to warders and to those 'in-and-outs' who look on the Joy as a home.

Convict D. 83222, Mountjoy prisoner, 1940s

In comparison to the other periods in Mountjoy's history the years 1924-1962 can be summed up in the phrase 'not a lot happened'. The numbers of prisoners declined, the prison regime became more lenient and Mountjoy's role in politics diminished. To those who have lived through the prison crisis of the last decades of the twentieth century this most recent period would seem the most alien.

The most striking aspect of Mountjoy between 1924 and 1962 was that the number of prisoners was incredibly low. When the Provisional Government took over the reigns of prison management from the British in January 1922, only 237 of Mountjoy's 900 cells were occupied.[1] This was the result of a

Prisoners in the modified borstal system exercising in Mountjoy in the 1920s.

number of factors. Various pieces of legislation reduced the reliance on the penalty of imprisonment. Thousands of young Irishmen, the normal clientele of Mountjoy, died in the Great War. In addition the British and then the Free State governments had been concentrated more on suppressing armed opposition than criminals during the War of Independence and Civil War. For a brief period after the Civil War there was a slight increase in numbers. This was blamed on people trying to take advantage of the uncertainty after the conflict and 'half-educated youths' whose morals came from 'the Streets and the Cinema'.[2] However, within a few years, the national daily average in prison was 740 (they were guarded by 86 prison officers[3]). Just over 300 were held in Mountjoy with the rest distributed between the remaining Free State prisons at Cork, Dundalk, Limerick, Portlaoise, Sligo and Waterford. Such was the decline in numbers that the General Prisons Board was rendered obsolete and in 1928 the Board, created in the 1870s to manage dozens of prisons holding a daily average of over 2,000 prisoners, was dissolved. The prisons were then managed by the Department of Justice.

Over the next three decades the numbers of prisoners in Ireland continued to decline. By 1955 there was a daily average of just 356 prisoners in the country[4] – 205 of these were in Mountjoy.[5] As the numbers of prisoners fell, so too did the number of prisons. In 1956 Cork and Sligo prisons closed. In the same year the Clonmel Borstal closed and the prisoners were transferred to a new borstal called St Patrick's in unoccupied wings of Mountjoy female prison. By the end of that year there were just the prisons at Mountjoy for men, women and juveniles, Portlaoise for convicts and Limerick for both men and women.

Ireland had one of the lowest rates of imprisonment in Europe (it was three times higher in England). The empty prisons reflected a near absence of crime in a remarkably stable society. The land question, the great social issue of the nineteenth century, had been resolved and a new farming class was settling into its role. Irish society was Catholic, rural and conservative. A strong sense of community ran through its fabric and life was governed by strict codes of behaviour. While this goes some way towards explaining the decline of imprisonment, emigration was also a major factor. Widespread poverty and the

Mountjoy prisoners working in a wing in 1923.

suffocating moral environment led thousands of Irish men and women to leave the country. Acting as the safety valve of Irish society, emigration siphoned off many members of the categories of people who filled prisons – the young, the disaffected and the marginalised. This emigration peaked between 1956 and 1961, when over 200,000 people left Ireland (five times the number of people who had been transported from Ireland to Australia). Although emigration removed some of those who might have ended up turning to crime, banishment and exile remained an option in the criminal justice system. Judges often gave criminals a choice between buying a ticket for the boat to England or going to prison. Prisoners were still encouraged to emigrate on release with some having their fares paid for them by the Discharged Prisoners' Aid Society. An indication of the rate of emigration of Mountjoy inmates is given in a 1959 survey of boys released from St Patrick's in 1957-8. Of the 99 surveyed twelve were back in prison, 35 were unemployed, twelve were in casual employment in Dublin while 36 were working in England.[6]

The decline in the number of women prisoners was even more dramatic than that of men. The main causes of their imprisonment were drunkenness – for which they almost always outnumbered men – and larceny – the most common crime for men. Although the British army garrisons had gone prostitutes continued to represent a high proportion of prisoners. In the 1935 Act that banned contraception in Ireland, provision was made for increasing sentences for what was termed 'common prostitutes'. However, female crime and prostitution remained closely linked. In 1946 a quarter of female prisoners were treated for venereal disease. Recidivism remained a particular characteristic of female prisoners. In 1954, 70 per cent had five previous convictions, compared to 28 per cent for men. However, by 1961 there had been a massive decline in the number of women prisoners. In 1961 women accounted for just five per cent of the Irish prison population.[8]

The Ireland of de Valera's 'comely maidens' was one in which female behaviour was strictly controlled. Fewer women crossed the line into criminality. Of those who did transgress, it can be assumed that when released from the Joy, many left the country fully aware that re-entering Irish society would be almost impossible. Equally, female emigration was particularly high in Ireland and young women without opportunities left at an alarming rate. At the same time alternatives to prison were also put forward for certain female crimes. Among these crimes was infanticide. In partial recognition of the mental anguish of this act, women convicted of infanticide were often sent to one of the Magdalen Asylums or mental institutions instead of prison.

The number of prisoners held in Mountjoy in the period 1924 to 1962 fell significantly, yet the number of executions increased as Mountjoy became the main place of execution in Ireland. Between 1922 and 1954 (not including political executions), there were 30 people judicially killed in Mountjoy. All were hanged for murder and each was buried in the prison. Just one of these was a woman. On 5 August 1925, Annie Walsh, who was described as being 'around 30', became the first woman executed in Ireland for 22 years. She was hanged in the women's prison at 8:45am. Forty-five minutes earlier her nephew, Michael Talbot, was hanged in the male prison. The two had been found guilty of murdering Walsh's 60 year-old husband, Edward, at Fedamore, Croom, County Limerick. She told the police that she had been in bed with her husband when her nephew, who was drunk, entered their bedroom, punched her husband and then shot him in the head. She said that Talbot spent the rest of the night in bed with her, holding her down by the throat. In Talbot's version of the story Annie Walsh had killed her husband with an axe, he had merely held the victim's arms for the second and fatal blow. He agreed that he spent the rest of the night in her bed but claimed it was with her consent. Both mentioned that the man had been killed for his insurance money. The next morning, after Talbot had left the house, Walsh went to the police.[9] It was reported that while the body was being guarded by the police Annie Walsh 'laughed, cried and prayed alternatively'. She was also heard to say, 'I am rid of the Walshes now; I will go back to my own people'.[10]

After independence the Free State used the services of Britain's hangmen. Members of the Pierrepoint family carried out all the criminal executions in Mountjoy. In this most unusual of dynasties Thomas, his brother Henry and Henry's son Albert all carried the title of Britain's 'Number One Executioner'. Each time a prisoner was sentenced to death in Ireland a letter was written to one of them requesting their services. Travelling to Ireland was always a difficult proposition for them. Hangmen were not popular in Ireland, especially in the case of political executions. The Pierrepoints travelled as light as possible (those on the look out for the hangmen often assumed they would be carrying the tools of their trade with them but these were kept in Mountjoy). Both Tom and Albert Pierrepoint carried revolvers on their trips to Ireland. When travelling they never discussed work for fear of revealing their identities but they did not skulk across the Irish Sea or make themselves inconspicuous. On the Holyhead boat they often joined in sing-songs. When Albert Pierrepoint was on his way to his first execution, which was in Mountjoy, he sang *The Rose of Tralee*.[11]

A previously undocumented chapter in the history of capital punishment in Ireland is the government's attempts to provide its own hangman in the 1940s. It was a delicate and secret matter but two letters remain in existence that shed light on this episode. One dates from 1941 and appears to be related to arrangements for a man, who was then a prospective hangman, to travel to Dublin. The purpose of the meeting seems to have been an interview for the job. In the letter the writer explained how he could be identified on his arrival in Dublin:

the leading campaigners was Sean MacBride. By the 1950s, international and national public opinion was turning away from the death penalty. Although the death penalty remained on the statute books (and the hanghouse at Mountjoy was readied on at least one subsequent occasion) the last execution took place in Mountjoy in 1954. On Easter Monday Albert Pierrepoint flew into Dublin from Manchester for the hanging of Michael Manning.[19] Manning, a 25-year-old carter from Limerick, was hanged in Mountjoy on 20 April for the murder of nurse Catherine Cooper (aged 65) in Limerick. Cooper had been found 'broken and battered' on the main Limerick-Dublin road on 18 November 1953. The next day the police confronted Manning. After some questioning, Manning, who had dried blood on his hands and sleeves, admitted to the killing. He gave the police a description of the attack, which he said took place while he was drunk:

> I saw a lady walking in front of me towards Limerick, on the left-hand side of the road. I walked behind her for a few minutes. I suddenly lost control of myself and jumped on her because I saw she was alone. She let a few screams, I knocked her down on the grass. I pulled her into the grass margin and stuffed grass in her mouth to stop her from roaring. She got quiet after five minutes, but she began to struggle again, and asked me to stop. She just said 'Stop, stop'. The next thing a motor car with lights stopped beside me. I got up and jumped over the ditch.

It emerged in court that there was a history of insanity in Manning's family. An uncle had died two years earlier in a mental home, an uncle of his mother had also died in a mental institution while at the time of the trial a cousin was a patient in a Dublin mental home.[20] However, after three hours deliberation, the jury returned a guilty verdict. 'Mr Justice Murnaghan then donned the black cap and sentenced him to death. Manning went slightly pale as the sentence was pronounced. His wife was outside the courtroom when the verdict was returned.'[21]

After the hanging, Manning's belongings were sent to his widow, Joan. A few days later the widow wrote to Governor Kavanagh. Her main purpose in writing was to request two copies of her husband's death certificate. She needed them to draw the pension. Of course she would pay for them if necessary. She also thanked the governor for the kindness he showed to both her and her husband. She wrote, 'we really adored each other and will until I join him in heaven some day. I can assure you Sir that Micheal [*sic*] is also praying for you all and he will return his thanks to you in another way'.[22]

The ending of capital punishment was just part of a trend in punishment which saw the criminal being treated more humanely. In 1895 the Gladstone Committee had begun the process of loosening the binds of prison life. The trend rapidly accelerated after the First World War. This was partly the result of the effect of imprisonment on Quakers who had been incarcerated as conscientious objectors. Appalled at the conditions in which they and other prisoners were kept, they also felt partially responsible – Elizabeth Fry was a Quaker and the model for the silent and separate system had come from the Quakers of Philadelphia. They declared that conditions were not what the reformers had originally intended and campaigned for their improvement. In 1924 George Bernard Shaw was invited to write the introduction to a book called *Imprisonment* which contained the thoughts of 'educated people' who had been imprisoned for their beliefs during the First World War. In it he lambasted the system of punishment centred on the prison. Shaw condemned the prison system as a 'horrible accidental growth' and not a deliberate human invention, and 'its worst features have been produced with the intention, not of making it worse, but of making it better'.[23] Imprisonment, he wrote, 'cannot be understood by those who do not understand freedom. But it can be understood well enough to have it made a much less horrible, wicked, and wasteful thing than it is at present'.[24] However, of more importance to the nature of imprisonment was the change in the relationship between the state and society caused by the First World War.

As hopes for quick, glorious campaigns faded and the Great War dragged on, European societies became almost entirely geared towards the war effort. People were called upon to fight, and die, in unprecedented numbers (even though conscription was not introduced in Ireland, nearly 50,000 Irishmen died in the fighting). The sacrifices necessitated by the war altered the terms of the social contract between the rulers and the ruled. While this was already changing – the institutions of 'civil society' such as the press and trade unions, were becoming increasingly powerful – the war speeded up the pace with which society was becoming 'democratic'. Indicative of this change was the liberation of women from the home to fill the posts vacated by men in the workplace, the call for 'homes for heroes' and the introduction in Ireland and Britain of virtual universal suffrage in the 1918 General Election. In future, society would be managed through an uneasy co-operation between the population and the government. Against this background, the conditions in which people were imprisoned were reassessed in terms of what was legitimate and justifiable in the modern age of mass democracy.

The silent and separate system went into terminal decline after the Great War. In 1922, while the new Irish prison system was in the throes of managing the Civil War, the English Prison Commissioners were busy reassessing silence. Experimenting with the complete abandonment of this policy, they inevitably reported few ill effects. The system was dropped 'on the general consideration that solitude has no beneficial effect, but on the contrary, does harm. The view has been held that it led to meditation over misdeeds, and repentance for them. But the commissioners think, on the contrary, that it usually leads to morbid introspection tendencies, to suicide, or to sullen, morose or revengeful feelings'.[25] In 1934 the system of silence and separation, which had been the reason for the construction of

214

Mountjoy, was abolished in Ireland. Nearly a century of prison practice had come to an end. However, its legacy continued for many years with 'old lags', unable to break ingrained habits, speaking furtively 'out of the corner of their twisted mouths'.[26]

The end of silence and separation may have been the most significant change in prison life but there were many others. In 1926 the General Prisons Board decided that the meagre prison diet was 'a relic of a past age in prison history in which it was mistakenly supposed that semi-starvation was a necessary element in the reformation of the criminal'.[27] A new and more substantial diet was introduced in Mountjoy in which Irish stew replaced suet pudding, bread replaced stirabout and tea replaced cocoa – according to one of Mountjoy's ex-prisoners, the joy with which that change must have been welcomed could only be realised by one 'who had suffered the cocoa'.[28] In 1927 the 'hideous plank bed' was abolished and each cell was supplied with a spring mattress on an iron frame. According to Mountjoy's Governor Kavanagh, this change 'was very welcome to the prisoners, although some of the old hands pretended that they had slept better on plank beds'.[29] Female cells were supplied with mirrors and the women were permitted to have cosmetics (before these concessions, according to Governor Kavanagh, 'it was pathetic to see some try to improvise a substitute for lipstick or rouge by dampening the red covers of their library books').[30] The women's coarse grey dresses were changed for cotton dresses in a variety of colours, while the heavy male uniform with wide black and grey stripes was replaced by a uniform of lighter material with a herringbone pattern.

The caged exercise rings were dismantled and the grounds of the female prison were laid out with lawns and flowerbeds. In winter, films were shown each week. In 1927 the first annual Mountjoy concert was staged. It was held each year on a Sunday near Christmas and was soon established as a key day in the prison calendar. Many of the top acts that were playing the Christmas season in the Dublin theatres filled the Mountjoy bill. Among those who graced its stage was the Army No. 1 Band (a perennial and popular feature), Jimmy O'Dea (who missed only two Mountjoy concerts in 30 years), Noel Purcell, Maureen Potter, Jack Cruise, the Bachelors and Kathleen Watkins. In January 1938, *The Irish Times*, under the headline 'Christmas Treat for Prisoners', reported that 'Jappe, the magician, performed a number of amazing conjuring tricks. The Whelan Sisters received loud applause for a beautiful display of step dancing'.[31] At the concerts the prisoners sat at the back while the invited guests and VIPs sat in front – evidently the prisoners liked it this way as, from this vantage point, they could watch both the show and the dignitaries.[32]

Despite the many changes introduced prison life was not completely transformed. Mountjoy prisoners continued to work at the same occupations as their nineteenth-century predecessors – tailoring, shoemaking, mailbag-making, woodcutting, baking, laundry work and basket-making. Those managing prisons were always keen to stress the improvements in prison life. They were less vocal about the deficiencies. Slopping out remained a nauseating daily routine. The majority still wore the prison uniform. The prisoners' underwear, shirts and socks were only washed every two weeks. The garments were washed together and sorted according to size so a prisoner was unlikely to get the same garments each time. In 1944 the medical officer wrote that one prisoner 'had discovered lice in his bed clothes. He actually produced these lice in a match box for inspection. This boy was clean in his own body and clothing when he came in here, and objected to the condition of the bed clothing'.[33] Another extract from the medical officer's journal stated that in many cases he found that the towels in the male prison 'were very dirty, and obviously used for some other purpose than cleaning the face and hands'.[34] In 1945 an article in the *Irish Catholic* stated that 'the Irish public is beginning to feel vaguely uneasy about the whole prison system as it now stands. More

ANNUAL CONCERT
MOUNTJOY PRISON
Sunday, 25th January, 1953

PROGRAMME

1. RECITAL BY NO. 1 ARMY BAND
   Conductor : CAPTAIN J. G. DOHERTY, B.Mus.
   MARCH : WASHINGTON POST .... Sousa
   SELECTION : THE DESERT SONG.... .... Romberg
2. AUSTIN GAFFNEY .... Baritone
3. PHYLLIS POWER .... Songs with Accordeon
4. KEVIN HILTON .... Entertainer
5. RORY O'CONNOR .... Irish Stepdancing
6. JOE O'REILLY .... Ventriloquist
7. DENIS FITZGIBBON .... " Din Joe "
8. NICK LEWIS .... Tenor
9. "CAPTAIN GREEN " Comedy Sketch
   DANNY CUMMINS, VERNON HAYDEN AND
   DERRY O'DONOVAN
10. JACK O'CONNOR AND LOUISE STUDLEY Solos and Duets
11. JIMMY O'DEA Takes up Nursing.
12. NOEL AND URSULA DOYLE .... Variety
13. JACK CRUISE .... Comedian
14. CECIL SHERIDAN and Members of Olympia Theatre
    Company .... Comedy Sketch
15. PHIL DONOHOE .... Songs at Piano
16. MAUREEN POTTER .... " Party Pieces "
17. NOEL PURCELL obliges.
18. CECIL SHERIDAN again.
19. BAND RECITAL : PART II.
    WALTZ .... " Destiny " (Baynes)
    SELECTION .... " Avenging and Bright "(Arr. Doyle)
    NATIONAL ANTHEM.
    Accompanist : ERIC BENSON.
    Compere : JACK CRUISE.

Programme from Annual Concert in Mountjoy Prison, 1953.

people than before are wondering if it is fulfilling its chief function of acting as an efficient deterrent to crime. It seems that our present system can never hope to do so'. Also in 1945, James Dillon TD called for 'the building of a new and more up-to-date prison than Mountjoy, leaving that site of famous and infamous memory to be incorporated into a housing scheme'.[35]

In 1945 *I Did Penal Servitude* was published. It was written by convict D. 83222. The author had worked for a charity, was addicted to gambling and had dipped into his employer's funds. He was sentenced to three years. *I Did Penal Servitude* opened the door on what had for many been the closed life of the Irish prison. Seán O'Faoláin, editor of the literary magazine *The Bell*, wrote in his introduction to the ex-convict's book, 'to read it is to be ashamed'. For O'Faoláin one of the most important aspects of the book was that it showed that prisons were not filled with 'patriots and incurables' but with men. He believed that its readers 'will be moved because they will suddenly realise this simple and forgotten fact'.[36]

Tracing D. 83222's progress through Sligo, Mountjoy and Portlaoise prison, *I Did Penal Servitude* detailed prison life from the viewpoint of an ordinary prisoner for the first time. The account is all the more moving, and important, for its lack of sentimentality. It is full of the humour, humanity and petty miseries of prison life. He described his public humiliation when waiting with two warders for a train to take him to prison – 'A crowd of people arrived for the train. Our seat was out on the platform. I could hear subdued talk behind me like the whispering at a wake'.[37] Describing the atmosphere in Mountjoy on the morning Harry Gleeson was hanged in 1941, he wrote:

> At last the day dawned. It was a shining summer morning, for Nature is no respecter of the macabre. From an early hour we, first offenders, were on our knees reciting Rosaries for the doomed man. As eight o'clock approached his time on earth became shorter; an hour, ten minutes, a minute. At last as the bell of a neighbouring church tolled the fatal hour we knew a life was passing

out. At that solemn moment every prisoner who retained a finer feeling or a semblance of sensibility shivered in his cell; while those old-timers who treated the tragic happening as an obscene joke, banging their stools against their cell doors, and shouting such cries as 'One off' or 'Another for the high jump', were the sewer rats of our economic latrines, whose subnormal state is not a slur on their progenitors but on the social system that suckled them. [38]

How the prison governor was viewed by warders:

In their eyes he is a strange god-like creature, so far removed from their ken that I doubt if they regard him as being flesh and blood at all. Dramatically they will recount some awe-inspiring remark of the Governor, and the other warders will drink in these words as if Jehovah himself had made some Olympian pronouncement.[39]

The prisoners in Mountjoy who vied for notoriety at their court cases:

When in December, 1944, 'Chinny' in a Dublin Court thanked the District Justice for giving him six months he concluded by saying: 'I hope to see you at the Christmas Concert in Mountjoy, my Lord!' This was reported in all the newspapers, and helped Noel Purcell to 'bring the house down' when it was included in the script of the *Mother Goose* Pantomime in the Theatre Royal.[40]

The day when the prisoners in Portlaoise were allowed to keep their cell doors open to listen to the radio broadcast of the All Ireland between Roscommon and Cavan:

I looked up and down from E4 to E1. Here were men doing sentences from six months to twenty years and life, all convicted of some crime, and still how human they were. No schoolboy at Croke Park had more enthusiasm. When Roscommon scored, how the convicts of the West cheered. When Cavan equalised, the guilty of the North-East raised the roof.[41]

The importance of Christmas cards:

When you get a Christmas card in freedom, very often you say, 'oh, damn, there's a card from Mrs So-and-So, to whom I forgot to send one. Now I'll have to send her a New Year Card!' At the best you exhibit your card until the Twelfth Day. In prison a Christmas card remains a treasure, not for days or weeks, but for years, and the sender is more truly thanked by the convict who receives it than anyone in freedom can realise.[42]

Prompted by the contents of *I Did Penal Servitude* the Irish Labour Party undertook a brief investigation of conditions in Portlaoise prison where D. 83222, a convict, had spent most of his sentence. Their widely-discussed report was published in booklet form as *Prisons and Prisoners in Ireland*, costing three pence. The report stated that the system was 'not the best system' – that in fact it was demoralising and outmoded. 'Nothing is done or, under the present system, can be done to improve morally or intellectually, the person sent to penal servitude.'[43] They felt that the time had arrived, 'when the grey ugliness of massive stone walls should disappear and persons sentenced to terms of penal servitude should be sent to a place of rescue rather than to dehumanising punishment'.[44]

The increased interest in prisons caused by *I Did Penal Servitude* and *Prisons and Prisoners in Ireland* accelerated the trend towards the improvement of conditions. At Christmas 1946, prisoners' families and friends were allowed to send them parcels containing fruit, cakes, sweets and other small luxuries. In the following year they were allowed to receive these once a month (the Society of Friends filled the gap for those with neither friends nor family to send parcels).[45] Chairs replaced stools in cells. In January 1946, the numbers of letters and visits to prisoners were increased. From July prisoners were unlocked from 7:00am to 7:30pm on Sundays and holidays. In August lights were allowed in the cells until 10:00pm instead of 8:30. Remission for local prisoners was increased from one-sixth to one-fourth of a sentence. Again in 1946, according to one Mountjoy report, an interesting development was 'the holding by the prisoners themselves of a few concerts on Sunday

evenings, with
"QUESTION TIME" as part
of the programme. In
spite of the dearth of talent, we understand they
have been very enjoy-
able'.[46] In terms of
importance the granting
of the privilege to
smoke was regarded as
the greatest concession
to prisoners. 'Next to
the loss of liberty', not
being allowed to smoke
was regarded as 'the

Vegetables growing in front of handball alley at Mountjoy Prison in the 1950s.

greatest deprivation suffered by the average prisoner'.[47] After
some deliberation it was decided that prisoners could have 30
cigarettes a week. Four were smoked each day from Monday to
Saturday and six were rationed for Sundays. Each day the
warders doled out the cigarettes and, as prisoners could not be
trusted with matches, the warders were called on to light their
cigarettes.[48] In 1947 the prison rules were updated. Up to the
time of writing, these rules still govern the day-to-day management of Irish prisons.

According to Governor Kavanagh, the changes in prison
life during this period were 'unspectacular but significant'. Of
his own efforts Kavanagh recalled after his departure from the
service:

I have always considered and tried to put into operation one single rule above all others: that everybody, prisoners and staff,
should behave sensibly, especially the Governor, and that the rules
should be invoked only when absolutely necessary. If I had any
policy in mind on taking over charge of Mountjoy it was that
everything possible should be done to help each inmate to recov-
er and retain his self-respect by treating him as a person in his own

221

right and not as a unit in a category, and by degrees to try and make the drab life of a prisoner a little brighter.[49]

Despite the improvements Ireland still lagged far behind international standards. A United Nations resolution on prisons declared that all prisoners should be treated with humanity and respect, that the essential aim should be reformation and that unconvicted prisoners should be kept separate from the convicted. In the run up to the passing of the 1960 Criminal Justice Bill, Captain Peadar Cowan, a former political prisoner in Mountjoy, wrote a booklet called *Dungeons Deep*. In it, Cowan painted a depressing picture of the Department of Justice's neglect of prisons. Each day two shillings and two pence was spent on each prisoner's diet – less than half the daily allowance in the mental homes.[50] Some ate their meals off enamel plates that were so rusted that the food leaked through holes.[51] After meals the plates were washed in warm water, without soap or detergent.[52] Prisoners were not supplied with bath towels. They took baths on sheet-changing days so they could dry themselves with clean sheets.[53] Cowan had nothing but good comments about the staff. What he did object to was the stingy management of the Department of Justice. Perhaps what best sums up the indignity of being a prisoner in Ireland was Cowan's clown description of a prisoner dressed in prison uniform:

> The majority of prisoners are short-term and consequently dressed in old worn clothes and boots. The old clothing is often stained, torn, dirty, ill-fitting and trampish looking. It is not unusual to see a newly-admitted short-term prisoner with torn trousers, either too small or too large, and without buttons on the fork. Some prisoners have half-mast trousers and others have them rolled up at the bottoms to prevent them dragging on the ground. The boots issued to short-term prisoners are often derelict and of different sizes. Many of them, through being worn by prisoners for whom they were much too big, have an Arabic turn up at the toes. The used shirts issued are sometimes buttonless, torn and ill-fitting

and now and again one may see a prisoner's belly and chest bare from the navel to the throat.[54]

However, the changes were driven by a desire to make prison life, if not comfortable, then more humane. The philosophy at work was a reverse one that was more concerned about what the prison should not do than about what it could do. It was summed up in the belief of English Prison Commissioner Alexander Paterson that prisoners were sent to prison as punishment, not for punishment. However, many continued to argue that punishment was the only thing the prison did effectively.

Prisons like Mountjoy had been vast cauldrons over which prison reformers, like alchemists, experimented with various concoctions to achieve criminal reform. Many ingredients were thrown in. Silence, religion, education, work, kindness and cruelty were all mixed in differing quantities. In Mountjoy, during the quiet years, education was being neglected but religion was still given an important role. Members of both the Legion of Mary and the St Vincent de Paul visited prisoners; on St Patrick's Day there was a special blessing in the borstal and the boys were given shamrock. There were frequent rosary classes. After the Second World War, Mountjoy's Catholic chaplain, John Kelly, was asked his views on religion and criminal reform. He concluded that although Catholic doctrine insisted that the root causes of crime were to be found in original sin, 'the psychologists are right in drawing attention, even though they exaggerated, to bad social conditions such as slums, dire poverty, bad housing, etc., and the elimination of these evils would be a great help towards reducing imprisonment'.[55] When the various penal prescriptions and recipes failed to find the elusive goal, the role of the prison in the criminal justice system was not challenged. The prisons remained but they were empty vessels containing only the faintest residue of the great purpose for which they had been originally conceived.

Generations of Dublin children grew up singing rhymes about Mountjoy. They went to bed early under threat that if they did not behave themselves they would end up in the Joy. However, apart from the games and fears of children, Mountjoy Prison receded from the forefront of Irish life. Mountjoy's role in society had diminshed. Fewer people were being sent there and the thoughts and ideas that made up its daily life were much less grandiose. A further change was in the area of politics.

Between 1924 and 1962 republicans represented an almost constant political population in Mountjoy. In 1925, Seán Russell and eighteen other IRA men escaped from Mountjoy. In 1927 a number of leading republicans (including Seán MacBride) were briefly held in connection with the assassination of Kevin O'Higgins. During the Second World War large numbers were interned and four were executed in Mountjoy for attacks on the police – Patrick McGrath and Thomas Harte in September 1940, Maurice O'Neill in April 1942 and Charles Kerins (hanged for the killing of Detective Sergeant O'Brien) on 1 December 1944. The executions of these men sealed the bitter division between de Valera and his former supporters. At the end of December 1956 the first of the IRA border raiders were imprisoned in Mountjoy. In 1957 J.J. McGirl was elected TD for Sinn Féin while in Mountjoy.

The prison remained part of the Irish political landscape and it was rare for Mountjoy to be without a political prisoner at any one time. However, after the Civil War, Mountjoy played a minor role in politics. Its number of political prisoners was generally small and the causes they represented had become marginal to most people. In 1928 Síghle Humphries, a republican prisoner in Mountjoy, wrote in her journal, 'Prison is the only house in a slave state in which a free man can abide with honour'.[56] It was a sentiment that most political prisoners would have echoed. However, in the same year a letter sent to her in Mountjoy read: 'You and your brave comrades deserve the highest gratitude from the ungrateful Irish. People are so selfish these times. When I see the interest they take in shows and boxing and Atlantic flights it disgusts me. Nothing at all about the sacrifices for Ireland.'[57] Over the next three decades no major republican movement grew up around prisons and prisoners.

The political history of Mountjoy after the Civil War pales in comparison to previous periods. However, the most unusual political prisoners in later years were the ten German spies held during the Second World War. Among these was Guenther Schuetz, alias Hans Marschner. Schuetz was almost fluent in English and had trained in Paris for intelligence work in English-speaking countries. In July 1940, he was parachuted into Wexford with a suitcase containing, among other things, a transmitter and *Just a Girl*, a novel by Charles Garvice that was to be used to send coded messages. He was captured soon after landing and interviewed by Army Intelligence. In the notes of this interview his landing is described:

> At first he had no sensation of falling, then the parachute opened, and for some little time he felt as if he was travelling upwards. It was a lovely night, and the clouds and a distant mountain flooded in moonlight, made the most beautiful sight he had ever seen. Then houses and trees began to rush upwards against him, and he landed, stunned with nose bleeding, in a field.[58]

Schuetz was captured the day after landing and was sentenced to seven years. He was initially held in Mountjoy with the other German agents (they were held in the Infirmary, separate from the republican prisoners who were seen as their natural allies). Although he often complained of being treated as a criminal he was particularly unhappy with his comrades' company. Shuetz was cultured and intellectual (one order he sent to Easons bookshop from Mountjoy was for Dante's *Divine Comedy*, 3 volumes of Shakespeare, Goethe's *Wilhelme Meister* and Victor Hugo's *Notre Dame*).[59] The others were largely uncouth, unrefined and openly antagonistic to Schuetz. Walter

Simon, alias Karl Anderson, subjected him to 'incredible insults and threats' while Willy Preetz, described in an official file as a 'proper thug' and an 'old lag', stole Schuetz's watch.[60] Schuetz, longing to be free from this unpleasant company, planned his escape.

The escape was organised with the help of IRA prisoners held in the main prison building – a convict employed as a wardsman in the Infirmary acted as a go-between. Safe houses were organised and detailed maps of the area immediately around Mountjoy were sent in via a republican prisoner. Incredibly, Governor Kavanagh approved the purchase of his escape outfit – Schuetz had tricked Kavanagh into buying a set of women's clothes for him on the pretext that he would bring them back to his fiancée in Germany when the war was over. On the night of 15 February 1942, Schuetz, having sawed through the bars on his window, made his way to the exterior wall accompanied by Jan Van Loon, a Dutch prisoner. Schuetz got over the wall (Van Loon was captured within the grounds of the prison). With a reward of £500 put up for his capture, Schuetz 'collected a mythology round himself equal to that of the Loch Ness Monster, having been reported seen in a dozen different locations'. Meanwhile, back in Germany, Schuetz was promoted to Captain. After six weeks on the run, he was captured in the home of Caitlín Brugha (widow of Cathal Brugha). Schuetz was returned to the company of his comrades who had been transferred to Arbour Hill after the escape. From there he wrote to Cáitlín Brugha's daughter Noinín, then interned in Mountjoy, of his unhappiness at being away from her:

> I need not tell you that the first few weeks were terrible and I was feeling just rotten but gradually the wounds are healing and I have not lost my sense of humour. How I do miss you every evening when the paper comes, I mean the crosswords, without your assistance it is a hell of a job, I can assure you.[61]

In the autumn of 1942 the spies were transferred from Arbour

GARDA SIOCHANA

£500
REWARD

The above sum will be paid to any person giving information resulting in the arrest of **HANS MARSCHNER**, German internee who escaped from custody at Mountjoy Prison on the night of 15th February, 1942

30 yrs. of age, 5ft. 9ins., complexion pale, hair dark brown, eyes brown, scar between eyes and on left cheek. Speaks English well.
Information may be given to any Garda Station.

Proportionate rewards will be paid for information concerning this man which will assist the Garda in locating him.

The 'WANTED' poster for Hans Marschner.

Hill to an internment camp in Athlone to sit out the remainder of the war. In September 1946, they were released and informed that if they wished they could remain in Ireland. Naturally reluctant to return to a Germany very different to the one that they had served, they began to set up new lives in Ireland. However, in the spring of the following year they were rounded up and prepared for repatriation. Most were returned to their homeland in 1947 to have their war careers investigated (they were flown from Baldonnel aerodrome by the United States' Air Force). Among these was Max Weber Drohl who remained in contact with Governor Kavanagh for a number of years. In June 1947, just a few days after he was released from custody in Germany, he sent Kavanagh the first piece of correspondence. It was a postcard of Nuremberg addressed to 'The Honourable Governor of "Mountjoy Prison"'. Two years later Weber Drohl wrote:

> Things here, have not improved hardly any, and we are not living at all, but just existing and barely able to crawl from one day to another, and I would be very glad and thankful, if I would be back in Mountjoy again, as a guest of dear old Ireland again and get enough to eat, instead of having to live here and stare in the Ruins, from morning till night, with a gnawing stomach.[62]

Among those not immediately returned to Germany was former Mountjoy escapee Guenther Schuetz. In 1946, while he was on parole in Dublin, Schuetz met Irishwoman Una Mackay. The two were married in May 1947. Later that month Schuetz was sent back to Germany where his new wife joined him. He later returned to Ireland to live (as did Van Loon, the man who had tried to escape from Mountjoy with him). The most senior German agent, Dr Herman Goertz, did not make it back to his homeland. Goertz had a history of anti-communism dating back to 1919 when he enlisted in the reactionary right-wing force, the Freicorps. He feared that if returned to Potsdam, then under the control of the Soviets, he would be executed.[63] On 23 May 1947, after a period out on parole, he was summoned to Dublin Castle and told that he would be taken to Mountjoy and then repatriated. Goertz committed suicide in the Aliens Office of Dublin Castle by taking cyanide. He was buried in Deansgrange cemetery, draped in the swastika.

The prisoner who is perhaps most associated in the popular mind with Mountjoy is Brendan Behan. In March 1942 he was lodged in Mountjoy for a few days after his release from borstal in Liverpool. In April he was arrested after a shoot-out with detectives near Glasnevin and was sentenced to fourteen years. He spent his first eighteen months in Mountjoy, was transferred

1961 unveiling by Eamon de Valera of monument to Republicans executed and buried in Mountjoy during the War of Independence.

to Arbour Hill and then released in an amnesty at the end of the war. Behan was back in Mountjoy on two further occasions for less politically motivated crimes – in 1948 (assaulting a Garda and using profane and obscene language) and in 1954 (drunk and disorderly). Behan was one of Governor Kavanagh's favourite prisoners. He later wrote that Behan was, 'Gay, witty, amusing, always in good humour, and his strong voice with its slight stammer, could often be heard above all others in the exercise yard or from one of the "D" Wing landings'.[64] During his first stay in Mountjoy, Behan made a career choice between being a revolutionary and being a writer. While confined in Mountjoy he began to write seriously for the first time, with Governor Kavanagh supplying him with pen and paper. Kavanagh also arranged for the writer Seán O'Faoláin to meet the young boisterous prisoner and help develop his obvious talent. In April 1942, O'Faoláin published Behan's first serious article, 'The Experiences of a Borstal Boy', in *The Bell* literary magazine. In Mountjoy Behan wrote his first play. Entitled *The Landlady*, it was supposed to be staged by republican prisoners. However, during rehearsals, fighting broke out between the actors and other political prisoners, angry at the foul language in the play. This project was abandoned.[65]

If Mountjoy played a part in shaping the life of Behan, Behan played no small role in rooting Mountjoy in the minds of Irish people. His best known play *The Quare Fellow* is set in Mountjoy at the time of the execution of Bernard Kirwan in 1943. Kirwan had been found guilty of killing his brother – according to one of Behan's characters, 'He bled his brother into a crock, didn't he, that had been set aside for the pig-slaughtering and mangled the remains beyond all hope of identification'. Throughout the play a prisoner in 'the digger' – the punishment cell – sings *The Old Triangle*. There are few Irish people who have not at one time or another found themselves at a party or in a pub in some part of the world belting out the refrain, if not the verses, of this song, which has entered the national subconscious and become part of what it is to be Irish.

Throughout almost the entire period covered by this chapter the management of the prison was in the hands of Seán

Sean Kavanagh's Mountjoy committal card from 1921.

Governor Kavanagh leaving Mountjoy on his last day.

Kavanagh, the longest-serving governor in the history of Mountjoy Prison. Born in Tralee, County Kerry, he became active in Sinn Féin after the 1916 Rising. During the War of Independence he worked in intelligence under Michael Collins. Arrested in January 1921, he was imprisoned in Kilmainham Gaol. However, after the escape of Ernie O'Malley, Frank Teeling and Simon Donnelly in February, he was moved to Mountjoy. Released after the Treaty was signed, his parting words at the gates of Mountjoy, which were often quoted in later years, were 'mind this place till I get back'. In August 1922 he was made deputy governor of Newbridge Internment Camp and in March 1923 the governor of Hare Park Internment Camp. At the end of the Civil War, he left the army and was appointed deputy governor of Mountjoy. In 1927 he was appointed governor of Limerick but the next year returned to Mountjoy as governor. Apart from a brief period in 1933, when he was transferred to Portlaoise, Kavanagh remained at the helm of Mountjoy until his retirement in 1962. In fact all of his family life was held inside the walls of Mountjoy. The events of three generations of the Kavanagh family happened in the Joy. Wedding receptions were held in the governor's garden and the grandchildren spent their summer holidays in the Joy. After retiring, he vacated his quarters and moved to Rathgar. One would have thought the change would have been welcomed but his wife, after years of peace and quiet in Mountjoy, could not get used to the noise that came with living on a street.

Epilogue: Anatomy of a Crisis

In 1997 I paid my first visit to Mountjoy prison. My aim was to try to step back in time and make a connection with Mountjoy's nineteenth-century past. Having researched Mountjoy's history for over two years and worked in Kilmainham Gaol Museum, I thought I was well prepared for the exercise. I was wrong. During the visit my thoughts were completely overrun with contemporary images.

During the un-lock of prisoners after lunch Seamus Cramer, an assistant chief officer and my guide for the afternoon, brought me into the male prison. When we stopped in the Circle the noise and movement of staff and prisoners made it feel like Dublin airport at Christmas. Seamus assured me, in a crowded-pub voice, that what looked like chaos was actually quite organised; from a booth which looked like a lost and found point, prisoners' visits were administered; prisoners queuing to my right were waiting to buy something at the prison shop; others waited to go to their workshops. Seeing my poorly-disguised unease, he assured me that I would be fine. I half believed him.

During the course of the afternoon we visited nearly every part of the prison. Present in most was the peculiar smell of Mountjoy. It is not an overpowering stench but a cloying smell that lodges in the nostrils and seeps into clothes. It is a curious mixture of decay, cigarettes, piss-pots in cells, daily slop-out, toilets at the end of corridors, underwear changed once a week, hundreds of people working and living at close quarters that mixes with the smell of food, disinfectant and detergents. Besides the smell of the prison, one is constantly made aware of the pressure on the prison. On the day of this first visit there were 767 prisoners in Mountjoy. There are about the same amount of prison employees. This sheer weight of numbers has translated into spatial demands. Every square inch of space has been allocated to some purpose. There is not a blade of grass in the male complex and the only areas left underdeveloped are the prisoners' exercise yards. Here the prisoners walk, sit in a corner or play football. If I were a poet I would have come up with a metaphor for the hundreds of white and orange plastic footballs that have met their end on the razor wire that lines the tops of the walls. The annual budget for footballs must be considerable.

In a room along the administration corridor leading to the Circle from the front gate, the daily count of prisoners is kept. Besides the regular counts of prisoners that are taken at set times throughout the day, every movement of a prisoner in or out (on Temporary Release, to hospital, to court, on bail) is recorded. At the end of each 24-hour period, the day in the life of the Joy is a series of entries covering several pages. On one side of this room hang countless handcuffs. On the other side are scores of sets of keys. Calls for handcuffs and keys and notifications of prisoner movements are continuous. There is constant action. In a control room separate from the cell complex, an officer sits quietly monitoring the prison's radio communications and closed circuit televisions. There is a small switch on the wall. While it looks for all the world like an innocent light switch there is a small sign underneath that reads 'GENERAL ALARM'. In the basement of B wing a dozen prisoners share a cell only intended for prisoners arriving late at night. I look in through the spy hole and one of the prisoners shouts 'Fuck off!' The walls in the padded cell are regularly washed to remove excrement and blood. Each day two cells on each landing are randomly searched for proscribed articles (the prisoners are strip-searched). In a section of the hospital a drug treatment unit puts a small group of prisoners through a detoxification programme. Another building, known as the Separation Unit, houses those who for their own safety cannot be housed with the bulk of prisoners (i.e. sex offenders and others likely to be attacked).

The main structures in Mountjoy date back to the Victorian era. Many talk about Victorian conditions in Mountjoy. However, during my numerous visits, getting a sense of its more distant past was very difficult. There were brief glimpses. The original prison buildings, both male and female, are solid, dignified and almost beautiful manifestations of misplaced Victorian ideals and values. Some of the old-style cell indicators are still outside the doors of cells. The requirement under the 1840 Prison Act that prisoners should be able to communicate with a member of staff is now fulfilled by a red-light system – a prisoner in their cell presses a button and a light on a board in the Circle informs the officer. On the wall of the Circle the prison triangle hangs in a frame – surely one of the most bizarre pieces of Irish heritage. The hang-house at the end of D wing is a chilling reminder of past policies.

It is easier to imagine Mountjoy's past when there are no prisoners. At night the wings are empty. The prisoners are silent in their cells, the warders looking through the spy holes. In the chapel of the original female prison, now in St Patrick's, I had the greatest sense of the past. From my research, the atmosphere seemed incredibly familiar to me. It was just as I had imagined and I could nearly see Superintendent Lidwell and one of her longest-serving prisoners, Catherine Hennessy, in the seats. But moments like these were few and far between.

The Joy was originally built to house prisoners before trans-portation. During almost 55,000 nights of continuous business in Mountjoy has been used for several different purposes – to confine drunks and prostitutes, to hang murderers, to suppress political dissent. Reflecting the demands and needs of society in the approach to its 150th anniversary, Mountjoy Prison once again reinvented itself. Mountjoy in the 1990s was an assault on the senses, an administrative nightmare and a logistical labyrinth.

***

It might seem strange to have ended the main body of this book at a time when the number of prisoners in Mountjoy was at an all time low, President John F. Kennedy had not yet visited Ireland and ex-Mountjoy prisoner Seán Lemass was Taoiseach. However, history ends where current affairs begin and it is in the early 1960s that we need to look for the start of the latest episode in the history of Mountjoy. It is a period characterised by a series of crises in crime and punishment in Ireland for which the name of Mountjoy has been synonymous.

This book finished at the end of the quietest period in Mountjoy's history. The years since Governor Kavanagh left his position have been a period of great change in Ireland. The country has gone through a process of modernisation. Since the early 1960s, practically every aspect of life in Ireland has changed almost beyond recognition. A rural society has become urban. A poor country has become wealthy. A culture based on community and Church has become fragmented and less religious. This modernisation has entailed both positive and negative aspects. From the experience of other countries it seems that one by-product of this process is the significant increase in the number of prisoners.

Between 1961 and 1964, the Irish prison population increased by 25 per cent. Although the increase may have been modest, it was the first significant rise in more than 100 years. It was also an ominous sign of what was to come. Until the end of the century prison numbers rose almost continuously. As they rose, so too did concern. An early response to the increase was the introduction in 1964 of an embryonic prison welfare service. In 1970 a Prison Act was passed which had, as its expressed aim, the rehabilitation of the offender. Legalising the detention of convicted persons in places 'other than prisons' it led to the opening of Loughan House for juvenile offenders and the Training Unit at Mountjoy (a self-contained prison with a relaxed regime for prisoners nearing the end of their sentence). It also led to the opening of what were called, more than 100 years after Lusk, Ireland's first open prisons at Shanganagh Castle and Shelton Abbey.

In 1961 Mountjoy held a daily average of 189 prisoners. In 1973 this number had increased to over 400. While political prisoners associated with the Northern Ireland Troubles accounted for around 100 of these, the bulk of the increase came from ordinary prisoners. In 1973 a Prison Study Group, funded by the Department of Psychiatry in University College Dublin, was established to find out the facts about Irish prisons. It was the first outside investigation into prisons since the Labour Party visited Portlaoise in 1946. During the course of their investigations they encountered a virtually closed system. The Department of Justice did not communicate with them and they were denied access to the prisons. Despite these obstacles the group published a report documenting the banality of prison life. It was also highly critical of the prison system and of Mountjoy in particular. Medical facilities were primitive. Prison education was virtually non-existent. Prison discipline was based on a process of degrading the inmate. There was a lack of willingness to investigate alternatives to prisons. At the same time there was confusion over the role of prisons in Irish society (should they rehabilitate or punish?). The prisons also gave little value for money. Each year it cost over £3,000 to keep a prisoner with 'no apparent results' – two out of three were recidivists.

As the 1970s progressed, conditions in Mountjoy deteriorated. One prison officer stated that 'there was nothing right about it'. The regime was strict and uncompromising for both prisoners and staff. Two attitudes serve well to illustrate the point. A prisoner found exercising was deemed to be either planning an escape or an attack on a prison officer. A warder speaking to a prisoner in a friendly tone was put on report for 'undue familiarity'. While both staff and prisoners were virtually without rights it was also a case of 'them' and 'us'. The atmosphere was one of oppression, rebellion and violence. The ordinary prisoners followed the example of the political prisoners who had fought the authorities to gain such extra privileges as more cigarettes and increased visits. On the other side a semi-official 'kicking-squad' dealt with unruly prisoners. The atmosphere was ugly yet if an officer was not seen to wade into a fight he could be branded a coward and deemed unsuitable for the position. A Prisoners' Revenge Group was established to target and intimidate staff.

By the end of the 1970s the prison population was twice the 1960 level, while the total prison budget for the country had risen from less than £1 million in 1971 to over £13 million. When Pope John Paul II visited Ireland in 1979 he addressed the bishops on the subject of prisoners: 'My dear brothers, do not neglect to provide for their spiritual needs and to concern yourselves also about their material conditions and their families.' Four years later the Council for Social Welfare published its report, *The Prison System*. In the report the Council stated that they were convinced 'that to a large extent it [imprisonment] is not effective, for while it "incapacitates" offenders for their period of detention it does not guarantee their reform in the long run; and that the extension of its use, as is frequently advocated in the interest of "law and order", will not achieve the desired result'. The final lines called on churchmen to help people 'to overcome their natural feelings of anger and revulsion and their desire for retribution, so that they can act towards the perpetrators of crime in conformity with the demands of the Gospel'.

In 1980, at the request of the Prisoners' Rights Organisation (an organisation set up to campaign for the civil rights of prisoners), Sean MacBride, a founder member of Amnesty

International, chaired an independent Commission of Inquiry into the Irish Penal System. MacBride was joined by some of the most capable people in Irish society. Among them was Patrick McEntee, Senior Counsel at the Irish Bar, Michael D. Higgins and Gemma Hussey (future government ministers) and Mary McAleese (later President of Ireland). Over a period of eighteen months the Commission received over 50 submissions (the Department of Justice again refused to take part). Its findings were published in 1982. In the preface to the report it was written, 'Neither the moral decadence of the age, nor the climate of violence in which we live could excuse our failure to scrutinise the effectiveness, or otherwise, of our existing penal system'. The report painted a depressing picture. Symptomatic of the attitude towards prisoners was the very low status given to education. Since it was introduced in the 1820s prison education has been recognised as a key element in the improvement of prisoners. In 1978 the education budget was a mere £35,000. More than twice this sum was spent on 'Post Office Services', while seven times more was spent on 'Travelling and Incidental Expenses'. In the daily routine, scrubbing floors and washing dishes were regarded as more important than education. Despite the platitudes about reform by prison administrators the commission came to the conclusion 'that imprisonment in Irish society is seen as a method of protecting society and punishing offenders'.

During the 1980s the crisis escalated remorselessly. A crime wave increased crime levels to seven times that of the 1940s. Reflecting external events, the daily prison population increased by over 60 per cent between 1980 and 1985. In 1984, nearly a century after it ceased operations as a criminal prison occupying the second stage of the Crofton system, Spike Island re-opened. While this attracted much publicity, Mountjoy epitomised the crisis. When issues of crime and punishment were discussed, Mountjoy inevitably came up. In 1983 a major prison officer strike (there were many small disputes during the industrial warfare of this period) and prisoner riot focused attention on the Joy. In the same year the long-standing principle of single cell accommodation was abandoned. The cornerstone of prison administration since the nineteenth century was overturned by statute. Doubling up became a nightly feature of Mountjoy life.

Spurred by rising prison numbers and the sour relations between staff and management, Taoiseach Garret Fitzgerald asked Dr T.K. Whitaker to chair an Inquiry into the Penal System in 1984. Whitaker had been the mastermind behind the first Programme for Economic Recovery in 1958, and at various times had been Governor of the Central Bank, President of the Economic and Social Research Institute and Chancellor of the National University. He was an eminent figure to lead the first serious attempt by the state to address the prison problem. The Whitaker Inquiry was also the first major government inquiry into the Irish prison system since the Cross Commission had heard Charles Stewart Parnell give evidence about his imprisonment in Kilmainham Gaol during the Land League campaign. In almost record time the Whitaker Report was published in 1985. It stated that the 'current mood in Ireland is one of serious concern about crime, particularly in its more violent manifestations: rape, murder, robbery with violence, attacks on elderly people, wounding and intimidation. The present level of crime is considered intolerable and there is a clamant demand that the authorities do more to discharge effectively their fundamental duty of maintaining law and order'. The report addressed the popular view that Irish prisons had become too much like holiday camps and that 'a little more experience of harsh and punitive conditions would reduce the crime wave'. However, it stated that 'It would be a strange holiday camp indeed which did not permit association with the opposite sex, which required its residents to work at labour not of their choice, locked them up for sixteen hours a day, insisted on solitary dining, offered crude and insufficient toilet facilities, provided no beer, no money, no privacy, restricted and censored letters, limited and supervised visits, confiscated watches, recycled clothing and subjected its occupants to random searches in the prison'. The report called for a dramatic overhaul of the system. Among the main recommendations were limiting the use of imprisonment as a penalty in favour of alternative forms of punishment and the establishment of a Prisons Board to take over the management of prisons. Readable, thorough and comprehensive, it immediately became a landmark in the history of the prison in Ireland. The Whitaker Report changed perceptions and began to shift the emphasis in prison administration. However, as much was left undone, 'but it says in the Whitaker report' became a familiar refrain in prison discussions.

When the Whitaker Report was being compiled, the crisis in Mountjoy was taking a new and grimly depressing twist. As heroin ravaged deprived areas of Dublin and other Irish cities, Mountjoy – ever the cracked mirror of society – was forced to confront the problem. The atmosphere in the Joy began to change from one of simmering violence to one of despair at wasted lives. 'Tough guys' were replaced by 'junkies' whose thoughts were pathetically ever on their next score. One ex-Mountjoy prisoner whose prison career went back to the 1960s recalled an instance when one of these new type of prisoners asked him what he was in for. When he replied that he had been caught with £70,000 worth of 'gear' the other prisoner became very excited. He pleaded to be supplied with some. The old timer was momentarily confused at the request, for while he was talking about computers the other was talking about heroin. Other Mountjoy memories are less amusing. With drugs came Aids. When the first prisoner to die of Aids left Mountjoy to be brought to hospital both staff and prisoners of Mountjoy saw themselves as possible future victims. At the time of the Whitaker Report the first prisoner to die of a drug overdose in prison was found in his Mountjoy cell. An abiding memory of one prison officer was the sight of one prisoner injecting another in the neck with heroin.

By the 1990s, crime and punishment became one of the most important social and political issues. Indictable crime had increased from 72,782 offences in 1980 to over 100,000 in 1995. In 1998 there was a daily average of 2,728 prisoners in Ireland. Crime stories sold newspapers. Cases of violent assaults and sex attacks were daily fare. Politicians fished for votes with promises of crackdowns on crime while well-known criminals with Chicago style nicknames – the 'General', the 'Penguin', the 'Monk' – seemed untouchable. The killing of journalist Veronica Guerin was one of the most significant events. Floral tributes piled up outside Dáil Éireann. People had become frustrated at the apparent immunity of the criminals. Temporary Release (TR) almost completely undermined public confidence. First introduced in the 1960 Criminal Justice Bill as a scheme to allow prisoners out of prison for special occasions – i.e. Christmas – by the 1990s it came to be the method by which the Department of Justice kept Mountjoy prison operating. Numbers in the Joy's 500 male cells exceeded 750 prisoners. As one prisoner was committed another was released to make space. The 'revolving' prison door turned the sentence of imprisonment into some sort of sick Orwellian joke. Prisons in general, and Mountjoy in particular, were no longer fulfilling even their most basic role – keeping people out of circulation. Another problem was the escalating costs associated with the overtime bill for prison officers. The public felt it was getting very little value for money from its prison service. For prison officers the taking of five of their number hostage in 1997 was one of the grimmest events of the period.

For many the first in-depth insight into Mountjoy came with the three-part television series, *The Joy*. In recent years a number of publications have shed light on the Mountjoy experience. The most consistent and productive writer on prison matters has been Paul O'Mahony. In 1995 he published *Crime and Punishment in Ireland*. In 1996 came *Criminal Chaos*. In the chapter 'Trapped by Imprisonment', he outlined the Irish over-reliance on imprisonment as a sanction against criminals. The next year his *Mountjoy Prisoners: A Sociological and Criminological Profile* was published by the Department of Justice. It was the first comprehensive survey of prisoners in Mountjoy. O'Mahony found that, among other things, just one-fifth of the Mountjoy population had been married, 50 per cent of prisoners had left school before the legal school-leaving age of fifteen, 21 per cent had more than twenty previous convictions, 42 per cent had used heroin in Mountjoy during their current imprisonment, one-fifth said they used heroin daily in the Joy and 48 per cent of prisoners claimed to have been assaulted at some point in their prison career by either a prisoner or prison officer.

Prisoners have recently been telling their own stories. Paul Howard's *The Joy* is the prison journey of 'a recognized heroin addict with HIV, [who] has spent almost all of his adult life inside. As a teenager he was first in St Patrick's Institution ... and then in the main prison itself. St Pat's was his primary school, Mountjoy his secondary school. All of the offences for which he was committed to the prison involved robberies to get money to buy drugs.' In the *Junkyard*, edited by Marsha Hunt, prisoners like 'Demo', 'Fiddler', 'Yogi', Paul, 'Botzy' and the 'Quiet Man' tell of their childhood, family life, 'the score', and criminal and prison life. As Hunt states, 'They sing a strangled and haunting tune with a repetitive refrain'. Like Gotzy says, 'Drugs, drugs and more drugs'. These publications tell of a period in Mountjoy's history very different from 'The Quiet Years' that preceded it.

During this period Mountjoy's governor, John Lonergan, has become one of the most recognisable media figures in Ireland. Lonergan entered the prison service in 1968. During his prison career he has worked in Limerick, Shanganagh, Loughan House, the Training Unit, Portlaoise and Mountjoy Prison. Governor of Mountjoy since 1992 (he was also governor between 1984 and 1988), he has been the single most important influence on the prison. After years of suspicion he introduced an open and humanitarian attitude towards prisoners and staff. Today there is a relatively easy-going atmosphere in Mountjoy. Prisoners have been given a greater status in the scheme of things. At the same time the prison officers have been encouraged to interact with the prisoners. They have ceased being mere disciplinarians. Many have become positive agents in the prison.

Governor Lonergan's influence in the prison has been immense. But he is perhaps best known for his efforts to influence the outside world. While recognising that his responsibility is to manage prisoners, he also believes that society should take its share of the responsibility. Early on in his Mountjoy career he came to the conclusion that neither he, nor the prison, would be used as a scapegoat for society's problems. He regularly points out to the general public that, 'They're your prisoners. They're your prisons. They're only there because you want them to be there. They're there in your name. They are also part of your responsibility and you are not going to throw all that responsibility over to me and say "it's your fault that A, B and C is happening".' To help educate the public about the nature of imprisonment he has thrown the doors of the prison open to the media, interested groups and school tours. Supported by the Department of Justice, Equality and Law Reform, many people have been given reasonable access to see for themselves just what is being done in their name. However, mice still scuttle down the wings at night and prisoners still commit suicide.

As I write this epilogue the news is saturated with coverage of a suicide in Mountjoy. At 4am this morning a prisoner was found hanging by a sheet. He was 25 years old and serving his first prison sentence. He had stolen a coat worth £40. Despite tragic events such as this suicide, the sense of crisis in Mountjoy and the prison system in general seems to be abating. To an extent the system has caught up with events that had been outside its control. Improvements have certainly been made, with more spent on the education and welfare of prisoners and greater accountability. In 1995 the Department of Justice set out over 53 specific proposals. Among the most important changes have been the establishment of a Prisons Board to manage prisons and the construction of new prisons. For decades the prisons were managed through a section of the Department of Justice. During 'The Quiet Years' this was adequate but as numbers and problems multiplied the small section dealing with prisons was overwhelmed with the issues that faced them. Many thought it remarkable that these civil servants, without special knowledge of prison administration, managed at all. The new Prisons Board harks back to the General Prisons Board dissolved in 1928. The first Director General of the Board is Sean Aylward. Responsible for the overall operations and management of prisons, he is answerable to the Minister for Justice.

In the last few years the number of prison places in Ireland has increased dramatically. A new female prison has been built at Mountjoy and a remand facility constructed at Clover Hill. A new prison has been opened at Castlerea and another prison is under construction in Portlaoise. Such additions may give the system a certain amount of breathing space to bring in further changes (one of the most talked about changes is the proposed re-introduction of in-cell sanitation in the male prison at Mountjoy). But no one is really too sure about the end result. This period of prison construction in Ireland is the first since the introduction of the separate system in the 1840s. This current phase of construction stands in stark contrast to previous ones, that were supported by penal philosophy. The current situation is different. While the extra places will improve conditions and ease the crippling overcrowding problem, few believe they will result in any significant decline in crime. Hardly anyone has confidence in the ability of the prison to change people on a sufficient scale. The recent crisis in the Joy showed once again that the prison has 'failed'. The overcrowding in Mountjoy is strong evidence of this fact. However, one must be careful. The issues of punishment and crime have always been complex. It seems today that they are more complex than ever. The prison has never done what it was supposed to do. While alternatives to the prison are put forward (one of the latest is the idea of community-based 'restorative justice' put forward by the Irish Penal Reform Trust), society seems transfixed by the prison. However, with more prisons being constructed infatuation with them is set to continue – the prison is dead, long live the prison. After 150 years of Mountjoy, that is nearly 55,000 nights of continuous business, it would take a brave person to bet against another 55,000 nights of life in Mountjoy Prison.

ENDNOTES

Chapter One: The Birth of the Prison in Ireland

1. Ekirch, A. Roger, *Bound for America, the Transportation of British Convicts to the Colonies, 1718-1775*, Oxford, 1987, p. 25.

2. Shaw, George Bernard, *Imprisonment*, issued by the Department of Christian Social Service of the National Council of the Protestant Episcopal Church, Brentano's, New York, 1925, p. 40.

3. 1782 Report of Committee enquiring into the state of Gaols and Prisons in this Kingdom, *House of Commons Journals* (Ire), X(2) 1782 pp. dxxxiii-dxxxv, p. dxxxiii.

4. 1783 Report from the Committee appointed to enquire into the present state, situation and management of the public prisons, gaols and bridewells, of this kingdom, *House of Commons Journals* (Irl), XI 1783-5, pp.cxxx-cxxxi, p. cxxxi.

5. The Parliamentary Register (Irl) III (2) 1783-4, p. 90.

6. *The Times*, 10 April 1787.

7. 1783 Report from the Committee appointed to enquire into the present state, situation and management of the public prisons, gaols and bridewells, of this Kingdom, *op cit.*, p. cxxxi.

8. *Kilmainham Papers*, National Library of Ireland, (NLI), Manuscript (Ms.) 11655.

9. 1785 Report from the Committee appointed to enquire into the present State, Situation and Management of the public Prisons, Jails and Bridewells, of this Kingdom, *House of Commons Journals* (Irl) XI (2) 1783-5, p. ccccxv.

10. *The Parliamentary Register* (Irl) III (2) 1783-4, p. 88.

11. 1785 Report from the Committee appointed to enquire into the present State, Situation and Management of the public Prisons, Jails and Bridewells, of this Kingdom, *op. cit.*, p. ccccxv.

12. 1783 Report from the Committee appointed to enquire into the present State, Situation and Management of the public Prisons, Jails and Bridewells, of this Kingdom, *op cit.*, p. cxxxi.

13. 1787 Report of Committee appointed to enquire into the present State, Situation, and Management of the Public Prisons, Gaols and Bridewells, *House of Commons Journals* (Irl) XII 1786-8 (2), dxxiv.

14. 1793 Report of Committee appointed to inquire into the Present State and Situation of the Public Gaols and Prisons, *House of Commons Journals* (Irl) XV (2) 1792-4, pp. ccccvii-ccccix, p. ccccviii.

15. Ignatieff, Michael, *A Just Measure of Pain*, The MacMillan Press, London, 1978, p. 81.

16. A Lecture by the Rev. H. W. Bellows, John Howard: His Life, Character, and Services, in Edward Pears (ed.) *Prisons and Reformatories at Home and Abroad*, Being the transactions of the International Penitentiary Congress Held in London July 3-13, 1872, Her Majesty's Prison, Maidstone, 1912, pp. 772-832, p. 788.

17. John Howard, *The State of Prisons in England and Wales*, 1777, p. 2.

18. *Walker's Hibernian Magazine* (hereafter *W.H.M.*), April 1790.

19. Howard, *op. cit.*, p. 66.

20. MacDonagh, Oliver, *The Inspector General, Sir Jeremiah Fitzpatrick and the Politics of Social Reform, 1783-1802*, Croom Helm, London, 1981, p. 53.

21. *Ibid.* p. 22.

22. Fitzpatrick, Jeremiah, *An Essay on Gaol Abuses*, Dublin, 1784, p. 43.

23. *Ibid.* p. 44.

24. *WHM*, November 1786.

25. *WHM*, October 1787.

26. *WHM*, May 1787.

27. *WHM*, October 1789.

28. *WHM*, July 1790.

29. *WHM*, May 1787.

30. *WHM*, December 1788.

31. *WHM*, July 1800.

32. *WHM*, July 1800

33. *WHM*, June 1785.

34. *WHM*, July 1789.

35. *WHM*, August 1787.

36. *WHM*, January 1792.

37. *WHM*, August 1787.

38. *WHM*, January 1786.

39. *WHM*, November 1799.

40. *WHM*, February 1786.

41. Henry, Brian, *Dublin Hanged*, Irish Academic Press, Dublin, 1994, p. 14.

42. *WHM*, November 1788.

43. Henry, *op cit.*, p. 13.

44. Collins, Henry, ed., Tom Paine, *The Rights of Man* (1791), Penguin, London, 1976, p. 268.
45. *WHM*, December 1788.
46. *WHM*, October 1790.
47. Henry, *op cit.*, p. 17.
48. *WHM*, February 1786.
49. See McGowan, James, The body and punishment in Eighteenth Century England, *Journal of Modern History*, December 1987, 651-679.
50. Foucault, Michel, *Discipline and Punish*, Penguin, London, 1977, p. 232.
51. Evans, *op cit.*, p. 113.
52. Report on State of Gaols and Prisons, *House of Commons Journals* (Irl) XII (2) 1786-8, p. dccxxxiii.
53. 1787 Committee appointed to enquire into the Causes why the Law respecting Gaols and Prisons has not been complied with in the County and City of Dublin, *House of Commons Journals* (Irl) XII (2) 1786-8, p. dxxxiv.
54. 1793 Report of the Committee appointed to inquire into the Present State and Situation of the Public Gaols and Prisons, op cit., p. ccccviii.
55. Fitzpatrick, (Sir) Jeremiah, *Thoughts on Penitentiaries*, Dublin, 1790, p. 41.

Chapter Two: Mountjoy: Ireland's Model Prison
1. Inspector General of Prisons, Report on General State of Prisons of Ireland *House of Commons Parliamentary Papers (HCPP)* 1819, xii.453, p. 6 and p. 12.
2. Howard, John, *The State of Prisons*, 1777, p. 242.
3. Association for the Improvement of Prisons, First Report, Dublin, 1819, p. 8.
4. Inspectors General of Prisons, Third Report, *HCPP* 1825 xxii.223, p. 14.
5. Inspectors General of Prisons, Fifth Report, *HCPP* 1826-27 xi.335, p. 14.
6. Evans, Robin, *The Fabrication of Virtue*, Cambridge University Press, Cambridge, 1982, p. 42.
7. A Statement on the Objectives of the Association for the Improvement of Prisons and of Prison Discipline in Ireland, Dublin, 1819, p. 4.
8. *Ibid.*, p. 5.
9. Association for the Improvement of Prisons, Third Report, Dublin 1822, p. 68.
10. Report of the Select Committee on Laws Relating to Prisons, *HCPP*,

1822 iv.67 p. 3.

11. Palmer, Major James, *A Treatise on the Modern System of Governing Gaols, Penitentiaries and Houses of Correction*, Dublin, 1832, p. 16.

12. Anon., *Queries on the State of Prisons*, Dublin, 1810, p. 7.

13. *Ibid.*, p. 10.

14. *WHM*, February 1786.

15. Association for the Improvement of Prisons, Fifth Report, Dublin, 1822, p. 68.

16. *Ibid.* p. 41.

17. Association for the Improvement of Prisons, Third Report, *op cit.*, p. 9.

18. Observations on the Expediency of Erecting Provincial Penitentiaries in Ireland, London, 1821, p. 15.

19. Association for the Improvement of Prisons, Third Report, *op cit.*, p. 13.

20. Society for the Improvement of Prison Discipline and for the Reformation of Juvenile Offenders, *Inquiries Relative to Prison Discipline*, London, 1818, p. 113.

21. Inspectors General of Prisons, Report in General State of Prisons of Ireland, *HCPP* 1819 xii.453, p. 7

22. Fitzpatrick, *op cit.*, 1784, p. 102.

23. Association for the Improvement of Prisons, Fifth Report, *op cit.*, p. 15.

24. Society for the Improvement of Prison Discipline and for the Reformation of Juvenile Offenders, *op. cit.*, p. 101.

25. Evans, *op cit.*, p. 117.

26. Returns of Reports by the Inspector-General of Prisons and Superintendent of Convict Service, on Complaints forwarded to the Irish government, between 1836 and 1842, *HCPP* 1843 xlii. 483, p. 41.

27. Evans, *op cit.*, 1982, p. 276.

28. Wilson, A., *Outlines of a Plan for the Improvement of Prison Discipline*, Dublin, 1830, p. 10.

29. *Ibid.*, p. 25.

30. *Ibid.*, p. 13.

31. Inspectors General of Prisons, Seventh Report, *HCPP* 1829 xiii.421, p. 7.

32. Wilson, *op cit.*, p. 26.

33. Hughes, Robert, *The Fatal Shore*, Pan Books, London, 1988, p. 86.

34. Costello, Con, *Botany Bay: The story of the Convicts Transported from Ireland to Australia*, Mercier Press, Cork, 1987, p. 161.

35. *Ibid.*, p. 162.

36. Chief Secretary's Official Registered Papers (*CSORP*), 1846 G7224.

37. *CSORP*, 1846 G12952.

38. *CSORP*, 1847 G8196.
39. *CSORP*, 1847 G5458.
40. Inspectors General of Prisons, Twenty-eighth Report, *HCPP* 1850 xxix.305, p. vii.
41. Inspectors General of Prisons, Twenty-seventh Report, *HCPP* 1849 xxvi.373, p. 5.
42. Inspectors General of Prisons, Twenty-eighth Report, *op. cit.*, p. ix
43. Shaw, *op. cit.*, p. 9.
44. Inspectors General of Prisons, Twenty-eighth Report, *op. cit.*, p. viii.
45. *Ibid.*, p. xv.
46. *CSORP*, 1849 G8196.

Chapter Three: Mountjoy Opens – the Moral Sewer Closes
1. Priestley, Philip, *Victorian Prison Lives, English Prison Biography 1830-1914*, Methuen, London, 1985, p. 29.
2. *CSORP* 1852, G1467.
3. Inspector General of Prisons, Forty-seventh Annual Report, *HCPP* 1868-9 xxix.221, p. 148.
4. Holtzendorff, Franz Von, *The Irish Convict System*, Dublin 1860, p. 54.
5. Evans, *op cit.*, p. 363.
6. Gibson, Charles B., *Irish Convict Reform*, Dublin 1863, p. 9.
7. *Ibid.*, p. 3.
8. *Ibid.*, p. 9.
9. Evans, *op cit.*, p. 391.
10. *CSORP*, 1850 G1769.
11. *CSORP*, 1846 G7224.
12. Inspector of Government Prisons, Annual Report for 1850, *HCPP* 1852 xxv.249, p. 57.
13. *Ibid.*, p. 72.
14. 1st Annual Report of the Directors of Convict Prisons, *HCPP* 1854-5 xxvi.609, p. 33.
15. Government Prisons Office Incoming Correspondence (hereafter GPO Corr.) 1852, 2032.
16. *CSORP*, 1852 G1799.
17. Inspector of Government Prisons, Annual Report for 1851, *HCPP* 1852-3 liii.277, p. 36.
18. Inspector of Government Prisons, Annual Report for 1850, *op. cit.*, p. 36.
19. 2nd Annual Report of the Directors of Convict Prisons, *HCPP* 1856 xxxiv.1, p. 52.

20. Inspector of Government Prisons, Annual Report for 1850, *op cit.*, p. 60.

21. Inspector of Government Prisons, Annual Report for 1851, *op cit.*, p. 53.

22. 3rd Annual Report of the Directors of Convict Prisons, *op cit.*, p. 69.

23. Inspector of Government Prisons, Annual Report for 1850, *op cit.*, p. 60.

24. Inspector of Government Prisons, Annual Report for 1851, *op cit.*, p. 19.

25. Inspector of Government Prisons, Annual Report for 1852, *HCPP* 1854 xxxii.477, p. 11.

26. 1st Annual Report of the Directors of Convict Prisons, *op cit.*, p. 17.

27. Inspector of Government Prisons, Annual Report for 1852, *op cit.*, p. 26.

28. *CSORP*, 1850 G3736.

29. *CSORP*, 1850 G2486.

30. *CSORP*, 1851 G4369.

31. GPO Corr. 1852, 1924.

32. Correspondence Relative to the Management and Discipline of Convict Prisons, *HCPP* 1854 (2) viii.167, p. 21.

33. *Ibid.*, p. 22.

34. Hughes, *op cit.*, p. 572.

35. Shaw, A.G.L., *Convicts and the Colonies*, Melbourne University Press, Melbourne, 1981, p. 353.

36. 1st Annual Report of the Directors of Convict Prisons, *op cit.*, p. 3.

37. *Ibid.*, p. 4.

38. *Ibid.*, p. 3.

39. Crofton, Sir Walter, *Convict Systems and Transportation*, 1863, p. 4.

40. Correspondence Relative to the Management and Discipline of Convict Prisons, *op cit.*, 6.

41. *Ibid.*, p. 3.

42. *Ibid*, p. 5.

43. *Ibid.*, p. 12.

44. *Ibid.*, p. 7.

Chapter Four: The Convict Question Solved

1. 1st Annual Report of the Directors of Convict Prisons, *HCPP*, p. 6.

2. *Ibid.*, p. 9.

3. *Ibid.*, p. 2.

4. *Ibid.*, p. 6.

5. *Ibid.*, p. 6.

6. Holtzendorff, Baron Von, *The Irish Convict System*, Dublin, 1860, p. 21.
7. 4th Annual Report of the Directors of Convict Prisons, *HCPP* 1857-8, xxx.389, p. 15.
8. *Ibid.*, p. 51.
9. *Ibid.*, p. 48.
10. Clay, Rev. W.L., *Our Convict Systems*, London, 1862, p. 43.
11. 3rd Annual Report of the Directors of Convict Prisons, *op cit.*, p. 70.
12. 1st Annual Report of the Directors of Convict Prisons, *op cit.*,p. 33.
13. *Ibid.*, p. 7.
14. Correspondence Relative to the Management and Discipline of Convict Prisons, *op. cit.*, p. 17.
15. Holtzendorf, *op cit.*, p. 70.
16. Gibson, *op cit.*, p. 11.
17. Sheehy, David, *Prison Papers*, Dublin, 1888, p. 41.
18. 2nd Annual Report of the Directors of Convict Prisons, *op. cit.*, p. 48.
19. Priestley, *op. cit.*, p. 122.
20. Four Visiting Justices of the West Riding Prison at Wakefield, *Observations on the Treatment of Convicts in Ireland*, London, 1862, p. 3.
21. *Ibid.*, p. 4.
22. 4th Annual Report of the Directors of Convict Prisons, *op cit.*, p. 39.
23. *Ibid.*, p. 23.
24. *Ibid.*, p. 39.
25. *Ibid.*, p. 44.
26. 1st Annual Report of the Directors of Convict Prisons, *op cit.*, p. 7.
27. Clay, *op. cit.*, p. 44.
28. 4th Annual Report of the Directors of Convict Prisons, *op cit.*, p. 51.
29. 2nd Annual Report of the Directors of Convict Prisons *op cit.*, p. 59.
30. Holtzendorff, *op cit.*, p. 47.
31. Clay, *op cit.*, p. 44.
32. *Ibid.*, *op cit.*, p. 6.
33. Hughes, *op cit.*, p. 488.
34. Whately, Richard, Archbishop of Dublin, *Thoughts on Secondary Punishments in a Letter to Earl Grey*, 1832, p. 36.
35. Holtzendorff, *op cit.*, p. 114.
36. *The Union*, December 24, 1857.
37. Gibson, *op cit.*, p. 33.
38. 5th Annual report of the Directors of Convict Prisons, *HCPP* 1859 (II) xiii pt. (II). 103, pp. 110-1.
39. Holtzendorf, *op. cit.*, p. 91.
40. *Clerical Journal*, November 23, 1857.
41. *The Morning Herald*, December 24, 1857.
42. *The Freeman's Journal*, October 17, 1857.

43. *Cornhill Magazine*, April 1861.
44. Four Visiting Justices, *op. cit.*, p. 1.
45. Wines, E.C., *The State of Prisons and of Child Saving Institutions in the Civilized World*, Cambridge, 1880, p. 236.
46. Holtzendorff, *op. cit.*, p. 92.
47. 4th Annual Report of the Directors of Convict Prisons, *op cit.*, p. 15.
48. Four Visiting Justices, *op. cit.*, p. 14.
49. Holtzendorff, *op. cit.*, p. 111.
50. *The Union*, December 24, 1857.
51. Pears, *op cit.*, p. 657.
52. *CSORP* 1853, 7242.
53. 5th Annual Report of the Directors of Convict Prisons, *op. cit.*, p. 89.
54. *Ibid.*, p. 90.
55. Four Visiting Justices, *op cit.*, p. 9.
56. Carpenter, Mary, On the Treatment of Female Criminals, *Fraser's Magazine*, January 1863, p. 42.
57. Taylor, Fanny, *Irish Homes and Irish Hearts*, London, 1867, p. 55.
58. Four Visiting Justices, *op cit.*, p. 8.
59. Carpenter, *op cit.*, 42.
60. 5th Annual Report of the Directors of Convict Prisons, *op cit.*, p. 90.
61. Taylor, *op cit.*, p. 54.
62. *Ibid.*, p. 57.
63. *Ibid.*, p. 56.
64. Wines, *op cit.*, p. 237.
65. *Ibid.*, p. 238.
66. Holtzendorff, *op cit.*, p. 158.
67. Taylor, *op cit.*, p. 53.
68. Wines, *op cit.*, p. 237.
69. Four Visiting Justices, *op cit.*, p. 15.

Chapter Five: Mountjoy Prison Life

1. GPO Corr. 1867, 110^1/2 *Mountjoy Male Prison (MMP)*.
2. GPO Corr. 1868, 760 *Mountjoy Female Prison (MFP)*.
3. Shaw, George Bernard, *Imprisonment*, Issued by the Department of Christian Social Service of the National Council of the Protestant Episcopal Church, Brentano's, New York, 1925, p. 4.
4. Cook, Charles, *The Prisons of the World*, London, 1891, p. 127.
5. 16th Annual Report of the Directors of Convict Prisons, *HCPP* 1870 xxxviii.539, p. 13.
6. Clay, *op cit.*, p. 43.
7. Priestley, *op cit.*, p. 164
8. Gibson, Edward, Penal Servitude and Tickets of Leave, *Journal of the*

Statistical and Social Inquiry Society of Ireland, April 1863, pp 332-343, p. 334.

9. McConville, Sean, The Victorian Prison: England, 1865-1965 in *The Oxford History of the Prison,* Morris, Norval and Rothman, David J., Oxford, 1995, pp. 131-167, p. 149.

10. Reports of the Royal Commission on Prisons in Ireland, Vol. II, Minutes of Evidence, *HCPP* 1884-5 xxxviii.259, p. 55.

11. Reports of the Commissioners appointed to enquire into the Working of the Penal Servitude Acts, Vol. III, *HCPP,* 1878-9 xxxviii.1, p. 829.

12. *Ibid.,* p. 830.

13. 24th Annual Report of the Director of Convict Prisons, *HCPP* 1878 xliii.641, p. 32.

14. 15th Annual Report of the Directors of Convict Prisons, *HCPP* 1868-9 xxx.413, p. 30.

15. GPO Corr. 1864 *MMP* (unnumbered).

16. GPO Corr. 1862 259 *MMP.*

17. GPO Corr. 1863 48 *MMP.*

18. O'Donnell, Peadar, *The Gates Flew Open,* Mercier Press, 1965, Cork, p. 7.

19. GPO Corr. 1857 385 *MMP.*

20. Sheehy, David, *Prison Papers,* Dubin, 1888, p. 48.

21. Milroy, Sean, *Memories of Mountjoy,* Dublin, 1917, p. 80.

22. *Ibid.,* p. 29.

23. Sigerson, George, *Political Prisoners Both at Home and Abroad,* London, 1870, p. 160.

24. 16th Annual Report of the Directors of Convict Prisons, *op. cit.,* p. 18.

25. 13th Annual Report of the Directors of Convict Prisons, *HCPP* 1867 xxxvi.273, p. 22.

26. Casey, John Keegan (ps. 'Leo'), *Religues,* collected and edited by Roe, Owen, (Davis, Eugene), Dublin, 1878, p. 109.

27. 13th Annual Report of the Directors of Convict Prisons, *op. cit.,* p. 22.

28. GPO Corr. 1872, 19 *MMP.*

29. Royal Commission on Prison Conditions in Ireland, Volume II, *op. cit.,* p. 20.

30. 18th Report of the Directors of Convict Prisons, *HCPP* 1872 xxxii.695, p. 33.

31. *Ibid.* p. 33.

32. GPO Corr. 1870 598 *MFP.*

33. Gibson, *op cit.,* p. 15.

34. 20th Annual Report of the Directors of Convict Prisons, *HCPP,* 1874 xxx.629, p. 31.

35. 15th Report of the Directors of Convict Prisons, *op. cit.*, p. 32.
36. Royal Commission on Prisons in Ireland, Vol. II *op. cit.*, p. 15.
37. GPO Corr. 1872, 19 *MMP.*
38. 20th Annual Report of the Directors of Convict Prisons, p. 36.
39. Penal Record (PEN) 1884/84.
40. 20th Annual Report of the Directors of Convict Prisons, *op cit.*, p. 30.
41. Falkiner, F. R., Our Habitual Criminals, *Journal of the Social Inquiry Society of Ireland,* August 1882, pp. 317-330, p. 327.
42. Report of the Inquiry into the Workings of the Penal Servitude Acts, Vol. III, *op cit.*, p. 935.
43. Report of the Inquiry into the Workings of the Penal Servitude Acts, Vol. I, *HCPP* 1878-9 xxxvii.1, p. liv.
44. Report of the Inquiry into the Workings of the Penal Servitude Acts, Vol. III, *op cit.*, p. 935.
45. J.M.G., *Irish Jails and British Jailers or Facts Versus Foreign Rule,* Dublin, 1872, p. 42.
46. English Prison Commissioners (PCOM, Public Records Offices, Kew, London), 7/386.
47. 13th Annual Report of the Directors of Convict Prisons, *op. cit.*, p. 46.
48. GPO Corr. 1872, 358 *MFP.*
49. 21st Annual Report of the Director of Convict Prisons, *HCPP* 1875.xxxix.613, p. 7.
50. Royal Commission on Prison Conditions in Ireland, *op. cit.*, p. 38.
51. GPO Corr. 1865, 40 *MMP.*
52. GPO Corr. 1859, 78 *MMP.*
53. GPO Corr. 1875, 1567 *MFP.*
54. 4th Annual report of the Directors of Convict Prisons, *op. cit.*, p. 48.
55. Ibid, p. 52.
56. 1st Report of the General Prisons Board, *HCPP* 1878-9 xxxiv.353, p. 105.
57. GPO Corr. 1862, 114 *MMP.*
58. *Cornhill Magazine,* April, 1861.
59. Taylor, Fanny, 1867, *Irish Homes and Irish Hearts,* London 1867, p. 56.
60. 24th Annual Report of the Director of Convict Prisons, *op. cit.*, p. 17.
61. 2nd Annual Report of the Directors of Convict Prisons, *op. cit.*, p. 66.
62. 23rd Annual Report of the Director of Convict Prisons, *HCPP* 1877 xlv.669, p. 36.
63. 4th Annual Report of the Directors of Convict Prisons, *op cit.*, p. 54.
64. *Ibid.*, p. 52.
65. 3rd Annual Report of the Directors of Convict Prisons, *op. cit.*, p. 70.
66. *Ibid.*, p. 74.
67. 23rd Annual Report of the Director of Convict Prisons, *op. cit.*, p. 17.

68. 3rd Annual Report of the Directors of Convict Prisons, *op. cit.*, p. 74.
69. 2nd Annual Report of the Directors of Convict Prisons, *op. cit.*, p. 65.
70. See GPO Corr. 1864, 556/566/1201 *MMP*, and, GPO Corr. 1869, 673 *MFP*.
71. See GPO Corr. 1862, 124 *MMP.*
72. Gibson, Edward, On Religious Toleration for Criminals, *Statistical and Social Inquiry Society of Ireland,* Journal Vol. iv, pp 443-5, January 1868, p. 444.
73. 13th Annual Report of the Directors of Convict Prisons, *op. cit.*, p. 20.
74. 1st Annual Report of the Directors of Convict Prisons, *op. cit.*, p. 39.
75. 3rd Annual Report of the Directors of Convict Prisons, *op cit.*, p. 71.
76. *Ibid.*, p. 70.
77. 10th Annual Report of the Directors of Convict Prisons, *HCPP* 1864 xxviii.481, p. 19.
78. 22nd Annual Report of the Director of Convict Prisons, *HCPP* 1876 xxxvii.643, p. 35.
79. GPO Corr. 1871, 113, *MMP.*
83. GPO Corr. 1861, 73 *MFP.*
84. GPO Corr. 1871, 288 *MMP.*
85. GPO Corr. 1859, 40 *MMP.*
86. Reports of the Commissioners appointed to Inquire into the Workings of the Penal Servitude Acts, Vol. III, *op cit*, p. 831.
87. Casey, *op. cit.*, p. 215.
88. 4th Annual Report of the Directors of Convict Prisons, *op. cit.*, p. 50.
89. 5th Annual Report of the Directors of Convict Prisons, *op. cit.*, p. 28.

Chapter Six: End of Reform
1. Wines, *op. cit.*, p. 44.
2. *The Economist*, 14 November 1857.
3. Crofton, Sir Walter, *The Criminal Classes and their Control: Prison Treatment and its Principles*, London, 1868, p. 11.
4. Wines, *op cit.*, p. 244.
5. *Freeman's Journal*, 17 October 1857.
6. 6th Annual Report of the Directors of Convict Prisons, *HCPP*, 1860, xxxvi.95, p. 7.
7. *Ibid.*, p. 14.
8. 20th Annual Report of the Director of Convict Prisons, *op. cit.*, p. 9.
9. 21st Annual Report of the Director of Convict Prisons, *op. cit.*, p. 10.
10. Crofton, Captain Walter, The Irish Intermediate Convict Prisons, a review of 'Notes on Colonel Jebb's Report on Intermediate Prisons', August, 1858, in the *Irish Quarterly Review*, Vol. VIII, pp. 1058-1102,

October, 1858, p. 1094.

11. An Irish Prison Chaplain, *Irish Convict Reform: The Intermediate Prisons, A Mistake*, Dublin, 1863, p. 52.

12. Royal Commission on Prison Conditions in Ireland, Volume II, *op. cit.*, p. 108.

13. Annual Report of the Inspector of Government Prisons for the year 1852, *HCPP* 1854, xxxi.477, p. 19.

14. 3rd Annual Report of the Directors of Convict Prisons, *op cit.*, p. 63.

15. 23rd Annual Report of the Director of Convict Prisons, *op cit.*, p. 6.

16. 2nd GPB, *HCPP* 1880 xxxv.211, p. 14.

17. Return of the Number of Male Convicts Discharged, *HCPP* 1864 xlix.27, p. 3.

18. 14th Annual Report of the Directors of Convict Prisons, *HCPP* 1867-8, xxxv.597, p. 19.

19. 15th Annual Report of the Directors of Convict Prisons, *HCPP*, 1868-9, xxx.413, p. 12.

20. 1st GPB, *op. cit.*, p. 15.

21. Reports of the Committee Appointed to Inquire into the Workings of the Penal Servitude Acts, Vol. III, *op cit.*, p. 777.

22. 20th Annual Report of the Director of Convict Prisons, *op. cit.*, p. 31.

23. Falkiner, *op cit.*, p. 318.

24. 4th GPB, *HCPP* 1882 xxxiii.661, p. 108.

25. Reports of the Committee Appointed to Inquire into the Workings of the Penal Servitude Acts, Vol. III, *op. cit.*, p. 837.

26. Wines, *op cit.*, p. 45.

27. 20th Annual Report of the Director of Convict Prisons, *op cit.*, p. 6.

28. GPB 1879, 7835.

29. Reports of the Royal Commission on Prison Conditions in Ireland, Vol. II, *op. cit.*, p. 340.

30. 24th Annual Report of the Director of Convict Prisons, *HCPP* 1878, xliii.641, p. 7.

31. 21st Annual Report of the Director of Convict Prisons, *op cit.*, p. 16.

32. GPO Corr. 1863, 17 *MMP.*

33. PCOM 7/249.

34. GPB 1906, 15434.

35. Bridges, Frederick, *Phreno-Physiometrical Characteristics of James Spollin, Who Was tried for the Murder of Mr. George S. Little, at the Broadstone Terminus of the Midland Great Western Railway, Ireland, on the 13th of Nov.*, 1856, London, 1858, p. iv.

36. Goring, Charles, *The English Convict* (abridged edition), *A Statistical Study,* His Majesty's Stationary Office, London, 1915, p. 15.

37. Report from the Departmental Committee on Prisons, *HCPP* 1895 lvi.1, p. 8.

38. GPB 1879, 13535.
39. GPB Corr. Register 1893, 680: January 16.
40. Return of Capital Convictions in Ireland 1859-1864, HCPP 1864 xlix.5, p. 5.
41. PCOM 8/212.
42. 36th Report of the GPB, *HCPP* 1914 xlv.711, p. x.
43. 33rd Report of the GPB, *HCPP* 1911 xxxix.779, p. vii.
44. 16th Report of the GPB, *HCPP* 1894 xliv.279, p. 3.

Chapter Seven: Neglected Biographies
1. *Convict Reference File (CRF)* 1859 H.8.
2. *CRF* 1870 D.9.
3. *CRF* 1870 D.20.
4. *CRF* 1856 A.6.
5. Gibbon, Edward, *The Decline and Fall of the Roman Empire*, Penguin Books, London, 1985, p. 115.
6. 28th Annual Report of the General Prisons Board, *HCPP* 1906 li.45, p. xvi.
7. 24th Annual Report of the General Prisons Board, *op. cit.*, p. 15.
8. 21st Annual Report of the General Prisons Board, *op cit.*, p. 16.
9. *CRF* 1873 J.3.
10. *CRF* 1870 B.1.
11. *CRF* 1872 O.15.
12. 23rd Report of the GPB, *HCPP* 1901 xxxii.597, p. 9.
13. *Ibid*, p. 17.
14. PEN, 1883/149.
15. Friedman, Lawrence J., *Crime and Punishment in American History*, Basic Books, New York, 1993, p. 233.
16. 33rd Report of the Inspectors General of Prisons, *HCPP* 1854-55 xxvi.307, pp. xxxviii-xxxix.
17. 13th Annual Report of the Directors of Convict Prisons, *op. cit.*, p. 47.
18. 20th Report of the GPB, *HCPP* 1898, xlvii.513, p. 11.
19. 35th Report of the GPB, *HCPP* 1913, xxxviii.451, pp. 2-3.
20. 29th Report of the GPB, *HCPP* 1907, xxxi.539, pp. 18-19.
21. Buckley, Margaret, *The Jangle of the Keys*, Dublin, 1938, p. 41.
22. 32nd Report of the Inspectors General of Prisons, *HCPP* 1854 xxxii.197, p. xv.
23. 1st Annual Report of the Directors of Convict Prisons, *op. cit.*, p. 14.
24. Falkiner, *op. cit.*, p. 318.
25. 2nd Annual Report of the Directors of Convict Prisons, *op. cit.*, p. 53.
26. 6th Annual Report of the Directors of Convict Prisons, *op. cit., p. 23.*.

27. Report of the Commission of Inquiry into the Reformatory and Industrial School System, 1934-6, Stationery Office, Dublin, 1936, p. 7.
28. First Report of the Inspector Appointed to Visit the Reformatory Schools of Ireland, *HCPP* 1862 xxvi.651, p. 6.
29. *Ibid* p. 5.
30. *CRF* 1857 K.2.
31. *CRF* 1857 D.23.
32. *CRF* 1862 Mc.6.
33. *CRF* 1859 H.11.
34. *CRF* 1872 W.15.
35. *CRF* 1882 M.72.
36. *GPB* 1895, 4776.
37. *GPB* 1895, 12728.
38. *GPB* 1909, 4295.
39. See *CRF* 1873 H.5.
40. See *CRF* 1902 J.13.
41. Waldron, Jarlath, *Maamtrasna, The Murders and the Mystery*, Edmund Burke, Dublin, 1992, p. 311.
42. See *CRF* 1896 D.72 and Wooton, Maria, *The Du Bedat Story: From Killiney to Kommetjie*, Tram Cottage Productions, 1999, Dublin.
43. See *The Times* 6 April, 1866, *The Irish Times* 20 April 1866, *CRF* 1863 L.8 and *CRF* 1866 L.6.
44. *The Irish Times*, 8 March 1901.
45. See *CRF* 1901 T.6.

Chapter Eight: Bastille I – 1865-1914

1. CRF 1857 H.15.
2. *The Times*, 12 June 1867.
3. Casey, *op. cit.*, p. 252.
4. Papers Concerning Political Prisoners 1865-1867, National Archives.
5. GPO Corr. 1865, 516 *MMP* and GPO Corr. 1866, 11 *MMP*.
6. GPO Corr. 1867, 367 *MMP*.
7. GPO Corr. 1866, 690 *MMP*.
8. GPO Corr. 1871, 149 *MMP*.
9. GPO Corr. 1866, 717 *MMP*.
10. O'Donovan Rossa, Jeremiah, *My Years in English Jails*, Ed. Seán Ua Cearnaigh, Anvil Books, 1967, p. 55.
11. *Ibid.*, p. 56.
12. *Ibid.*, p. 60.
13. Milroy, *op cit.*, p. 45.
14. Extracts from Letters from Untried Political Prisoners Confined in Mountjoy Male Prison 1867-8, National Archives.

15. J.M.G., *op. cit.*, p. 39.
16. *Ibid.*, p. 40.
17. Casey, *op. cit.*, p. 60.
18. GPO Corr. 1867, 564 *MMP.*
19. Crime Branch Special, 1894/S, National Archives.
20. Cook, Charles, *The Prisons of the World*, London, 1891, p. 127.
21. GPB 1892, 15801.
22. CRF 1899 F.18.
23. Letter written by James Connolly in Mountjoy Prison, 3 September 1913, Kilmainham Gaol Archives.
24. *Daily Sketch*, 16 October 1913.
25. Edwards, Ruth Dudley, *James Connolly*, Gill and Macmillan, Dublin, 1981, p. 110.
26. *Freeman's Journal*, 1 December 1913.
27. Lawrenson, Swanton Daisy, *Emerging from the Shadow, The Lives of Sarah Anne Lawrenson and Lucy Olive Kingston*, Attic Press, Dublin, 1994, p. 58.
28. GPB 1915, 7451.
29. GPB Suffragettes, File H, National Archives.
30. GPB Suffragettes, Folder 5, National Archives.
31. GPB Suffragettes, File C, National Archives.
32. GPB Suffragettes, File L, National Archives.

Chapter Nine: Bastille II – 1914-1924
1. GPB 1918, 1181.
2. GPB 1916, 1049.
3. Green, Max S., Our Ideals and Methods, *The New Ireland Review*, Vol. III March-August 1895, pp. 156-162, p. 156.
4. *The Irish Times*, 3 March 1922.
5. *The Times, 29 December 1922.*
6. See GPB Corr. Register, 4 May - 7 August 1919.
7. *The Times*, 28 September 1917.
8. *Daily Mail*, 1 October 1917.
9. GPB 1919, 1953.
10. GPB 1920, 4132.
11. Prisons Committee Minute Book 1916-20, Dublin City Archives.
12. *GPB* 1920, 4132.
13. RF 1934 16/121, Dept. of Justice Papers, National Archives.
14. *GPB* 1919, 4677.
15. Milroy, *op. cit.*, p. 4.
16. RF 1934 16/121, Dept. of Justice Papers, National Archives.
17. *GPB* 1919, 4677.

18. *GPB* 1921, 9210.
19. *The Irish Times*, 31 March 1919.
20. *GPB* 1919, 1234.
21. *Belfast Newsletter*, 1 January 1919.
22. *GPB* 1919, 4677.
23. Republican cartoon of escape from Mountjoy in 1919, Kilmainham Gaol Museum Archive.
24. War Office (WO), O35/56/B, Public Records Office (PRO), London.
25. WO/71/363.
26. O'Luing, Sean, Manuscript, NLI, Accession number 5140.
27. A note signed by fellow prisoners given to Patrick Moran the night before his execution, Kilmainham Gaol Museum Archive.
28. Last letter of Thomas Bryan, 13 March 1921, Kilmainham Gaol Museum Archive.
29. *Freeman's Journal*, 15 March 1921.
30. *Freeman's Journal*, 15 March 1921.
31. *GPB* 1921, 2221.
32. WO 71/360.
33. *The Irish Times*, 31 May 1921.
34. *The Irish Times*, 8 June 1921.
35. O'Mahony, Sean, *Frongoch, University of Revolution*, Dublin, 1987, p. 97.
36. *GPB* Hungerstrikers 7406 and 7451, NLI.
37. Buckley, *op. cit.*, p. vii.
38. *Ibid.*, p. 28.
39. *Ibid*, p. 40.
40. *Ibid.*, p. 51.
41. *The Trumpeter* magazine, Ms. 21121, NLI.
42. Dept. of the Taoiseach Files, S. 1884B, National Archives.
43. H17/3, Department of Justice Files, National Archives.
44. Dept. of the Taoiseach Files, S. 1369/3.
45. Dept of the Taoiseach Files, S. 1369/3.
46. Christina Doyle Collection, Ms. 5815, NLI.
47. Frank Gallagher papers, Ms. 18356 (2), NLI.

Chapter Ten: 1924-1962: The Quiet Years

1. Department of Justice Papers, H78/17, National Archives.
2. Annual Report of the General Prisons Board for the year 1923-24, p. vi.
3. Annual Report on Prisons for the year 1930, p. 6.
4. Annual Report on Prisons for the year 1957, p. 3.
5. Annual Report on Prisons for the year 1955, p. 21.

6. Annual Report on Prisons for the year 1958, p. 20.
7. Annual Report on Prisons for the year 1954, p. 5.
8. Annual Report on Prisons for the year 1961, p. 20.
9. *The Irish Times*, 10 July 1925.
10. *The Irish Times*, 11 July 1925.
11. Pierrepoint, Albert, *Executioner: Pierrepoint*, Coronet Books, London, 1977, p. 105.
12. Kavanagh Papers.
13. Kavanagh Papers.
14. Pierrepoint, *op. cit.*, p. 158.
15. Kavanagh Papers.
16. Pierrepoint, *op. cit.*, p. 158.
17. *Ibid*, p. 159.
18. *Ibid*, p. 160.
19. Kavanagh Papers.
20. *The Irish Times*, 16 February 1954.
21. *The Irish Times*, 18 February 1954.
22. Kavanagh Papers.
23. Shaw, op. cit., p. 42.
24. *Ibid*, p. 50.
25. PCOM 7/312.
26. D. 83222, *I Did Penal Servitude*, Metropolitan Publishing, Dublin, 1945, p. 200.
27. Department of Justice Papers, National Archives, RF 1934 16/129 (1).
28. *Irish Press*, 29 November 1938.
29. Kavanagh Papers.
30. Kavanagh Papers.
31. *The Irish Times*, 1 January 1938.
32. Kavanagh Papers.
33. Department of Justice papers 1934 16/49.
34. Department of Justice papers 1934 16/49.
35. Department of Justice papers RF 1934 16/74 Part 1A.
36. D. 83222, *op. cit.*, p. v.
37. *Ibid*, p. 19.
38. *Ibid.*, p. 99.
39. *Ibid*, p. 23.
40. *Ibid*, p. 80.
41. *Ibid*, p. 162.
42. *Ibid*, p. 185.
43. *Prisons and Prisoners in Ireland*, p. 13.
44. *Ibid*, p.14.
45. Department of Justice papers 16/450.

46. Annual Report on Prisons for the year 1946, p. 16.
47. Annual Report on Prisons for the year 1947, p. 17.
48. Department of Justice papers 16/470 Part A.
49. Kavanagh Papers.
50. Cowan, Peader, *Dungeons Deep,* 1960, p. 8.
51. *Ibid*, p. 10.
52. *Ibid*, p. 11.
53. *Ibid*, p. 16.
54. *Ibid*, p. 4.
55. Department of Justice Papers 16/423.
56. UCD Archives, Sighle Humphries Papers, P 106/1068.
57. UCD Archives Sighle Humphries Papers, P 106/1084/37.
58. Military Archives G2/1722.
59. Military Archives G2/1722.
60. Military Archives G2/X/0703.
61. Military Archives G2/X/0703 Part 1.
62. Kavanagh Papers.
63. Military Archives G2/1722.
64. Kavanagh, Sean, In Prison, in *The World of Brendan Behan*, ed. McCann, Sean, Four Square, London, 1965, pp. 67-70, p. 67.
65. O'Connor, Ulick, *Brendan Behan*, Granada, London, 1979, p. 74.

BIBLIOGRAPHY

A: *Manuscripts*
B: *Official Reports and Papers*
C: *Books*
D: *Articles*

A: *Manuscripts*

Sean Kavanagh Papers
Assorted collection of notes, letters, articles and files belonging to Sean Kavanagh, Governor of Mountjoy Prison 1927-1962.
Kilmainham Gaol Museum Archive
Republican cartoon of escape from Mountjoy in 1919.
A note signed by fellow prisoners, given to Patrick Moran the night before his execution.
Last letter of Thomas Bryan, 13 March 1921.
Letter written by James Connolly in Mountjoy Prison, 3 September 1913.
National Archives
i. Chief Secretary's Official Registered Papers (CSORP) – 1846 G7224, 1846 G12952, 1847 G5458, 1847 G8196, 1849 G8196, 1850 G1769, 1850 G2486, 1850 G3736, 1851 G4369, 1852 G1467, 1852 G1799, 1853, 7242.
ii. Convict Reference Files (CRF) – 1856 A.6, 1857 D.23, 1857 H.15, 1857 K.2, 1859 H.8, 1859 H.11, 1862 Mc.6, 1863 L.8, 1866 L.6, 1870 B.1, 1870 D.9, 1870 D.20, 1872 O.15, 1872 W.15, 1873 H.5, 1873 J.3, 1882 M.72, 1896 D.72, 1899 F.18, 1901 T.6, 1902 J.13.
iii. Crime Branch Special, 1894/S.
iv. Department of the Taoiseach Files – S. 1369/3, S. 1884B,
v. Department of Justice Files – H17/3, H78/17, Registered File (RF)

265

1934 16/49, R. F. 1934 16/74 Part 1A, R. F. 1934 16/121, R. F. 16/423, R. F. 16/450.

vi. Extracts from Letters from Untried Political Prisoners Confined in Mountjoy Male Prison 1865-7.

vii. Government Prisons Office (GPO) Correspondence – 1852/1924 Mountjoy Male Prison (MMP), 1852/2032 MMP, 1857/385 MMP, 1859/40 MMP, 1859/78 MMP, 1861/73 Mountjoy Female Prison (MFP), 1862/114 MMP, 1862/124 MMP, 1862/259 MMP, 1863/17 MMP, 1863/48 MMP, 1864 MMP (unnumbered), 1864/556 MMP, 1864/566 MMP, 1864/1201 MMP, 1865/40 MMP, 1865/516 (MMP), 1866/11 MMP, 1866/690 MMP, 1866/717 MMP, 1867/110^{1}/2 MMP, 1867/367 MMP, 1867/564 MMP, 1868/760 MFP, 1869/673 MFP, 1870/598 MFP, 1871/113 MMP, 1871/149 MMP, 1871/288 MMP, 1872/19 MMP, 1872/358 MFP, 1875/1567 MFP.

viii. General Prisons Board (GPB) Correspondence Register – 1893, 680: 16 January 1919, 4 May-7 August.

ix. GPB Hungerstrikers – Files 7406 and 7451.

x. GPB Files 1879/7835, 1879/13535, 1892/15801, 1906/15434, 1915/7451, 1916/1049, 1919/1234, 1919/4677, 1918/1181, 1919/1953, 1920/4132, 1921/2221, 1921/9210,

xi. GPB Suffragettes – Files C, H and L and Folder 5.

xii. Penal Records (PEN), 1883/149, 1884/84.

National Library

i. O'Luing, Sean, Manuscript, Accession number 5140, interviews with Mountjoy prisoners before their executions on 14 March 1921.

ii. Ms. 5815 – Christina Doyle Collection, containing typewritten documents dealing with Irish political prison conditions 1923-4.

iii. Ms. 11655 – Kilmainham Papers.

iv. Ms. 18356 – Frank Gallagher papers.

v. Ms. 21121 – The Trumpeter Volume 1, number 2, new series Mountjoy 3 December 1922. A Miscellany in various hands with a number of pieces written by Frank Gallagher.

Dublin City Archives

i. Minute book of Mountjoy Prison Committee 1916-1920.

University College Dublin Archives

i. Sighle Humphries Papers, P 106/1068, P 106/1084/37.

Military Archives

i. Files relating to German World War II prisoners – G2/1722, G2/X/0703.

Bibliography

Public Record Office, London
i. Prison Commissioner Files (PCOM) – 7/312, 7/249, 8/212.
ii. War Office Files (WO)– 35/56/B, 71/360, 71/363.

B: *Official Reports and Papers*

Pre-1800
1782 Report of Committee enquiring into the state of Gaols and Prisons in this Kingdom, *House of Commons Journals* (Ire), X(2) 1782 pp. dxxxii.-dxxxv.
1783 Report from the Committee appointed to enquire into the present state, situation and management of the public prisons, gaols and bridewells, of this kingdom, *House of Commons Journals* (Irl), XI 1783-5 pp. cxxx-cxxxi.
The Parliamentary Register (Irl) III(2) 1783-4 , p. 90.
1785 Report from the Committee appointed to enquire into the present State, Situation and Management of the Public Prisons, Jails and Bridewells, of this Kingdom, *House of Commons Journals* (Irl) XI (2) 1783-5, p. ccccxv.
1787 Report of Committee appointed to enquire into the present State, Situation and management of the Public Prisons, Gaols and Bridewells, *House of Commons Journals* (Irl) XII 1786-8 (2), p. dxxiv.
Report on State of Gaols and Prisons, *House of Commons Journals* (Irl) XII (2) 1786-8, p. dccxxxiii.
1787 Committee appointed to enquire into the Causes why the Law respecting Gaols and Prisons has not been complied with in the County and City of Dublin, *House of Commons Journals* (Irl) XII (2) 1786-8, p. dxxxiv.
1793 Report of Committee appointed to inquire into the Present State and Situation of the Public Gaols and Prisons, *House of Commons Journals* (Irl) XV 1793-4 (2), p. ccccviii.

1800-1922
Report of the Inspector General of Prisons, House of Commons Parliamentary Papers (*HCPP*) 1819 xii.453.
Abstract Reports of Inspector General of prisons 1815-1820, *HCPP* 1821 xx.159.
Annual Reports of the Inspectors General of Prisons, *HCPP* 1823-1878.

Annual Reports of the Inspector of Government Prisons, *HCPP* 1850-1852.

Annual Reports of the Directors of Convict Prisons, *HCPP* 1854-1878.

Annual Reports of the General Prisons Board, *HCPP* 1878-1921.

Correspondence Relative to the Management and Discipline of Convict Prisons, *HCPP* 1854 (2) viii.167.

First Report of the Inspector Appointed to Visit the Reformatory Schools of Ireland, 1862, *HCPP* 1862 xxvi.651.

Return of the Number of Male Convicts Discharged, *HCPP* 1864 xlix.27.

Return of Capital Convictions in Ireland 1859-1864, *HCPP* 1864 xlix.5.

Reports of the Commissioners appointed to inquire into the Working of the Penal Servitude Acts, Vol I, *HCPP* 1878-9 xxxvii.1 and Vol. III, *HCPP*, 1878-9 xxxviii.1.

Reports of the Royal Commission on Prison Conditions in Ireland, Vol. II, Minutes of Evidence, *HCPP*, 1884-5, xxxviii.259.

Report from the Departmental Committee on Prisons, *HCPP* 1895 lvi.1.

1922-present

Annual Reports on Prisons, Department of Justice.

Report of the Commission of Inquiry into the Reformatory and Industrial School System, 1934-6, Stationery Office, Dublin, 1936.

Rules for the Government of Prisons, Stationery Office, Dublin, 1947.

Report of the Committee of Inquiry into the Penal System (Whitaker Report), Stationary Office, Dublin, July 1985.

Mountjoy Prisoners: A Sociological and Criminological Profile, O'Mahony, Paul, Stationery Office, Dublin, 1997.

C: Books

An Irish Prison Chaplain, *Irish Convict Reform: The Intermediate Prisons, A Mistake*, Dublin, 1863.

Anon., *Observations on the Expediency of Erecting Provincial Penitentiaries in Ireland*, London, 1821

Barry, Tom, *Guerilla Days in Ireland*, *Irish Press* Limited, Dublin, 1949.

Bridges, Frederick, *Phreno-Physiometrical Characteristics of James Spollin, Who Was tried for the Murder of Mr. George S. Little, at the Broadstone Terminus of the Midland Great Western Railway, Ireland, on the 13th of Nov., 1856*, London, 1858.

Bibliography

Buckley, Margaret, *The Jangle of the Keys*, Dublin, 1938.

Casey, John Keegan (ps. 'Leo'), *Reliques*, collected and edited by Roe, Owen (aka Davis, Eugene), Dublin 1878.

Cook, Charles, *The Prisons of the World*, London, 1891.

Costello, Con, *Botany Bay: The Story of the Convicts Transported from Ireland to Australia*, Mercier Press, Cork, 1987.

D. 83222, *I Did Penal Servitude*, Metropolitan Publishing, Dublin, 1945.

Edwards, Ruth Dudley, *James Connolly*, Gill and Macmillan, Dublin, 1981.

Ekirch, A. Roger, *Bound for America, the Transportation of British Convicts to the Colonies, 1718-1775*, Oxford, 1987.

Evans, Robin, *The Fabrication of Virtue*, Cambridge University Press, Cambridge, 1982.

Fitzpatrick, Jeremiah, *An Essay on Gaol Abuses*, Dublin, 1784.

Fitzpatrick, Sir Jeremiah, *Thoughts on Penitentiaries*, Dublin, 1790.

Foucault, Michel, *Discipline and Punish*, Penguin, London, 1977.

Four Visiting Justices of the West Riding Prison at Wakefield, *Observations on the Treatment of Convicts in Ireland*, 1862.

Gallagher, Frank, *Days of Fear*, John Murray, London, 1928.

Gibson, Charles B., *Irish Convict Reform*, Dublin, 1863.

Goring, Charles, *The English Convict* (abridged edition), A *Statistical Study*, Her Majesty's Stationary Office, London, 1915.

Henry, Brian, *Dublin Hanged*, Irish Academic Press, Dublin, 1994.

Holtzendorff, Baron Von, *The Irish Convict System*, Dublin, 1860.

Howard, Paul, *The Joy, Mountjoy Jail: the Shocking, True Story of Life Inside*, O'Brien Press, Dublin, 1996.

Howard, John, *The State of Prisons*, 1777.

Hughes, Robert, *The Fatal Shore*, Pan Books, London, 1988.

Hunt, Marsha, (ed), *The Junk Yard*, Mainstream Publishing, Edinburgh, 1999.

Ignatieff, Michael, *A Just Measure of Pain*, MacMillan, London, 1978.

J.M.G., *Irish Jails and British Jailers or Facts Versus Foreign Rule*, Dublin, 1872.

Lawrenson, Swanton Daisy, *Emerging from the Shadow, The Lives of Sarah Anne Lawrenson and Lucy Olive Kingston*, Attic Press, Dublin, 1994.

MacDonagh, Oliver, *The Inspector General, Sir Jeremiah Fitzpatrick and the Politics of Social Reform, 1783-1802*, Croom Helm, London, 1981.

McGuffin, John, *Internment*, Anvil Books, Dublin , 1973.

Milroy, Sean, *Memories of Mountjoy*, Dublin, 1917.

O'Connor, Ulick, *Brendan Behan*, Granada, London, 1979.

O'Donnell, Peadar, *The Gates Flew Open*, Mercier Press, Cork, 1965.

O'Donovan Rossa, Jeremiah, *My Years in English Jails*, ed. Seán Ua Cearnaigh, Anvil Books, 1967.

O'Mahony, Paul, *Criminal Chaos, Seven Crises in Irish Criminal Justice*, Round Hall, Sweet and Maxwell, Dublin, 1996.

O'Mahony, Paul, *Crime and Punishment in Ireland*, Round Hall Press, Dublin, 1993.

O'Mahony, Sean, *Frongoch, University of Revolution*, Dublin, 1987.

Osborough, Niall, *Borstal in Ireland, Custodial Provision for the young adult offender 1906-1974*, Institute of Public Administration, Dublin, 1975.

Pierrepoint, Albert, *Executioner: Pierrepoint*, Coronet Books, London, 1977.

Priestley, Philip, *Victorian Prison Lives, English Prison Biography 1830-1914*, Methuen, London, 1985.

Shaw, A.G.L., *Convicts and the Colonies*, Melbourne University Press, Melbourne, 1981.

Shaw, George Bernard, *Imprisonment*, Issued by the Department of Christian Social Service of the National Council of the Protestant Episcopal Church, Brentano, New York, 1925.

Sheehy, David, *Prison Papers*, Dublin, 1888.

Sigerson, George, *Political Prisoners Both at Home and Abroad*, London, 1870.

Taylor, Fanny, *Irish Homes and Irish Hearts*, London 1867.

Waldron, Jarlath, *Maamtrasna, The Murders and the Mystery*, Edmund Burke, Dublin, 1992.

Wines, E. C., *The State of Prisons and of Child Saving Institutions in the Civilized World*, Cambridge, 1880.

Wooton, Maria, T*he Du Bedat Story: From Killiney to Kommetjie*, Tram Cottage Productions, Dublin, 1999.

D: *Articles and Pamphlets*

Anon., *Queries on the State of Prisons*, Dublin, 1810 – NLI.

Anon., *Observations on the Expediency of Erecting Provisional Penitentiaries in Ireland*, London, 1821.

Association (Society) for the Improvement of Prisons and of Prison

Discipline in Ireland, *A Statement on the Objectives of the Association*, Dublin, 1819 – NLI.

Association for the Improvement of Prisons and of Prison Discipline in Ireland, *Third Report*, for 1821, 1822 – NLI.

Association for the Improvement of Prison Conditions, *Fifth Report*, for 1823, Dublin 1824 – NLI.

Bellows, Rev. H.W., John Howard: His Life, Character, and Services, in Edward Pears (ed.) *Prisons and Reformatories at Home and Abroad*, (being the transactions of the International Penitentiary Congress Held in London July 3-13, 1872), Her Majesty's Prison, Maidstone, 1912, pp. 772-832 – Trinity College Dublin Early Printed Books.

Carpenter, Mary, On the Treatment of Female Criminals, *Fraser's Magazine*, January 1863 – NLI.

Council for Social Welfare, *The Prison System*, Dublin, 1983.

Crofton, Sir Walter, *The Criminal Classes and their Control: Prison Treatment and its Principles*, London, 1868 – NLI.

Crofton, Sir Walter, *Convict Systems and Transportation*, London, 1863 – NLI.

Crofton, Captain Walter, The Irish Intermediate Convict Prisons, a review of 'Notes on Colonel Jebb's Report on Intermediate Prisons', August, 1858, in the *Irish Quarterly Review*, Vol. VIII, pp. 1058-1102, October, 1858 – NLI.

Cowan, Peader, *Dungeons Deep*, 1960.

Falkiner, F.R., Our Habitual Criminals, *Journal of the Social Inquiry Society of Ireland*, August 1882, pp. 317-330 – NLI.

Gibson, Edward, Penal Servitude and Tickets of Leave, *Journal of the Statistical and Social Inquiry Society of Ireland*, April 1863, pp. 332-343 – NLI.

Gibson, Edward, On Religious Toleration for Criminals, *Statistical and Social Inquiry Society of Ireland*, Journal Vol. iv, January 1868, pp. 443-5 – NLI.

Green, Max S., Our Ideals and Methods, *The New Ireland Review*, Vol. III March-August 1895, pp. 156-162 – NLI.

Hinde, Richard S.E., Sir Walter Crofton and the Reform of the Irish Convict System, 1854-61, in *The Irish Jurist* Volume XII new series Part 1, pp. 115-147, Part 2 pp. 295-337, Summer 1977, University College Dublin.

Kavanagh, Sean, In Prison, in *The World of Brendan Behan*, ed. McCann, Sean, Four Square, London, 1965, pp. 67-70.

Labour Party, *Report on Certain Aspects of Prison Conditions in Portlaoighise Convict Prison*, The Labour Party, Dublin, 1946.

McConville, Sean, The Victorian Prison: England 1865-1965, in *The Oxford History of the Prison*, ed. Morris, Norval and Rothman, David J., Oxford, 1995, pp. 131-168.

McGowan, James, Nineteenth-Century Developments in Irish Prison Administration, *Research Discussion* Series, No. 12, Institute of Public Administration, Dublin, August 1977.

McGowan, J., The Body and Punishment in Eighteenth-Century England, *Journal of Modern History*, December 1987, pp. 651-679.

O'Donnell, Ian, 'Criminal Justice Review', *Administration,* vol. 47, no. 2 (Summer 1999), pp. 175-211.

Palmer, Major James, *A Treatise on the Modern System of Governing Gaols, Penitentiaries and Houses of Correction*, Dublin, 1832 – NLI.

Society for the Improvement of Prison Discipline and for the Reformation of Juvenile Offenders, *Inquiries Relative to Prison Discipline*, London, 1818 – NLI.

Whately, Richard, Archbishop of Dublin, *Thoughts on Secondary Punishments in a Letter to Earl Grey*, 1832 – Trinity College Dublin, Early Printed Books.

Wilson, A., *Outlines of a Plan for the Improvement of Prison Discipline*, Dublin, 1830 – NLI.

PERSON INDEX

Subject Index